RESISTING 12-STEP COERCION

HOW TO FIGHT FORCED PARTICIPATION IN AA, NA, OR 12-STEP TREATMENT

BY

STANTON PEELE, PhD, JD

AND

CHARLES BUFE

WITH

ARCHIE BRODSKY

SEE SHARP PRESS ◆ TUCSON, ARIZONA ◆ 2000

For information contact See Sharp Press, P.O. Box 1731,
Tucson, AZ 85702-1731.

Peele, Stanton.
    Resisting 12-step coercion : how to fight forced participation
in AA, NA, or 12-step treatment / Stanton Peele, Ph.D., J.D., and
Charles Bufe, with Archie Brodsky ; introduction by Thomas Horvath,
Ph.D., President of the American Psychological Association's Division
on Addictions. – Tucson, AZ : See Sharp Press, 2000.
    204 p. ; 23 cm.
    Includes bibliographical references and index.
    ISBN 1-884365-17-5

    1. Alcoholism — Treatment. 2. Alcoholism — Rehabilitation.
3. Alcoholics Anonymous. 4. Counseling — Moral and ethical aspects.
5. Informed consent (Medical law). 6. Twelve-step programs.
7. Alcoholism counselors — Professional ethics. I. Title II. Bufe, Charles.
III. Brodsky, Archie.

                    362.29286   99-91322
                                                              CIP

Contents

Appendices

Introduction

I am currently the President of the American Psychological Association's Division on Addictions (Division 50), the world's largest organization of addictive behavior psychologists. Unfortunately, even though the research conducted by the members of our Division and other psychologists forms most of the scientific foundation for addiction treatment, in practice scientific knowledge has little impact on addiction treatment in the United States, and psychologists typically play a small role in addiction treatment. Instead, we have a treatment system which is almost entirely based on an approach that has little evidence of success, and which attempts to treat human diversity with a one-size-fits-all approach. This approach is implemented primarily by drug and alcohol counselors who have far less training than psychologists or other mental health professionals.

Perhaps you have picked up this book because you are already familiar with how U.S. residents are coerced into 12-step groups (such as Alcoholics Anonymous) and into 12-step treatment. Even if you have not fully appreciated the irrationality and enormity of 12-step coercion, you probably have at least an intuitive sense that this coercion is wrong in several ways. If you're uncertain about this, it's understandable—don't almost all addiction professionals insist that 12-step recovery is the only approach that works?

This book can help to resolve any uncertainty you may have about mandated attendance in 12-step groups and 12-step treatment. *Resisting 12-Step Coercion* will explain in detail (with thorough documentation) how frequently 12-step coercion occurs, how and why it can be damaging, and how to prevent or resist it in practical ways. The material presented here will enable individuals faced with such coercion not only to evaluate their options, but also to understand what recourse they have in fighting imposed 12-step treatment.

This information is presented efficiently, yet with deep appreciation for the sufferings caused by 12-step coercion. When individuals become subject to coercive judicial or treatment systems, they are likely to be especially confused, self-doubting, and vulnerable. Great damage can be done at such times—times which call for careful assessment and options.

The authors offer a number of qualifications to their argument, and these are worth introducing here. Unless adjudicated incompetent, individuals are and should be held fully responsible for their behavior. Individuals should be free to choose to enter 12-step groups and 12-step treatment—just as they should be free to choose other self-help groups and treatments (or no treatment at all). What the U.S. needs is not to pare down existing treatment options, but to expand these options and to provide equal access to a variety of approaches, particularly those that have solid evidence of effectiveness. AA's spiritual approach is neither proven nor disproven by scientific study, nor is any other set of spiritual or religious beliefs; such beliefs are a separate matter from science. The central precepts of the disease concept of alcoholism have already been refuted or remain unconfirmed. In addition to its lack of scientific basis, there are also powerful public health arguments to be made for jettisoning the disease hypothesis—the foundation of 12-step treatment—as a basis of public policy.

I would add that whatever success does occur through 12-step attendance may be based more on the experience of social support than on "working the steps." Although for some working the steps may be the only road to success, the number of such individuals is probably very small. Most individuals would benefit from a variety of approaches, because, to simplify, success may be based more on making the decision to change than on the kind of help obtained after that decision. Nevertheless, getting help that reinforces the decision to change can be very beneficial, and can help to reduce the high relapse rates typical of all addictive behaviors. A substance-abusing individual needs careful personal (and possibly professional) assessment and information about a range of options, not dogma.

The primary responsibility for the current state of affairs in addiction treatment lies with present treatment providers, who continue to misinform the public about the diversity and effectiveness of treatment and support groups. In October, 1998, my associate Jeff Jones, CDAC, and I conducted a survey of San Diego alcohol providers (Horvath, 1999). In essence, we asked them where we could refer someone who clearly had problems from drinking, but who unequivocally did not want to attend AA. Forty-five percent stated that AA was the only approach, 47% stated that there were other approaches but that they were not effective, and only 8% (3 out of 38) got it right: there are alternative approaches and they can be helpful.

In my own treatment center, Practical Recovery Services, established in 1985, the matching of services to clients is the highest priority. We view our role as aiding a naturally occurring recovery process, and not as providing something without which the client would end up dead or in an institution. We use empirically supported treatments, or elements of them, as described in Chapter 2 of this book, as well as other psychological change techniques. Treatment is a collaborative dialogue—based on the individual's unique needs and state-of-the-science techniques for behavior change—that identifies addiction (and related) problems, and practical solutions for these problems.

SMART Recovery is an alternative support group (see Appendix B) which I feel privileged to serve, currently as president. SMART's volunteer meeting leaders offer support groups which focus on teaching participants how to build and maintain motivation, identify and cope with cravings, resolve old problems in new ways (rather than relying on addictive behavior), and build a balanced lifestyle (in order to prevent relapse). Rather than tell newcomers that "we are the only thing that works," we encourage them to attend a few meetings, try our methods, read our publications, and return if they find them helpful. We assume that individuals are competent to determine if SMART Recovery would likely be of help to them.

Managed care has had mixed results in changing addiction treatment. The overemphasis on inpatient treatment that was prevalent one to two decades ago has now stopped, and has been replaced with an emphasis on outpatient treatment. This has been good for most insured persons, although saving money rather than the insureds' welfare would appear to have been the insurance companies' primary motive.

But the 12-step approach is still dominant. Even the prospect of saving money has not overcome deeply ingrained practices. I have had several clients who requested and seemed likely to benefit from a short course of individual psychotherapy sessions of the type that have been well tested in the scientific literature. However, their case managers "knew" that an individual with moderate addiction problems could only benefit from an outpatient program which consisted of multiple weekly meetings for several months, and which was of course 12-step oriented. It did not matter that the program cost three times what I was proposing or that the program had little evidence of efficacy (vs. the references I provided for mine). Nor did it matter that the time requirements of the program were completely impractical for these particular individuals. If attempted, the 12-step outpatient program would have required undoing much of the clients' lives, in both their positive and negative aspects, rather than undoing the negatives while building on the positives. In the end, the clients became frustrated and left treatment, and precious moments of motivation were lost.

Stanton Peele, Charles Bufe, and Archie Brodsky have long been advocates for truth in the addiction field. Among them they have written over 20 books on various aspects of addiction and its treatment, beginning with Peele and Brodsky's 1975 classic, *Love and Addiction*. Bufe has also built See Sharp Press, a publishing house that presents addiction works that might not otherwise be seen. Without their leadership we would be much further behind than we are today. It is exciting to see them now present the information necessary to bring about what I believe is the single most needed change in the U.S. addiction treatment system: guaranteeing informed consent and choice of treatment and support groups. As the authors point out, this freedom of choice, like so many freedoms, will likely not be granted at first request. They provide here the rationale and tools for those who are willing to fight for it.

—A. Thomas Horvath, Ph.D., FAClinP

President, Practical Recovery Services, La Jolla (San Diego), CA
    www.practicalrecovery.com
President, 1999-2000, Division on Addictions, American
    Psychological Association
President, SMART Recovery
Author of *Sex, Drugs, Gambling and Chocolate: A Workbook for
    Overcoming Addictions* (1999)

Preface

In the United States today, people most often enter alcohol treatment and Alcoholics Anonymous because they are compelled to do so. There are a number of avenues for such coercion. First and foremost are the courts, which regularly sentence DWIs to 12-step programs. According to Constance Weisner (1990, p. 588) of the Alcohol Research Group in Berkeley, "In fact, many states have transferred much of the handling of DWI offenses to alcohol treatment programs." Not only DWI, but many other crimes are dealt with by referrals to the treatment system, which regularly includes participation in AA (or NA—Narcotics Anonymous) groups.

Inside of prisons, inmates are forced into AA groups and programs based on them. Sometimes the treatment is required as a part of sentencing. Often, it is made clear to the inmate that AA attendance is required in order to gain parole. In addition, other state-run programs—for example, social support programs—frequently require clients to undergo such treatment. The costs of refusal here are expulsion from the program and termination of benefits. Likewise, in family court cases, when alcohol problems are alleged, the court will mandate assessment and typically will also mandate treatment, often under threat of loss of child custody.

The same holds true for drugs and drug use as well, with the added problem that, since use of many drugs is illegal, any use at all of such substances, no matter how moderate, is automatically labeled "abuse," "addiction," or "chemical dependence." Anyone arrested for possession of such drugs is automatically labeled an abuser or addict; and a great many such people are forced into 12-step groups and 12-step treatment.

The trend in U.S. courts is ever more in this direction. The creation of drug courts as alternatives to ordinary court proceedings and the substitution of treatment for criminal sentencing are becoming the norm. In part, this development is an improvement over repressive sentencing of drug users. Nonetheless, such coerced treatment carries many of the negative consequences of jail sentences, and it has additional drawbacks in terms of personal freedoms and the right to define one's inner life.

Meanwhile, employee assistance programs and a wide variety of private and public employers likewise funnel people reported to have drug or alcohol problems into treatment—virtually always of the 12-step variety. Employees are told that they can either enter treatment "voluntarily" or lose their jobs. While this is not the same type of coercion as state-ordered treatment under threat of imprisonment, it is clearly not a free choice.

The disease model of alcoholism that underlies AA and 12-step treatment programs has an explanation of the need for such coercion: alcoholics are in "denial." This denial then becomes an all-purpose pretext for forcing people to do things that they don't want to do. Professional organizations—such as the American Society of Addiction Medicine—provide official medical sanction for this authoritarian tendency.

At the same time, all alcohol problems—from drunk driving, to drinking at work, to periodic excesses at parties—are labeled alcoholism or alcohol dependence, which is the basis on which individuals are coerced into alcoholism treatment programs and AA. Yet, many people in such situations need simply to be careful where they drink and how they consume alcohol—they are not clinically alcohol dependent or, in some cases, even alcohol abusers. Most in this group can resume drinking with appropriate safeguards.

Furthermore, many people, especially young people, display sometimes severe substance abuse problems, but then outgrow them. This process is so ordinary that it has been given the commonplace name, "maturing out." Maturing out will occur far more often than not —unless drug/alcohol treatment and education persuade many individuals who would otherwise do so that they cannot escape youthful drinking and drug excesses.

Since, as noted above, all illegal drug use is regarded as drug abuse, an employee found to have consumed marijuana will be forced to undergo treatment. A similar predicament holds for drivers found to have consumed marijuana, since there is no legal threshold for marijuana in the blood, as there is for alcohol. For people treated in these circumstances, the question immediately raised is, "treated for what?" Cannot people be moderate consumers of marijuana (or, for that matter, of cocaine or any other drug)? Once again, such treatment will almost invariably be 12-step treatment.

Much of the pressure for expanding coercive drug treatment is due, oddly enough, to the failure of current drug policies. Since there is a pervasive sense that we as a society are barking up the wrong tree with punitive laws that punish simple possession or use of drugs with imprisonment, treatment becomes an attractive alternative. Since many career felons use drugs and alcohol regularly as a part of deviant lives, the idea has taken hold that treating them for substance abuse in prison will improve their prospects of avoiding reimprisonment.

Not only is the imposition of treatment within the court system a popular plank in the drug policy reform movement's platform, but it is widely endorsed by the perpetrators of our current repressive drug policy. Thus, some radical drug reformers react favorably to the comment of drug czar Barry McCaffrey, "Treating offenders for drug addiction instead of just locking them up will reduce crime as well as prison costs" (Wren, 1999). Here is a policy everyone can agree with! Since supporters of this reform believe treatment helps people, and may in fact do so in some cases (although many fewer than claimed), forcing people into 12-step drug and alcohol treatment programs is thought to be benign, even a great humanitarian improvement over penal solutions. But what if this is not the case, as is made clear in the following examples:

- Helen Terry, a city employee in Vancouver, Washington, was ostracized on the job after she testified in support of a colleague's sexual-harassment suit. Terry never drank more than a glass of wine in the evening. Nonetheless, based on an unconfirmed report that she had drunk too much at a social event, her superiors ordered her to admit she was an alcoholic and to enter a treatment center under threat of dismissal. (Davidson, 1990)

- A ship's pilot was reported for having alcohol on his breath. The pilot said he had drunk several beers with dinner five hours before reporting for work. He was sent to a doctor, an addiction specialist who assessed him as alcohol dependent, was compelled to enter a residential treatment program or face dismissal, and was told he would have to attend AA several times a week and undergo other post-treatment supervision *provided by the assessing physician*. The pilot had never seen the report written by this assessor, which was sent directly to the pilot's employer; the pilot was not even aware that the doctor had been retained by the company. (See Appendix A.)

- A man had accumulated three DWI convictions during a difficult period in his life. These were discovered, 15 years later, by his employer (a federal agency). Although he was highly successful at work and no one there had ever suggested that he had a substance abuse problem, he was told to undergo treatment (which he had never done) and that henceforth he would have to abstain from alcohol if he wanted to keep his job.

- A young man working in a mail room tested positive for marijuana use in a random drug test. He was suspended from his job until he completed a drug treatment program. In the program, he was in constant conflict with his counselors because he refused to acknowledge—as required by the 12-step program—that he was powerless over his drug use: "I smoke grass once a month!"

- Dawn Green admitted she was drunk as charged when she was arrested for DUI in Middlesex County, New Jersey. A year later, her license was restored. Following its restoration, however, she was ordered to report for an alcohol assessment, the result of which was that she was assessed as alcohol dependent. "I said, 'How could I [be]? Except for the time I was arrested, I rarely drank more than a couple of glasses of beer or wine and that was a couple of times a month. And since I got pregnant, I haven't touched alcohol at all.' Green added, 'I paid for my mistake and I don't think it's fair to keep after me for a problem I had one night two years ago. . . . Every time I questioned anything they told me if I didn't [comply] I would get my license suspended and be sent to jail.'" (Peet, 1986)

Virtually any interaction between the individual and the state, or an employer, school, or anyone with power over a person's future, can involve compulsory treatment, especially since it is claimed to benefit the individual, to be an alternative to even harsher punishment, or to give people options they may not previously have had.

This book, in contrast, considers the range of drawbacks to an increasingly intrusive therapeutic state. What are these drawbacks?

- The person forced into treatment may not have a drug or alcohol problem and may only be a casual or controlled user whose use came to light in a compromising context.

- The treatment, especially 12-step treatment or groups, may be unacceptable to the person on religious or personal grounds.

- The treatment, especially 12-step treatment or groups, may be no more—or may be even less—successful than self-initiated efforts to change.

- The treatment may be superfluous after successful self-initiated change has occurred, sometimes long in the past.

- The dictated outcome—abstinence—may be unjustified in the individual case.

- Even where the treatment may potentially be beneficial, the state or employer may have no right, on First Amendment grounds, to compel a person to undergo treatment— particularly 12-step treatment or participation in 12-step groups.

This book is a response to the accelerating trend of coercing people into substance abuse treatment in the United States. It offers the potential victim of this massive system sound information with which to resist this pressure. It provides support for those who sense that something is amiss in their diagnosis, in the treatment they are ordered to undergo, and/or in their prognosis. If they find that the treatment they have been mandated to enter is offensive to them, and/or they question its likely efficacy, this book offers ample evidence that their suspicions are sound, and that these form legitimate reasons for resisting the ordered treatment. In particular, this book deals with the legal aspects of this problem, and the legal options available to the individual confronted with such a problem.

Readers will find that the news in this area is not entirely good. Legal strategies for resisting intrusions against the right of individuals to decide for themselves what is wrong with them and what to do about it are not always well mapped. Furthermore, the cost of avoiding treatment can be facing legal penalties for having committed a crime and/or for having endangered the safety of others (for instance, by drunk driving). *In no way is this book meant to excuse people from the operation of normal judicial sanctions for actions that endanger or harm others.* Indeed, in part we want to strengthen the norms of social disapproval; we are not inclined, for example, to excuse drug- and alcohol-related violence as a therapeutic problem in which perpetrators are blameless because they are supposedly powerless over their addiction.

Furthermore, in some areas, there is little or no legal protection against state and employer coercion of individuals. This is largely the case with compulsory drug testing, combined with a requirement of treatment, in private employment relationships. Even in areas where the courts have ruled clearly—such as the illegality of state-required 12-step treatment—the ability of individuals (such as those in prison or those from whom the state has taken children) to actually make use of these rulings is limited. In another area for which there is legal support—the requirement of informed consent about the nature of treatment, its outcomes, and potential alternatives—the principle is more often observed in the breach than in the practice.

Nonetheless, our view in writing this book is that compulsory treatment is wrong and ineffective. Our goal is to support—even to encourage—individuals to resist the therapeutic state. In no area is its emergence—once a science fiction topic, as in *A Clockwork Orange* —more real than in present-day substance abuse treatment.

—Stanton Peele

Morristown, NJ
December 1999

Foreword

As Stanton Peele notes in his Preface, there are myriad avenues by which individuals are forced into 12-step alcohol and drug treatment, and into 12-step groups such as Alcoholics Anonymous (AA) and Narcotics Anonymous (NA). The total number of such persons is in excess of 1,000,000 annually, and is likely closer to 1,500,000. Given that approximately 2,000,000 persons are treated annually in the United States, this means that a majority of those treated are coerced into it, as are a majority of newcomers to AA and NA.

What seems to have escaped general notice is that, given the number of those treated, if treatment were anywhere near as effective as treatment advocates claim, the number of alcohol abusers in this country would have plummeted to near zero over the last two decades —that is, in the period when 12-step treatment was instituted on a mass scale in this country. Yet the treatment of literally tens of millions of Americans has had *no discernible effect* on the rate of alcohol abuse in the United States.[1]

This is hardly surprising given the nature of the great bulk of treatment. Well over 90% of treatment facilities in this country are 12-step facilities, and, as we'll see, the treatment they provide consists

---

1. Marty Mann (1981), a cofounder of AA's educational front group, the National Council on Alcoholism (now the National Council on Alcoholism and Drug Dependence), traced the growing estimates of the number of alcoholics in the United States from 3 million in 1943 to 5 million in 1956 to 6.5 million in 1965 to "9.3 to 10 million alcoholics and problem drinkers" in 1975 (p. 3). This translates into an alcoholism rate of about 4.5% of the adult population (i.e., 18 or older) of the United States in 1956, and a combined alcoholism and problem drinking prevalence of about 6.5% in 1975. In 1992, the estimate for those with either alcohol dependence or abuse was about 7.5%, or about 14 million Americans (USDHHS, 1997). At its web site, the National Institute on Alcohol Abuse and Alcoholism currently lists a figure for 1995 of about 18.5 million alcohol-dependent and abusing individuals, or nearly 10% of the adult population (NIAAA, 1999b). When factored into the finding that more than half of Americans now abstain (Stinson et al., 1998), this would mean that 20% or more of all drinkers are alcohol abusers or alcohol dependent! Of course, these figures must be taken with a large grain of salt, but they're a good indication that the spending of tens of billions of dollars to subject tens of millions of our fellow citizens to 12-step treatment has had, at best, no effect whatsoever on the rate of alcohol abuse in this country.

primarily of religious indoctrination. As Chapter 3 shows, the religiosity of the 12-step approach is so obvious that it's amazing that anyone would deny it. Yet 12-step groups and individuals routinely and vehemently deny it, asserting that their program is "spiritual, not religious."

This denial of the obvious began at the time that AA separated itself from its parent Protestant evangelical group, the Oxford Group Movement. The motive then was to sidestep a possible ban by the Catholic hierarchy on Catholic participation in AA. That concern has long passed, but most AA members remain in deep denial about the religious nature of AA.[2]

At present, there are two primary reasons for this. The first is that the vast majority of AA members are ignorant of both the history of their organization and of what constitutes religion. As well, they're members of a very anti-intellectual organization in which questioning is considered a "disease symptom," and in which great emphasis is placed on unquestioning acceptance. (Two of the most popular AA slogans are "Utilize, don't analyze," and "Let go and let God.") So, most AA members hear the "spiritual, not religious" assertion at meetings and repeat it in parrot-like fashion.

The many AA members who own and staff 12-step treatment facilities, as well as those who staff AA's educational and medical front groups, have an additional motivation: *money*. Treatment is a multi-billion-dollar industry, and the honest admission that AA (and all other 12-step groups and treatment) is religious in nature would seriously jeopardize their access to that river of government and insurance industry cash.

The end result of all this is that ineffective, expensive religious indoctrination in the guise of treatment continues to be the norm in this country; at least tens if not hundreds of thousands of 12-step group members—many with little training beyond AA or NA membership—are employed in the treatment industry; many others, who own the treatment facilities, have profited handsomely; AA's good name as a voluntaristic organization has been severely tarnished; and the tens of billions of dollars spent over the last quarter century on 12-step treatment have had no discernible effect on the rate of alcohol abuse.

Another ugly truth is that AA true believers have largely managed to block forms of treatment that are both inexpensive and have good

---

2. There are exceptions to this rule, notably AA historian Dick B., who has written a series of books on AA's religious origins. For information on his works, go to http://www.dickb.com.

scientific evidence of efficacy. This continues to this very day, and is especially true of controlled-drinking therapies. In fact, 12-step professionals routinely vilify and blackball other professionals who dare to question 12-step orthodoxy, and especially those who have the courage to try to establish alternative treatment programs. There have been many ugly incidents of 12-steppers attacking controlled-drinking researchers, advocates, and clinicians with the cry, "They're *killing* people!" What makes this most ironic is that the large bulk of the scientific studies with control or comparison groups indicate that 12-step groups and treatment are themselves quite ineffective in dealing with alcohol and drug problems.

One of the reasons for this demonization of controlled drinking advocates (and of those who advocate decriminalization or legalization of drugs) is the demonization of alcohol and other drugs in 12-step ideology. Twelve-steppers do not regard drinking and drug problems as mere behavioral problems which individuals can—through hard work and persistence—learn to overcome.[3] Rather, in AA and all other 12-step groups, substance-abusing individuals are presented as *powerless* in themselves to deal with their problems; and the substances they abuse are presented as *powerful.* Perhaps the clearest example of this is found in *Alcoholics Anonymous*, AA's "Big Book," in which alcoholics are presented (in step 1 among other places) as "powerless," while alcohol is presented as "cunning, baffling, powerful!"[4] (Wilson, 1939, 1976, pp. 58–59).

The effect of this demonization is threefold: 1) It at least partially absolves substance abusers from responsibility for their actions ("I couldn't help it—I'm an alcoholic and the alcohol made me do it!"); 2) It discourages individuals from trying to overcome their own problems by presenting those problems as insoluble (without the direct intervention of God), and so could well serve to *increase* the number and severity of drug and alcohol problems; and 3) By presenting *substances* as evil and powerful, it provides the rationale for authoritarian governmental intrusion in the lives of individuals (who might easily fall prey to these evil, "cunning" substances).

---

3. In fact, if enough effort is put into changing other aspects of a person's life, or if those pieces fall into place through age and maturation, it may not take much effort to deal with a substance abuse problem—once it becomes inconsistent with how a person otherwise lives his or her life. (See Peele et al., 1991.)

4. The full sentence in the Big Book is "Remember, we deal with alcohol—cunning, baffling, powerful!" To see the true absurdity of this anthropomorphic statement, substitute another liquid for "alcohol," as in, "Remember, we deal with milk—cunning, baffling, powerful!"

This third effect has led (at least in part) to the so-called War on Drugs. This war has greatly increased government intervention in the lives of individuals, has grossly eroded civil liberties, has cost easily several hundred billion dollars (and likely over a trillion) over the last few decades, and has resulted in the imprisonment of millions of individuals—who hurt no one—for consensual "crimes" involving substances far less dangerous than alcohol or tobacco.

A great irony of this war on victimless crimes is that it has resulted in an increase in *real* crimes—crimes with victims. By greatly driving up the price of drugs, the government has ensured that addicts will need large amounts of cash to purchase drugs—thus ensuring vast amounts of property crime (which some blame on drugs rather than on government prohibition, ignoring the fact that outright addicts of such highly addictive drugs as nicotine and methadone don't commit property crimes to support their habits—due to the low cost of their legal drugs).[5]

One doubts that this was what Bill Wilson had in mind when he set the ball rolling by describing individuals as "powerless" and alcohol as "cunning, baffling, powerful!" But it's what he wrought.[6]

Those who originally promoted the 12-step concept of alcoholism and addiction (in medical guise, the "disease concept of alcoholism/ addiction") were quite probably well intentioned; they likely wanted to replace moralistic judgment of alcoholics and addicts with medical compassion for the "diseased." But their efforts have resulted in disaster for the nation—incredible expense, an utterly ineffective approach to addictions, and millions of ruined lives. In the face of all this, 12-steppers continue to assert—despite a great deal of contrary evidence—that their approach is the only way to deal with addictions. And a great many of them, shamefully, now advocate and willingly participate in the mass coercion of their fellow citizens into what were once proudly voluntaristic religious healing programs.

There is some good news, though. In recent years, several appeal- level courts have ruled that AA and other 12-step groups are religious in nature, and that the state's coercing individuals into attending such groups is a violation of the "Establishment Clause" of the First

---

5. As one wag put it, "No one ever pulled an armed robbery to buy a pack of Marlboros."

6. This is not to blame Bill Wilson and AA alone for the War on Drugs—this nation has always had more than its share of moralistic, intrusive busybodies, who deserve a large part of the blame—but it is to point out that the demonization of substances by 12-step groups and treatment professionals provides ideological justification for the destructive, authoritarian War on Drugs.

Amendment. The Supreme Court recently refused to hear the appeal of two such cases, so there is no Supreme Court decision on the subject (that is, there is no national binding precedent), and there isn't likely to be one any time soon. This means that reform will proceed piecemeal across the country, as those who advocate, order, and participate in coerced 12-step participation are quite unlikely to abandon their use of coercion until forced to do so.

Thus change will come only when individuals stand up for their rights. This book is dedicated to those brave individuals. And it is dedicated to giving them the information they need to successfully resist 12-step coercion.

—Charles Bufe

Tucson, AZ
December 1999

ACKNOWLEDGMENTS: I would like to thank those who were good enough to offer useful criticisms and suggestions during the writing of my portion of this book. These include Archie Brodsky, Stanton Peele, Lynaea Search, and Emmett Velten. I would also like to thank those who were good enough to provide research materials and/or other useful information to me. These include Archie Brodsky, J.A. Johnson, Stanton Peele, Guy Salamone, Bruce Tomaso, Lois Trimpey, and Emmett Velten. Finally, I would like to thank Earl Lee for help with the cataloguing of this book. If I've omitted anyone, my sincere apologies.

1

The Nature of the Problem

by Charles Bufe

This chapter provides an overview of the American alcoholism field. It provides an outline of current conditions and how these conditions arose. It briefly considers the following: 1) Definitions of alcoholism, alcohol abuse, and alcohol dependence; 2) Domination of 12-step groups in the self-help field; 3) Domination of 12-step treatment in the professional field; 4) The number of treatment facilities and the number of those treated; 5) The expense of treatment; 6) Avenues of coercion into 12-step groups and 12-step treatment; 7) The number of coerced persons; 8) The percentage of coerced persons who are alcoholics or addicts; 9) Origins and tenets of the disease concept of alcoholism; 10) Scientific evidence regarding the disease concept; 11) The nature of 12-step treatment.

What Is Alcoholism?

Before assessing the effectiveness of 12-step groups and 12-step treatment in dealing with alcoholism, it's first necessary to define the term. Since the word "alcoholism" was coined over 100 years ago, there has never been agreement about what it means. A great variety of definitions have been offered over the years, most dealing with level of consumption, physical dependence, and behavioral, legal, social and/or physical consequences; but all such definitions are, necessarily, arbitrary in at least some respects. One can see how imprecise such definitions are in the wildly varying estimates of the number of alcoholics in the United States given by various experts in recent years—some still cite the figure common to 1970s professional journal articles of 10 million alcoholics, while other estimates have run as high as 25 million (roughly 12% of the adult population). The National Institute on Alcohol Abuse and Alcoholism (1999b) estimates that there were 18.4 million alcohol abusers and alcoholics in 1995. Other estimates are even higher. G. Douglas Talbott, founder and past president of the American Society of Addiction Medicine, has claimed: "The old figure was 10,000,000 alcoholics. . . . It is way beyond that now, and as far as we are concerned, 22 million people have an alcohol problem related to the disease of alcoholism" (Wholey, 1984, p. 19). These estimates indicate that in the United States, despite great efforts, the level of alcohol abuse has not decreased, even though the rate of abstinence has increased (Stinson et al., 1998).

Because of the great, probably insurmountable, difficulties in arriving at a generally accepted definition of the term "alcoholism," addictions researchers and other professionals have largely abandoned it in favor of the somewhat more precise terms "alcohol abuse" and "alcohol dependence." These terms at least recognize that alcohol use and abuse run across a spectrum (or several spectrums, if you consider level of consumption, physical dependency, and behavioral, legal, social, and physical consequences separately) from teetotaler to physically dependent, physically damaged, heavy daily drinker. The American Psychiatric Association (APA) has, in fact, dropped the term "alcoholism" from its authoritative *Diagnostic and Statistical Manual of Psychiatric Disorders* (*DSM*) in favor of "substance dependence" and "substance abuse," thus treating alcohol dependence and abuse as the equivalent of tobacco or heroin dependence and abuse—and *not* as a separate disorder.[1]

Alcohol (Substance) Dependence

The current (fourth) edition of the *DSM* notes, "The essential feature of Substance Dependence is a cluster of cognitive, behavioral, and physiological symptoms indicating that the individual continues use of the substance despite significant substance-related problems. There is a pattern of repeated self-administration that usually results in tolerance, withdrawal, and compulsive drug-taking behavior" (APA, 1994, p. 176). *DSM-IV* defines the Criteria for Substance Dependence as follows:

---

1. A NOTE ON LANGUAGE: We use the terms "alcoholism" and "alcoholic" in the following pages as synonyms for "alcohol dependence" and "alcohol-dependent person." We use these terms in this restrictive sense and do *not* use them—as many 12-step adherents do—in reference to alcohol problems of all types, including mild abuse. We employ these terms simply because they're a convenient form of shorthand, familiar from long use.

A maladaptive pattern of substance use, leading to clinically significant impairment or distress, as manifested by three (or more) of the following, occurring at any time in the same 12-month period:

1. tolerance, as defined by either of the following:
   a. a need for markedly increased amounts of the substance to achieve intoxication or desired effect
   b. markedly diminished effect with continued use of the same amount of the substance

2. withdrawal, as manifested by either of the following:
   a. the characteristic withdrawal syndrome for the substance
   b. the same (or a closely related) substance is taken to relieve or avoid withdrawal symptoms

3. the substance is often taken in larger amounts or over a longer period than was intended

4. there is a persistent desire or unsuccessful efforts to cut down or control substance use

5. a great deal of time is spent in activities necessary to obtain the substance (e.g., visiting multiple doctors or driving long distances), use the substance (e.g., chain-smoking), or recover from its effects

6. important social, occupational, or recreational activities are given up or reduced because of substance use

7. the substance use is continued despite knowledge of having a persistent or recurrent physical or psychological problem that is likely to have been caused or exacerbated by the substance (e.g., current cocaine use despite recognition of cocaine-induced depression, or continued drinking despite recognition that an ulcer was made worse by alcohol consumption).

(APA, 1994, p. 181)

DSM-IV then, on the same page, goes on to refine the diagnosis, providing the distinction, "With Physiological Dependence: evidence of tolerance or withdrawal" or "Without Physiological Dependence: no evidence of tolerance or withdrawal."

Alcohol (Substance) Abuse

DSM-IV notes, "The essential feature of Substance Abuse is a maladaptive pattern of substance use manifested by recurrent and significant adverse consequences related to the repeated use of substances" (APA, 1994, p. 182).

It defines the Criteria for Substance Abuse as:

A. a maladaptive pattern of substance use leading to clinically significant impairment or distress, as manifested by one (or more) of the following, occurring within a 12-month period:

   1. recurrent substance use resulting in a failure to fulfill major role obligations at work, school, or home (e.g., repeated absences or poor work performance related to substance use; substance-related absences, suspensions, or expulsions from school; neglect of children or household)

   2. recurrent substance use in situations in which it is physically hazardous (e.g., driving an automobile or operating a machine when impaired by substance use)

   3. recurrent substance-related legal problems (e.g., arrests for substance-related disorderly conduct)

   4. continued substance use despite having persistent or recurrent social or interpersonal problems caused or exacerbated by the effects of the substance (e.g., arguments with spouse about consequences of intoxication, physical fights)

B. the symptoms have never met the criteria for Substance Dependence for this class of substance.

(APA, 1994, pp. 182–183)

These are now the standard terms and definitions used by researchers, academics, and a great many practitioners. Many others, however, continue to use the outdated, less precise term, "alcoholism." These include the mass media, 12-step groups, especially Alcoholics Anonymous (AA), and a great many 12-step professionals and paraprofessionals (members of AA and Narcotics Anonymous [NA] who work in 12-step treatment centers).

The reasons for continued use of this outmoded term vary. They include: 1) simple ignorance of modern terminology, and the reasons for its use—this is usually the case with reporters and other journalists; 2) habit; 3) identity maintenance—members of AA (and, especially, AA treatment professionals and paraprofessionals) have often (re)constructed (in AA) their identities around alcoholism as the core of their being (Rudy, 1986), and are very protective of that identity; 4) ideology—the term "alcoholic" is a binary term (one is either alcoholic or nonalcoholic), and such a black-and-white definition is essential to the disease concept of alcoholism, the ideological underpinning of abstinence-demanding 12-step treatment.

The Number of Alcohol Abusers

Specifying the number of alcohol abusers in this country is a very complicated question, and because of the subjective nature of even many of the best-defined criteria (such as those in the *DSM*), any answer will necessarily be at least somewhat arbitrary. There have, however, been many attempts to provide an answer. The U.S. Department of Health and Human Services estimated in 1997—based on the 1992 Census Bureau-conducted National Longitudinal Alcoholism Epidemiological Survey (NLAES)—that about 14 million Americans, roughly 7.5% of the adult population, are alcohol-dependent or abusing (USDHHS, 1997). If you believe the figures of the National Institute on Alcohol Abuse and Alcoholism, then the total is 18.4 million; that is, 11.2 million alcohol-dependent and 7.2 million alcohol abusers (NIAAA, 1999b). Just how arbitrary these figures are can be seen by comparing them with the results of similar, previous surveys. The 1988 National Health Interview Survey, for instance, found a combined rate of alcohol abuse and dependence of 6% using the same *DSM-IV* criteria as the NLAES, but a rate of 8.6% using the criteria of the previous edition of the *DSM*, the *DSM III-R* (USDHHS, 1997, p. 19). These figures jibe reasonably well with the Addiction Research Foundation (ARF) estimate of the number of alcohol-dependent persons in Ontario, Canada: 5.4% (ARF, 1998).

The Dominance of 12-Step Groups

Alcoholics Anonymous (AA), Narcotics Anonymous (NA), and the 12-step treatment derived from them are mass phenomena in the United States. They dominate—and nearly monopolize—the addictions self-help and treatment fields.

As of January 1, 1999, Alcoholics Anonymous had approximately 51,000 groups and 1,167,000 members in the United States, comprising roughly two-thirds of all AA members in the world (AA, 1999, p. 1). AA is by far the largest of all addictions self-help groups in America. Narcotics Anonymous is the next largest, with 16,000 groups and (through extrapolation—assuming that the average NA group is the same size as the average AA group) approximately 373,000 members (NA, 1998, p. 1). For the purposes of our analysis, they can be considered as one, because NA is for all practical purposes a carbon copy of AA. Its ideology, core beliefs (as codified in the 12-steps), and structure are virtually identical to AA's. For example, the NA 12 steps differ in only two words (in the first and twelfth steps) from AA's 12 steps.

Between them, AA and NA have a combined membership in excess of 1.5 million; combined AA and NA membership probably outnumbers the combined membership of the five major non-12-step self-help groups (Moderation Management, Rational Recovery, SMART Recovery, Secular Organizations for Sobriety, and Women for Sobriety) by a ratio of at least 50 to one.[2]

The Dominance of 12-Step Treatment

The 12-step approach is every bit as dominant in the treatment field as it is in the self-help field. A large, recent survey of alcohol treatment providers reported that 93% of the 450 facilities it surveyed utilized the 12-step approach (Roman & Blum, 1997, p. 24). Breaking this figure down, the percentage of inpatient-only facilities utilizing

2. This is due in part—in addition to the far longer history of AA, created half a century before the other groups—to AA's and NA's insistence that theirs is a program for life, and that addicts will die if they don't attend AA or NA, while three of the five major alternative self-help programs (Moderation Management, Rational Recovery, and SMART Recovery) specifically advise members to leave after a relatively short period of time (no more than one-and-a-half years in SMART, for example), and the other two major alternative programs (Secular Organizations for Sobriety and Women for Sobriety) do not advise members on how long they should attend, leaving that to the judgment of the individual.

the 12-step approach was, unsurprisingly, 96%; the percentage of facilities offering both inpatient and outpatient treatment utilizing the 12-step approach was 95%; and the percentage of outpatient-only facilities using the 12-step approach was 90% (e-mail message, J.A. Johnson, Research Coordinator, Center for Research on Behavioral Health and Health Services Delivery, University of Georgia, November 4, 1998).

It's worth noting that all of the 450 facilities surveyed treated both alcohol and drug abuse, but that only 2.4% of them offered segregated alcohol and drug programs (Roman & Blum, 1997, p. 6). This is powerful testimony to the integration of alcohol and drug abuse treatment programs, and to the dominance of the 12-step approach in treating all forms of substance abuse. As well, writers sympathetic to the 12-step movement confirm that the 12-step approach pervades the entire treatment industry. One such writer, Gregory B. Collins, MD, states:

> In spite of some confusion about roles, boundaries, philosophies, and objectives, the relationship between AA and treatment has been clear: AA is not treatment as stated in the Traditions of AA; treatment is not AA, i.e., it accepts payment. Overlap is in principles. Nonetheless, this union has brought forth the modern alcoholism treatment industry as we know it with its hospital-based programs, free-standing residential treatment facilities, halfway houses, outpatient centers, and support groups. The unifying philosophical principle remains the Twelve Steps and Twelve Traditions of AA, bolstered further by the disease model of alcoholism . . .
>
> (Collins, 1993, pp. 34–35)

Another professional notes that, ". . . all kinds of interconnections between professional treatment and AA exist, and the Twelve Steps have been adopted as an important component of professional treatment programs. The United States is the clearest representative of this type of *hegemony* of AA" (Mäkelä et al., 1996, p. 186, emphasis in original).

Still another indication of the pervasiveness of the 12-step approach to addictions treatment can be found in the journal article, "Help-seeking and recovery by problem drinkers" (Tucker & Gladjso, 1993), which compared 161 individuals—members of AA who had not been formally treated and individuals who had gone through formal treatment. The researchers conducting the study ran into an interesting problem: they were unable to include a comparison group of treated subjects who had not been exposed to AA, because almost all of their treated subjects *had* been exposed to AA in treatment: "Few subjects had received alcohol treatment without also having participated in A.A., so a treatment-only group was not included" (Tucker & Gladsjo, 1993, p. 532).

Thus the 12-step model dominates the treatment industry. If you (or one of your clients) are sentenced to or otherwise coerced into treatment, it will almost surely be 12-step treatment.

The Number of Facilities and the Number of Those Treated

Just as the 12-step approach is pervasive in the treatment industry, treatment is a pervasive influence in contemporary American society. There are approximately 15,000 treatment facilities (inpatient and outpatient combined) (Substance Abuse and Mental Health Services Administration [SAMHSA], 1999, p. 112) treating approximately 2,000,000 persons annually. SAMHSA's Treatment Episode Data Set (TEDS) reports 1,477,881 admissions in 1997 (SAMHSA 1999, p. 47), but those data are quite incomplete; they do not include any admissions from Arizona, Indiana, Mississippi, Puerto Rico, or West Virginia, and are not complete for, apparently, all other states. SAMHSA reports, "In general facilities reporting TEDS data are [only] those that receive State [sic] alcohol and/or drug agency funds . . . [and] TEDS also does not include data on facilities operated by Federal [sic] agencies" (SAMHSA, 1999, pp. 4–5). Taking into account such inadequacies, SAMHSA estimates that there were 2,207,375 admissions in 1997 (SAMHSA, 1999, p. 114). This is the total number of estimated *admissions*; but because some individuals were likely admitted to more than one substance abuse program in 1997, the total number of *persons* treated is almost certainly somewhat lower. In any case, given that the SAMHSA data attempt to treat transfers from one program to another as single admissions, it seems likely that at the very minimum 2,000,000 persons were treated in 1997.

The Cost of 12-Step Treatment

Twelve-step treatment is also very expensive. The National Treatment Center Study (NTCS) placed the daily cost of adult inpatient treatment at an average of $509 among the facilities it surveyed, while the cost per day of detox treatment ran to an average of $586, and adolescent treatment to an average of $592 per day

(Roman & Blum, 1997, p. 20). This adds up quickly. One study placed the average cost to a Midwestern manufacturing plant at $4665 per treated employee (in 1985 dollars, the equivalent of approximately $7100 in 1999) (Holder & Blose, 1991, p. 190). More recently, the Substance Abuse and Mental Health Services Administration reported that treatment in correctional centers costs an average of $24 per day, with an average of 75 days of treatment for a total of $1800 per client; long-term residential care costs an average of $49 per day, with an average stay of 140 days, for a total cost of $6800; and short-term residential treatment costs an average of $130 per day, with a "typical stay of 30 days" (SAMHSA, 1997c, p. 3). The large difference between average costs as reported by SAMHSA and by the National Treatment Center Study is probably due to SAMHSA's inclusion of many publicly funded facilities, while the NTCS surveyed only facilities which receive a majority of their funds from private sources (e-mail message, J.A. Johnson, November 6, 1998).

The total cost of 12-step treatment to taxpayers and insurers is staggering. Estimates range from a low of $3.6 billion annually for treatment in the late 1980s (Nace, 1993, p. 437; Huber et al., 1994, p. 1663, put the total at $3.8 billion in 1989) to a high of $10.5 billion in "direct costs" ("specialty organizations, short-stay hospitals, office-based physicians, other professional services, nursing homes, support costs") in 1990 (USDHHS, 1997, p. 388). This figure agrees with the Institute of Medicine estimate of $10 billion in treatment costs in 1990 (USDHHS, 1994, p. 15). More recently, the *New York Times* (Morrow, 1998, p. D1) estimated current costs at $5 billion per year. These estimates are all for alcohol treatment alone. They do not include the costs of drug treatment. Another glimpse at how expensive treatment is can be gained by looking at state treatment spending alone (including channeled federal funds), which ran to $2.52 billion in 1992 (USDHHS, 1995, p. 57).

Avenues of Coercion

There are several common ways in which individuals are coerced into 12-step group participation or into 12-step treatment:

1) It is very common for the courts to place criminal defendants in diversion programs featuring 12-step treatment and/or AA/NA participation in lieu of prosecution in alcohol- and drug-related cases, with prosecution deferred only as long as the coerced person remains in treatment and/or attends AA or NA.

2) It is equally common for the courts to mandate 12-step treatment or AA/NA participation as a condition of probation for such persons after conviction for an alcohol- or drug-related offense.

3) Penal institutions often coerce prisoners into AA/NA attendance and/or 12-step treatment under threat of denial of parole or early release.

4) Parole officers routinely coerce those they supervise into AA or NA participation under threat of reimprisonment.

5) Employers often coerce "impaired" employees into 12-step treatment—frequently through Employee Assistance Programs (EAPs)—under threat of job loss.

6) State bar associations and medical associations routinely coerce "impaired" lawyers, doctors and nurses into 12-step treatment (and, later, AA or NA as "aftercare") through professional diversion programs under threat of disbarment or loss of professional certification.

7) It is fairly common for parents to force their teenage children into 12-step treatment, often through direct physical force or through coercive "interventions." (The child is cornered by several adults, including some from a treatment institution, and is then browbeaten—sometimes for hours—until he or she "agrees" to go into treatment.)

8) Several jurisdictions, including Michigan (Meredith, 1999) and New York City, have begun to require drug testing of welfare recipients in order to force them into treatment. Those who refuse to be tested, or who test positive and refuse treatment, must forfeit their benefits.

These practices cover a majority of cases of 12-step coercion, but hardly all cases. A great many other individuals are coerced into AA, NA, or 12-step treatment. These include liver transplant candidates, children removed from parental custody, parents in child-custody cases, members of the military with substance abuse problems . . . and the list goes on.

Coercion Into Alcoholics Anonymous

While it's very difficult to estimate the total number of individuals coerced annually into AA, NA, or 12-step treatment, a number of reliable sources indicate that the total is very high—almost certainly above 1,000,000. One can glimpse the importance of coercion to AA and NA—and its contribution to their growth—in AA's membership figures. Since the late 1970s, AA has conducted periodic membership surveys, generally once every three years. (For this reason the AA surveys are normally referred to as "triennial surveys.") In these surveys, AA asks its members what factors were most important in bringing them to AA. The findings of AA's 1996 survey were quite revealing. They indicated that *probably in excess of 40% of AA's current members were coerced into attendance* (AA, 1997).[3]

In addition, given that over 1,000,000 Americans per year are coerced into alcohol treatment (which almost always means coerced

---

3. Unfortunately, it's difficult to be more exact, because AA asked its members to name the three most important factors in bringing them to AA. But, even given its limitations, it is possible to extrapolate a reasonable estimate from the data.

I arrived at the 40+% figure as follows: 16% of those attending AA were openly coerced by the courts or penal system. I started with this as a baseline figure, because it involves undisguised coercion. Other "important factors" came to a total of 241%. To arrive at the coercive total percentage, I added the full 40% listed for treatment facilities (clients are almost invariably coerced into AA attendance by treatment facilities), three quarters of the 16% listed for counseling agencies (counseling agencies often make counseling contingent on AA attendance), the full 9% listed for "employer or fellow worker" (undoubtedly, almost all of them were coerced into treatment by EAPs or professional diversion programs), 7% out of the 39% listed for family (the *National Treatment Center Study Summary Report* indicates that 17.5% of inpatient clients are adolescents, almost none of whom would enter treatment voluntarily), and half of the 8% listed for health care providers (who sometimes make treatment contingent on AA attendance). This yields a total of 65%, which I divided by 2.41, which yields a figure of roughly 27%. Adding that 27% to the 16% who were outright coerced by the legal and penal systems yields a total of 43% of current AA members who belong to the organization primarily as a result of some type of coercion. Of course, this method is inexact, but it does yield a reasonable ballpark figure. And if that figure of 43% is correct, it means that 500,000 of AA's current members were coerced into attendance.

into AA as well), it seems certain that a large majority of newcomers to AA are coerced into attendance (and then leave as quickly as they can through AA's "revolving door"). This conjecture fits well with AA's self-reported new member dropout rate of 95% in the first year (Alcoholics Anonymous, n.d., p. 12, Figure C-1).

Coercion Into Narcotics Anonymous

It seems likely that the percentage of NA members coerced into attendance is even higher than that of AA members coerced into attendance, because of the illegality of many recreational drugs in this country. Whereas with alcohol one must sometimes demonstrate a pattern of abusive behavior or get a DUI in order to be forced into AA or treatment, those who use illegal drugs are often arrested for simply possessing small amounts of drugs. As well, no matter in what manner such persons use drugs, they are—in part because of 12-step-induced abstinence hysteria—automatically assumed to be drug abusers, or even drug dependent, and therefore fair game for coercion into NA or 12-step treatment. (According to drug war dogma, there is no such thing as, for instance, moderate marijuana use—despite the experience of many millions of casual users.)

NA's own figures bear this out. They reveal that "47% of our members were introduced to Narcotics Anonymous through a treatment facility or while incarcerated," and that "24% were introduced by a community professional (doctors, *attorneys*, clergy, *judges*)" (NA, 1998, p. 5, emphasis added). Given the penchant of 12-step groups for the use of euphemism, one can reasonably assume that those "introduced" to NA by judges and (district?) attorneys were actually coerced into attendance through either pre-trial diversion programs or as a condition of probation. This would bring the coerced percentage to well above 50% of NA members.

Coercion Into 12-Step Treatment

An indication of what percentage of clients are coerced into 12-step treatment is provided by the Substance Abuse and Mental Health Services Administration's Treatment Episode Data Set. A recent TEDS survey reports, "TEDS 1995 admissions show a *high rate of self-referrals (69% for heroin) and a high rate of referral by the criminal justice system for marijuana (49%), PCP (47%), and alcohol-only (46%)*" (SAMHSA, 1997a, p. 3, emphasis in original). To put this in further perspective, in 1995 only 20% of those treated for marijuana abuse were individually referred, and only about 33% of those treated for drug abuse of all types were individually referred (SAMHSA, 1997a, p. 46). This low percentage of individual referrals combined with the very high percentage coerced by the criminal justice system provides good evidence—taking into account the many other avenues of coercion —that a majority of individuals in 12-step drug treatment are coerced into it.

Moreover, given that 46% of those treated for alcohol-only abuse in 1995 were directly coerced into it by the criminal justice system, and that only 28% of those treated for alcohol-only abuse were individually referred (SAMHSA, 1997a, p. 46), it's certain—given the many other types of coercion beyond the criminal justice system— that a sizable majority of those in 12-step alcohol-only treatment are coerced into it. This becomes even more obvious when one realizes that "individual" referral "includes self-referral due to pending DWI/DUI" (SAMHSA, 1999, p. 103). As to relative size, those treated for "alcohol only" abuse made up 30% of total admissions in 1995 (SAMHSA, 1997a, p. 47; SAMHSA, 1997b, p. 26). As for those treated for "alcohol with secondary drug" abuse, 34% were directly coerced into attendance by the criminal justice system, while only 31% of such persons were individually referred (SAMHSA, 1997b, p. 46). (No figures were given for "drug with secondary alcohol" abuse.) Those treated for both alcohol and drug abuse made up just over 46% of those treated (SAMHSA, 1997b, p. 26).

The most recent SAMHSA data indicate a similar level of coercion. In 1997, alcohol-only and alcohol-with-secondary-drug admissions comprised 48% of all admissions, with 42% of those admitted being directly coerced by the criminal justice system, and only 27% being individually referred (derived from SAMHSA, 1999, p. 67, Table 3.4). In addition, in 1995 those admitted for marijuana use comprised 10.5% of all admissions, but by 1997 that percentage had risen to 13% (SAMHSA, 1999, p. 47, Table 2.1), with fully 52% of such admissions being directly coerced by the criminal justice system. (An indication of the increasing use of drug courts is that the percentage of admissions for marijuana use more than doubled between 1992 and 1997, from 6% of admissions to 13% of admissions, according to SAMHSA, 1999, p. 47.)

Given that approximately 2,000,000 Americans per year enter treatment, these figures mean that—considering the many other avenues of coercion—almost certainly *over 1,000,000 of our fellow citizens are coerced into 12-step treatment annually.* And the total could be considerably higher than that.

A great many other people—almost certainly hundreds of thousands—are coerced into AA or NA attendance (though not necessarily 12-step treatment) through judicial diversion programs or as a condition of probation or parole. So, the total number of those coerced annually into AA, NA, and 12-step treatment combined likely far exceeds 1,000,000, and could reach as high as 1,500,000.

This is, quite simply, a staggering number.

Are Coerced Persons Really Alcoholics?

The multi-billion-dollar 12-step treatment industry treats at the very minimum one million coerced clients annually, a great many of whom do not meet the diagnostic criteria for alcohol abuse, let alone alcohol dependence. One of the largest groups of coerced clients, DUI offenders, is illustrative. The National Highway Transportation Safety Administration (NHTSA) reports that "approximately 20% of all licensed drivers drive while intoxicated . . . during any given 1-year period" (NHTSA, 1996, p. 1, citing Nichols, 1990), and that at least 50% of those arrested for DUI offenses do not meet the clinical criteria for alcohol abuse or alcohol dependence (NHTSA, 1996, p. 1).

Thus the application of the term "alcoholism" to everyone with *any* alcohol-related problem whatsoever (including the social drinker who has one too many on New Year's Eve and gets a DUI citation) is clearly inappropriate. But it helps to ensure a steady, profitable stream of coerced clients to treatment programs; it helps to reinforce the alcoholic identities of the professionals and paraprofessionals running 12-step treatment programs; and it allows (indeed, implicitly demands) the use of one-size-fits-all, abstinence-demanding 12-step treatment for everyone who steps through the doors of a treatment center. Never mind (as we'll see later) that 12-step treatment doesn't work very well. And never mind that every single one of the testable premises underlying 12-step treatment's ideological basis (the disease concept of alcoholism) is demonstrably false.

The Disease Concept of Alcoholism

Origins of the Disease Concept

The disease concept of alcoholism is the cornerstone of 12-step treatment, and is intimately tied to AA. In fact, it is largely a *product* of AA. It was first propounded (in "modern" terms) in two articles by

Yale researcher E.M. Jellinek published in 1946 and 1952. It was later put in what retired University of California professor Herbert Fingarette calls its "canonical" form (Fingarette, 1988, p. 20) in 1960 in Jellinek's book, *The Disease Concept of Alcoholism.* Jellinek's articles and book have been amazingly influential during the latter half of the 20th century. They have provided the "scientific" rationale for AA and 12-step treatment.

Jellinek's influence is amazing, however, not because of his work's supposed scientific value, but rather because it has virtually *no* scientific value. Jellinek based his writings not on experimental studies with control groups and random assignment of subjects, not on epidemiological studies with matched comparison groups, not on longitudinal studies, not even on retrospective studies of a random sample of the population, but, rather, on one retrospective study of a small sample of self-selected Alcoholics Anonymous members, with no comparison group.

Jellinek's data came from an AA-designed questionnaire distributed through the monthly magazine, *The Grapevine,* which functions as an internal AA organ. Thus all of the replies Jellinek received came from self-selected AA members—that is, members of an organization with a rigid, uniform view of alcoholism. Jellinek received 158 questionnaires, of which he discarded 60 because they were either completed by women, were incomplete, or had been completed by AA members who had pooled their answers. Jellinek went on to interpret the answers on the remaining 98 questionnaires at great length, producing impressive looking graphs and thousands upon thousands of words of explication. His works remain a mainstay in the scientific arsenal of 12-step proponents.

But the fact remains: Jellinek's work was a retrospective study based on a small, exclusively male, self-selected sample of AA members. It's little wonder that the answers they gave Jellinek mirrored the view of alcoholism one finds at virtually every AA meeting.

The Central Tenets of the Disease Concept

The AA-generated theory (more accurately, a weak hypothesis), the disease concept of alcoholism, has several central tenets:

1) the disease of alcoholism is progressive—it inevitably worsens if left untreated;

2) the disease is an entity unto itself—it exists independently of an alcoholic's family, work, economic, and social situations;

3) alcoholics cannot recover from their disease—the best that they can do is arrest it by remaining abstinent;

4) alcoholics are powerless to deal with their disease without outside assistance;

5) alcoholics experience loss of control if they take so much as one drink—the AA folk saying, "one drink, one drunk," expresses this belief succinctly;

6) loss of control is the result of uncontrollable craving;

7) the disease of alcoholism is characterized by denial.

Inevitable Progressivity and Spontaneous Recovery

Almost all of these central tenets of the disease concept are demonstrably false. In regard to inevitable progressivity, the supposed powerlessness of alcoholics to recover (let alone recover unaided), and loss of control, scientists have known for decades that alcoholism disappears faster than can be explained by mortality among individuals older than 40. One researcher reports, "In the statistics available on alcoholics in Victoria [State, Australia] predicted prevalence and actual prevalence do approximate each other, but only until the age of 40 years is reached, after which the actual prevalence increasingly falls below the predicted prevalence with increasing age" (Drew, 1968, pp. 957–958). He concludes: "The reported evidence demonstrates that alcoholism tends to disappear with increasing age. Although morbidity and mortality may account for a large part, a significant proportion of this disappearance is probably due to spontaneous recovery. . . . It is interesting that this type of observation has been so generally ignored while the concepts of 'irreversibility' and 'loss of control' have generally and tenaciously been accepted . . ." (Drew, 1968, p. 965).

Scientists have also known for decades that significant numbers of alcohol abusers "spontaneously" [4] recover (Cahalan, 1970; Fillmore,

---

4. The term is in quotation marks because there are often definite reasons for "spontaneous" recovery. These include very dangerous or very embarrassing incidents which shock an alcohol abuser into quitting; a gradually growing existential

1974; Fillmore, 1975; Knupfer, 1972; Saunders et al., 1979). The meta-analysis estimate of 3.7% to 7.4% per year (Smart, 1975/76, p. 284) fits reasonably well with the available longitudinal study-derived data on mortality of alcohol abusers (Finney & Moos, 1991) and with the results of the massive National Institute on Alcohol Abuse and Alcoholism (NIAAA)/Census Bureau study, the National Longitudinal Alcohol Epidemiological Survey (NLAES) (Dawson, 1996). Finney and Moos surveyed 12 longitudinal studies of alcohol abusers, and reported an average mortality rate of 2.15% per year for the treated abusers, during an average follow-up time of 11.3 years. (The single study of "generally untreated alcohol abusers," Öjesjö, 1981, reported an annual mortality rate of 1.7%, a lower percentage than reported by all but one study of treated abusers.)

The NLAES was conducted in 1992 by Census Bureau field workers who did face-to-face interviews with roughly 43,000 Americans age 18 and over, concerning the use of alcohol and other drugs over the respondents' lifetimes. The respondents included "4,585 adults with prior *DSM-IV* alcohol dependence" (Dawson, 1996, p. 771). That is, these individuals were serious alcohol abusers, persons who would be termed alcoholics in common parlance. "To be included in this analysis, an individual had to have satisfied the criteria for prior-to-past year *DSM-IV* alcohol dependence by meeting at least 3 of the 7 *DSM-IV* criteria for dependence" (Dawson, 1996, p. 772).

The results of this huge retrospective study lend powerful new evidence that a great many, indeed a large majority of, alcoholics—and, remember, this was a study of alcohol-*dependent* persons, not mere alcohol *abusers*—spontaneously recover, with the percentage steadily rising as time passes. The NLAES reported that 20 or more years after the "onset of dependence," 90% of surviving, untreated formerly alcohol-dependent persons were either abstinent (30%) or "drinking without abuse or dependence" (60%) (Dawson, 1996, p. 773). Given that there appears to be little difference in mortality rate between treated and untreated alcoholics (Finney & Moos, 1991; Vaillant, 1995), and that the mortality rate of the cohort from which the alcohol-dependent persons in this survey was sampled was probably in the 2%-per-year range, one can at least roughly calculate the percentage of untreated alcoholics who recover without undergoing treatment or participating in AA.

Assuming an average mortality rate of 2.15% per annum (as

---

awareness of the seriousness of the problem, which leads to the same result; and religious conversion. See Tuchfeld (1981) for a more thorough discussion of this matter.

derived from the Finney & Moos study),[5] a straightforward calculation reveals that 57% of those who first exhibited alcohol dependence 20 years before the NLAES should still have been alive at the time of the study. Given that 90% of the untreated subjects[6] were either abstinent or drinking socially without problems, one arrives at the tentative conclusion that at least 51% (.57 X .90) of the cohort from which the NLAES subjects were drawn were alive and recovered at the time of the study.[7] (Given that alcohol-related mortality declines with age, the percentage could be higher.)

But even if the recovery rate were only 51%, that is still better than it sounds. The reason for this is that significant numbers of those who died did so as a result of non-alcohol-related causes. The average mortality rate in the United States is roughly 1.3% per year (spread out over all ages). Given that alcohol problems tend to be concentrated in the younger age groups, it would be reasonable to expect that the mortality rate in a non-alcohol-abusing population in the same age range as alcohol abusers would be lower than average. If it were 1% per year, then a non-alcohol-abusing comparison group to the subjects in the NLAES would show an approximately 80% survival rate over a 20-year period. Comparing this 80% with the 51% of

---

5. The mortality rate was quite possibly lower than this, given that alcohol-related mortality appears to decline with age (Drew, 1968).

6. "Treatment" in this study includes not only formal treatment, but also participation in AA. Thus these untreated recovered subjects had been neither in formal treatment nor had they participated in AA.

7. This is, of course, a rough approximation given that the figures are for 20 or more years, not merely for 20 years. But given the very high estimated death rate (2.15%) over a very long period (20 years), and that one would expect such a death rate to decline in the middle and latter years of this period, the calculated recovery rate is reasonable, and perhaps conservative, though of course inexact. The data for those surviving and recovered 10 to 20 years after onset of dependence support this view.

The NLAES reported that 10 to 20 years after the onset of dependence, 80% of surviving, untreated formerly alcohol-dependent persons were either abstinent (16%) or drinking without abuse or dependence (64%) (Dawson, 1996, p. 773). Assuming an average mortality rate of 2.15% per annum, a straightforward calculation reveals that 68% of the cohort who first exhibited alcohol dependence an average of 15 years before the NLAES should have been alive at the time of the study. Given that 80% of the untreated subjects were either abstinent or drinking without problems, one arrives at the tentative conclusion that 53% (.68 X .80) of the 10-to-20-year cohort from which the NLAES subjects were drawn were alive and recovered at the time of the study. Correcting this for non-alcohol-related mortality of 1% per year (as below in the text) one arrives at a spontaneous recovery rate of 66% for untreated, formerly alcohol-dependent persons 15 years after the onset of dependence.

recovered formerly alcohol-dependent persons in the NLAES yields a spontaneous recovery rate of 64%, corrected for non-alcohol-related mortality. Of course, these numbers are tentative, but—even assuming a mortality rate higher than the already very high 2.15%—they still provide powerful evidence that the supposed inevitable progression of the disease of alcoholism exists only in the minds and solemn pronouncements of 12-step true believers. It also provides powerful evidence that the supposedly inevitable loss of control experienced by alcoholics likewise exists only in the minds and pronouncements of 12-step proponents.

The Loss of Control Myth

Clinical experiments further disprove the loss-of-control supposition. Since the 1960s, researchers have conducted controlled experiments designed to discover whether inevitable loss of control and the trigger effect really exist. (The classical disease concept posits that any amount of alcohol consumption, no matter how minute, triggers loss of control in alcoholics.) The results of these experiments have been uniformly negative.

There have been a large number of studies conducted in clinical situations in which alcohol was made available to alcoholics, often with them earning it through the performance of menial tasks. Many of these studies also offered rewards either for not drinking or for moderate consumption, and/or penalties (such as being kicked out of comfortable surroundings) for excessive consumption. The results of these studies have been remarkably uniform: in such clinical settings, the vast majority of alcoholics control their drinking. One review of over 50 such studies concludes, "within a hospital or laboratory environment, the drinking of chronic alcoholics is explicitly a function of environmental contingencies" (Pattison et al., 1977, p. 100). Such experiments have been attacked by the 12-step establishment as meaningless, because they did not take place in the "real world." But as Herbert Fingarette points out:

> ... if these drinkers were able to control their drinking in these special settings, one of two explanations must hold. Either (1) the careful observers in the special settings are noticing behaviors that careful observers would also detect in everyday situations or (2) the change in setting from home to hospital indeed radically affects alcoholics' self-control and drinking patterns.
>
> Either of these explanations undermines the classic loss-of-control conjecture. If the first explanation holds, then loss of control is a

stereotype born of faulty observation and a misunderstanding of drinkers' behavior. If the second explanation holds, then it is the social setting, not any chemical effect of alcohol, that influences drinkers' abilities to exert control over their drinking.

(Fingarette, 1988, p. 37)

This is powerful testimony against the disease-concept precept that alcoholism is an entity unto itself, existing independently of the alcoholic's social situation.

Further confirmation that alcoholism is *not* an independent entity can be found in studies of the Community Reinforcement Approach to alcohol abuse (CRA). The fundamental underlying tenet of CRA is that alcoholism is not an entity unto itself, but, rather, is highly influenced by social, economic, relationship, recreational, and family situations. Proceeding from this premise, CRA programs help an alcoholic develop better ways of meeting his or her needs than by drinking. One study describes CRA as follows: "An operant reinforcement approach was used . . . that rearranged community reinforcers such as the job, family and social relations of the alcoholic" (Hunt & Azrin, 1973, p. 91).

The authors continue, "The results showed that the alcoholics who received this Community-Reinforcement counseling drank less, worked more, spent more time with their families and out of institutions than did a matched control group of alcoholics who did not receive these procedures." These results were not trivial: "The mean percent of time spent (1) drinking was 14 per cent for the reinforcement group and 79 per cent for the control group; (2) unemployed was 5 per cent for the reinforcement group and 62 per cent for the control; (3) away from family . . . was 16 per cent for the reinforcement group and 36 per cent for the control group; (4) institutionalized was 2 per cent for the reinforcement and 27 per cent for the control group" (Hunt & Azrin, 1973, p. 97).

A later study combining the Community Reinforcement Approach with disulfiram (Antabuse) showed even more impressive results. At the six-month follow-up, the control group was drinking on 16.4 days per month versus 0.9 days for the CRA group; and the control group was intoxicated 10 days per month versus 0.4 days for the CRA group (Azrin et al., 1982).[8] Significantly, the control group in both of these

---

8. Despite these extremely encouraging results, there was no further investigation of CRA and alcohol abuse in the United States until the late 1990s (ongoing in Albuquerque, New Mexico, and involving University of New Mexico researchers).

studies was comprised of individuals (matched to those in the Community Reinforcement Approach groups) who had undergone only conventional 12-step treatment.

The Trigger Effect

There have also been direct investigations of the supposed chemical trigger effect (leading to loss of control) of alcohol consumption. Again, the results of these controlled experiments have been consistently negative. They typically involve giving alcoholics drinks either containing or not containing alcohol, and then measuring consumption based on expectations. One of the most famous—and methodologically sound—of these studies was conducted by University of Washington researcher Alan Marlatt in the early 1970s.

In the experiment, Marlatt et al., under the guise of a taste test, gave four groups of alcoholic subjects either straight tonic water or tonic water with a small amount of vodka mixed in. (The amount was small enough that it was not detectable through taste.) One group was given tonic water and told that it was tonic water. A second group was given tonic water mixed with vodka and told that it was tonic water. A third group was given tonic water and told that it was tonic water mixed with vodka. And a fourth group was given tonic water mixed with vodka and told that it was tonic water mixed with vodka. In other words, the researchers told two of the groups the truth about what they were drinking, and they lied to the other two groups about it. The results flatly contradicted the expectations of the disease theory and its loss-of-control myth: *regardless of what they were actually drinking,* the groups that *believed* they were drinking a vodka mix drank *more* than the groups that *believed* they were drinking only tonic water. Thus expectation was the trigger—*not* the presence (or absence) of alcohol (Marlatt et al., 1973).

Denial

Thus far we've seen that the available scientific evidence negates the first six premises of the disease concept (listed above on pp. 31–32). So, we're left with the seventh, denial. This premise is unique in that it cannot be scientifically tested (or, at least, no one has devised a means of doing so).

One suspects that this lack of interest is due in large part to the premises of CRA, which are in direct contradiction to those of the dominant 12-step/disease model.

The disease-concept assertion that denial characterizes and is a major symptom of alcoholism is just that: an assertion—and a particularly asinine one at that. Everyday experience will show this: a great many alcoholics go to AA and 12-step treatment for help (in itself an admission of a problem), yet many of them continue to drink abusively, often while attending AA and working the steps. Are they in denial?

Another problem with the concept of denial is that it is useless as a diagnostic symptom. For, even if everyone who is an alcoholic is in denial about their problem (which, as we've just seen, isn't true), those who are *not* alcoholic will also deny that they are alcoholic. Thus reliance upon denial as a diagnostic symptom undoubtedly leads to many false positives.

It's also worth noting that denial is a Catch-22 accusation: if you admit that you're an alcoholic, you're an alcoholic; if you deny that you're an alcoholic, you're in denial—strong evidence that you *are* an alcoholic. Either way you lose. Just as many innocent people lost the last time denial of a charge was accepted as evidence of its truth—at witchcraft trials in the Middle Ages.

Denial does have its uses, though. It's a very handy weapon with which to badger coerced, recalcitrant clients in 12-step treatment facilities, and with which to badger coerced, recalcitrant newcomers at AA and NA meetings.

12-Step Treatment

The disease concept of alcoholism is the ideological underpinning of the $10-billion-a-year treatment industry, and the edifice erected upon it is entirely worthy of its foundation.

Twelve-step treatment is, in reality, institutional AA and NA. To put this another way, the primary goal of 12-step treatment is the introduction of clients to AA or NA, with the purpose being to push clients into joining AA or NA and attending their meetings for the rest of their lives. Twelve-step advocates can sometimes be surprisingly forthright about this:

(1) Treatment does not "cure" the disease—the expectation is that by instituting an achievable method of abstinence the disease will be put into remission. (2) All therapeutic efforts are directed at helping the patient reach a level of motivation that will enable him or her to commit to this abstinence program. (3) An educational program is developed to assist the patient in becoming familiar with the addictive

process, insight into compulsive behaviors, medical complications, emotional insight, and maintenance of physical, mental, and spiritual health. (4) The patient's family and other significant persons are included in the therapeutic process with the understanding that the therapeutic process does not occur in a vacuum, but rather in interpersonal relationships. (5) *The patient is indoctrinated into the AA program and instructed as to the content and application of the 12 steps of the program.* [emphasis added] (6) Group and individual therapy are directed at self-understanding and acceptance with emphasis on how alcohol and drugs have affected their lives. (7) There is insistence on participation in a longitudinal support and follow-up program based on the belief that, as in the management of all chronic disease processes, maintenance is critically important to the ultimate outcome of any therapy. This follow-up usually consists of ongoing support provided by the treatment facility as well as participation in community self-help groups such as AA, Narcotics Anonymous (NA), Opiates Anonymous (OA), and the like.

(G.A. Mann, cited by Collins, 1993, p. 35)

Two other pro-12-step writers, in a journal article describing inpatient treatment, note: "Information about self-help groups such as AA specifically need[s] to be covered during treatment because they form the backbone of a successful recovery program" (Warner & Mooney, 1993, p. 99).

So, AA forms the "backbone of a successful recovery program." But what exactly goes on in 12-step treatment? One study of AA, done in collaboration with the World Health Organization, describes 12-step inpatient treatment as follows:

Institutional 12-step treatment consists of an intensive program for a period of up to four or six weeks. Patients attend lectures on AA, read AA literature, and go to AA meetings at the institution or outside. AA members visit the institution and talk about their personal experiences. Key positions in the treatment personnel are often held by recovering alcoholics who are doctors, psychologists, nurses, and particularly, so-called alcoholism counselors. The latter are recovering alcoholics with varying degrees of formal training. In the course of the institutional program, the patient goes through the first four to five Steps of AA. A common formulation is that institutional 12-step treatment is an introduction to AA, where the real recovery should take place.

(Mäkelä et al., 1996, p. 195)

This closely jibes with descriptions by former clients of 12-step treatment. One such client described his 35-day stay in a "Minnesota Model"[9] 12-step treatment facility to me as follows: "We'd get up in the morning, do calisthenics, eat breakfast, and then go to group therapy, which was basically working the steps. After lunch, we'd have a lecture [in which 12-step/disease-concept ideology was presented as established fact], and then after dinner, we'd go to an AA meeting." This is a relatively benign description.

Another former client, a physician, describes her stay in a 12-step inpatient facility in darker terms:

> For anyone who has not been in a 12-step rehab, the daily program is brutal. Mine lasted from 7:30 AM to 10:00 PM. Essentially there was no time to think. If anyone was in his or her room for more than a few minutes, staff went in and announced that "isolating was just going to cause stinking thinking, so get out of your room." Every patient was expected to be at meals exactly on time, and to participate in all scheduled events. Late arrivals resulted in the loss of the minimal telephone contact we were allowed with the outside world. Almost every group, meeting and lecture began with the Serenity Prayer, and ended with the Lord's Prayer . . . I was told that "addicts do not like following rules," so many arbitrary rules were imposed to essentially break us of the bad habit of thinking independently. They wanted to break my will, so that I would "snap," and become one of them, obedient and grateful to the program. . . .
>
> I was told from the moment that I arrived . . . [that if I] didn't complete their "simple program," there was a 100% chance I would drink again, and would lose my career and my family, and would ultimately die from drinking.
>
> . . . I was not allowed to question anything about AA, especially the religious aspect . . . They kept telling me that my thinking was stinking, that my intelligence was a liability and was causing my problems, and

9. One group of researchers describes "the generic 'Minnesota Model' program" that continues to dominate American addictions treatment: "a milieu advocating a spiritual twelve-step (AA) philosophy, typically augmented with group psychotherapy, educational lectures and films, and relatively unspecified general alcoholism counseling, often of a confrontational nature" (Miller et al., 1995, p. 32). Other researchers describe the Minnesota Model as "a therapeutic model which integrated into a single program of care on-site AA meetings and systematic counseling in '12-step work,' with traditional medical interventions such as benzodiazepine detoxification and disulfiram therapy" (Schmidt & Weisner, 1993, p. 388). They go on, "Though precursors of the Minnesota Model have been traced back to the 1950s, it was in the 1980s that the approach became widespread, emerging by the end of the decade as the most widely employed of all alcohol treatment modalities in the nation" (p. 388).

that I had better check my psychiatric knowledge at the door and stop thinking.[10]

(Bartlett, 1997, pp. 4–5)

This then is 12-step inpatient treatment. Twelve-step outpatient treatment is essentially a watered-down version of 12-step inpatient treatment: counseling sessions with 12-step professionals and para-professionals, the purpose of which is to badger clients into over-coming their "denial," accepting the disease concept, "working the steps," and participating in AA (or NA) meetings; and for some coerced clients that means "90 meetings in 90 days." The authors of a study of 12-step outpatient drug treatment describe it as follows:

> Patients were counseled that cocaine addiction was a treatable but incurable disease. They were asked to attend at least one self-help meeting every week in addition to their regularly scheduled sessions. The regularly scheduled sessions consisted of both supportive and confrontative therapy, didactic lectures, and videos on cocaine dependence, AIDS, the disease model of addiction, and the self-help orientation. During the ninth week of treatment patients were asked to bring a family member to treatment to address family issues emanating from addiction. In the latter weeks of treatment, an aftercare plan was developed and counseling was provided on relapse prevention based on the 12-step model. Finally, patients were expected to identify a sponsor from a local self-help group [read CA or NA—only 12-step groups have sponsors—C.B.] by the final week of treatment.
>
> (Higgins et al., 1991, p. 1220)

This is a good description of normal 12-step outpatient treatment, and the 12-step treatment utilized in this study was in fact designed to be as typical as possible of what one would find at treatment facilities.

But what is the experience of 12-step treatment like for those coerced into it? Archie Brodsky and Stanton Peele describe a typical case, that of a married woman in her 50s called "Marie." She received a DUI citation after being stopped at a police checkpoint, and chose to pay $500 to attend 12-step outpatient treatment rather than lose her license for a year:

---

10. Chris Cornutt, a former paraprofessional counselor at a 12-step inpatient treatment facility, told me in an E-mail message on March 13, 1997 that patients "are virtually trapped in a Kafka nightmare once they admit themselves. If they voice any disagreement to you, they risk the wrath of the treatment team. Other patients 'turn them in' for non-AA or conflicting ideas. 'Narcing' on your fellow patients is a sign that you are working a good program and is heavily promoted."

Marie's treatment consisted of weekly counseling sessions, plus weekly A.A. meetings, for more than four months. . . . At A.A. meetings, Marie listened to ceaseless stories of suffering and degradation, stories replete with phrases like "descent into hell" and "I got down on my knees and prayed to a higher power." For Marie, A.A. was akin to a fundamentalist revival meeting.

In the counseling program . . . Marie received the same A.A. indoctrination and met with counselors whose only qualification was membership in A.A. These true believers told all the DWIs that they had the permanent "disease" of alcoholism, the only cure for which was lifetime abstinence and A.A. membership—all this based on one drunk-driving arrest!

In keeping with the self-righteous, evangelistic spirit of the program, any objection to its requirements was treated as "denial." The program's dictates extended into Marie's private life: She was told to abstain from all alcohol during "treatment," a proscription enforced by the threat of urinalysis. As Marie found her entire life controlled by the program, she concluded that "the power these people attempt to wield is to compensate for the lack of power within themselves. . . . I find it unconscionable that the criminal justice system has the power to coerce American citizens to accept ideas that are anathema to them. It is as if I were a citizen of a totalitarian regime being punished for political dissent."

(Brodsky & Peele, 1991, [On-line], p. 4)

Another story one of us (S.P.) recently received at his web site[11] further illustrates the degrading effects of 12-step treatment and "aftercare" (AA or NA participation) on non-addicted alcohol and drug users:

About 3 months ago I took a hair drug test at work. The test showed positive for marijuana. I had been using marijuana for a few years and only used a small amount each night before bedtime. After having severe migraines for years I turned to it as a last resort (I had used Imitrex, Vicodin, among other painkillers almost daily and Covera HS) and it helped considerably, almost completely eliminating the migraines.

Upon failing the drug test I was subject to being terminated by my employer if I didn't enter an Employee Assistance Program. I had to go through a four-hours-a-day/four-days-a-week program for three weeks at a rehab facility, even though I still believe I was using the marijuana for relief of my migraines and sleeping disorders. I did not abuse the drug or use it recreationally.

---

11. http://www.peele.net

After the hospital rehab program I've been forced to go to at least four AA meetings a week in order to be in compliance with my employer's EAP. People laughed at my marijuana habit at the first AA group I went to—one guy told me, "In LA we used to smoke marijuana after our AA meetings." I went to another AA group and admitted I was a marijuana addict. Afterwards, a lady came up to me and said, "You should say you are an alcoholic, you will be accepted better." I told her I don't drink alcohol and never developed a taste for it because of my migraines. So now I'm going to my third group, where I just say I'm an addict so I will be accepted by the group.

After about ten meetings I became so depressed I lost all my energy and I just lay around and have gained 20 lbs. I'm single, and recently have found myself thinking that life is no longer worth living.[12]

These descriptions of inpatient treatment, outpatient treatment, and aftercare are not unusual horror stories. Rather, they are typical of the experiences of the one million-plus Americans coerced into 12-step treatment and 12-step groups every year.[13]

Given the nature of 12-step treatment and 12-step groups, their results aren't terribly surprising.

---

12. One indication of the out-of-control state of 12-step treatment providers is that almost 5% of those admitted to treatment for marijuana use are subjected to detoxification—for supposed dependence on a non-physically addictive drug with, of course, no physical withdrawal symptoms (SAMHSA, 1999, p. 66, Table 3.4).

13. For further examples of such stories, see Bufe (1998), Peele (1989), Ragge (1998), Rebecca Fransway's upcoming *12-Step Horror Stories*, and virtually any issue of *The Journal of Rational Recovery*.

2

The Efficacy of 12-Step Groups and 12-Step Treatment

by Charles Bufe and Stanton Peele

The massive American treatment enterprise is based on the belief that alcohol and drug abuse can be treated away, and that we know how—and are currently able—to do so. Despite continuous efforts to establish its validity, this fundamental idea has not been shown to be true. Instead, research has repeatedly questioned whether the standard elements of U.S. substance abuse treatment work, and indeed, sometimes indicates that they do more harm than good. Consider that, after several expensive treatment experiences and many vows of abstinence, professional golfer John Daly resumed drinking and gambling. What had he learned in treatment? "It's sad, but I think it's great to be free," Daly told *Golf World* magazine. "Granted, I could go out and lose everything [by] gambling and drinking, but there's no sense in denying it. It's in my blood." Daly, like many, got the message that he had a disease for which he was not personally responsible.

This chapter will review the extensive research on substance abuse treatment. This research shows: 1) no clinical study has found the *sine qua non* of alcoholism treatment in the U.S., Alcoholics Anonymous, to be effective; 2) the most effective alcohol and drug treatments, as indicated by clinical trials, are rejected by U.S. treatment providers; 3) when standard substance abuse treatments have been compared to no or minimal treatment, they produce results no better than no or minimal treatment; 4) the U. S. government conducted the most expensive trial of psychotherapy ever done and found that minimal treatment, which places responsibility for allaying alcoholism on the drinker, is as good as the most elaborate 12-step treatment and cognitive/skills training; 5) a massive federal survey of American drinkers found that most alcoholics in the U.S. do not enter treatment, a higher percentage of *un*treated than treated alcoholics are in remission, and most untreated *and* treated alcoholics continue to drink, only the untreated do so with better results; 6) coerced treatment of prison inmates and probationers is actually counterproductive; 7) finally, there is no replacement for individual motivation and the provision of sufficient resources for those who want to improve their lives and cease addiction and substance abuse.

The Efficacy of AA and NA

There have been a number of controlled studies of AA and 12-step treatment, but there have been no scientifically valid, generalizable studies of NA. That is, there have been no studies of NA featuring random assignment of subjects and no-treatment control groups, or even comparison groups given other treatments, nor have there been longitudinal studies with matched comparison groups. There have been a number of uncontrolled, ungeneralizable (by their very nature) studies of 12-step groups (especially AA); and 12-step partisans love to quote such studies (and anecdotal evidence) as if they demonstrate the efficacy of 12-step programs.[1] The reason that the results of such uncontrolled studies *cannot* be generalized was put well by Holder et al. in an important 1991 article in the *Journal of Studies on Alcohol*:

> Prior reviews of the alcoholism treatment outcome literature have suggested that evidence from controlled clinical trials is considerably more consistent than the cumulative evidence of uncontrolled case studies and group designs. Positive uncontrolled reports can be found for virtually every treatment that has been tried for alcoholism, in-

---

1. George Vaillant, in his *Natural History of Alcoholism Revisited* (1995), provides a good example of this approach. In his lengthy discussion of Alcoholics Anonymous (Vaillant, 1995, pp. 254–269), Vaillant—who calls "the treatment system of AA" "the most exciting alcohol program in the world" (p. 350)—discusses anecdotal evidence and uncontrolled studies at length, but does not mention the only two controlled studies of AA's effectiveness ever conducted (Brandsma et al., 1980; Ditman et al., 1967). He even writes as if these controlled studies do not exist, stating, "controlled studies of AA have proven too difficult to carry out"—even though the Ditman et al. study is listed in his bibliography—and he goes on, "naturalistic [i.e., uncontrolled] studies offer evidence that AA is effective" (Vaillant, 1995, p. 268). He doesn't mention AA's self-damning *Comments on A.A.'s Triennial Surveys* monograph (Alcoholics Anonymous, n.d.), either, even though he himself is a member of AA's General Service Board.

cluding psychosurgery, respiratory paralysis and the administration of LSD. . . . Positive or negative outcomes may be attributable not only to the treatment offered, but to a host of confounding factors including patient selection criteria, expectancies, additional treatment components and posttreatment factors. Uncontrolled trials also offer no basis for comparison of outcomes. Is a 40% success rate a triumph or a disgrace compared with what would be expected from no treatment or alternative treatments? . . . Controlled trials in general, and randomized clinical trials in particular, are commonly employed as the standard of evidence for specific effectiveness of medical treatments.

(Holder et al., 1991, p. 52)

NA's Effectiveness

So, ignoring the ungeneralizable, uncontrolled studies cited by AA's and NA's supporters, and the self-serving, gross overestimates of treatment effectiveness by treatment providers, what are we left with? As regards NA, nothing. There is no scientifically valid evidence of NA's effectiveness. To put this another way, those being coerced into NA are being coerced into a program for which there is no scientific evidence of efficacy.

NA, however, is merely a clone of AA, as can be demonstrated by comparing the heart of both programs, the 12-steps of AA and NA, which differ by only single terms in steps 1 and 12. As well, NA borrowed its organizational structure and its meeting structure directly from AA. Further confirmation of the essentially identical nature of AA and NA can be seen in the integration of drug and alcohol 12-step treatment. The *National Treatment Center Study Summary Report* states that, "Only 11 of the 450 programs (2.4%) offer segregated treatment programming for patients with alcohol problems and patients with drug problems" (Roman & Blum, p. 26). Thus, NA can legitimately be regarded as a clone of AA, and one can reasonably expect that the efficacy of NA will be approximately that of AA.

AA's Effectiveness

As for AA, there are scientifically valid studies, but not many. Two, to be exact—and they are of particular interest to the purposes of this book because they both involved coerced clients. Because of their importance, we'll consider them at some length.

The Ditman Study

The first of these studies was conducted in San Diego in 1964 and 1965, and its subjects were 301 "chronic drunk offenders," who were defined "as having two drunk arrests in the previous three months or three drunk arrests in the previous year" (Ditman et al., 1967, p. 64). These offenders were randomly assigned to a no-treatment control group, a group assigned to go to AA as a condition of probation, and a group assigned to clinic treatment (type not specified) as a condition of probation. Those assigned to AA needed to provide proof of attendance in the form of signed statements from AA meeting secretaries attesting to their presence. All of these individuals were followed for at least a full year after their convictions. The primary outcome measure the investigators used was the number of rearrests during the year following conviction. The results were that 69% of those assigned to Alcoholics Anonymous were rearrested; 68% of those assigned to clinic treatment were rearrested; and 56% of the no-treatment control group was rearrested. Although this may sound striking, the investigators noted, "the chi-square tests . . . failed to reach statistical significance" (Ditman et al., 1967, p. 66). Their study summary reads, "No statistically significant differences between the three groups were discovered in recidivism rate, in number of subsequent rearrests, or in time elapsed prior to rearrest" (p. 64). To put this another way, this study provided evidence that AA is no more effective than no treatment at all.

The Brandsma Study

The second study, published in book form under the title *Outpatient Treatment of Alcoholism* (Brandsma et al., 1980), was a carefully designed, sophisticated, NIAAA-funded study of AA and three alternative therapies: lay-led Rational Behavior Therapy (similar to today's SMART Recovery program); professionally conducted one-on-one Rational Behavior Therapy (today called Rational Emotive Behavior Therapy); and professionally conducted one-on-one, traditional (Freudian-based) insight therapy. This study, like the Ditman et al. study, featured random assignment of subjects and a no-treatment control group. The researchers indicate that there were very few differences between the various groups, and that "the random assignment procedure was successful" (p. 70).

After screening, 260 clients were accepted for the study; 184 were court-coerced and were participating in the study as a condition of probation, and 76 were self-referred. The authors characterized the participants "as representative of the 'revolving door' alcoholic court cases in our cities" (p. 63).

Upon entering the study, the subjects were randomly assigned to one of the four treatment groups, or to a no-treatment control group. Treatment was scheduled to last up to a year, and the subjects were monitored during that time, with an outcome assessment after they completed treatment. They were then reinterviewed 3, 6, 9, and 12 months after the outcome assessment. The authors used several different outcome measures, including number of drinking days per 90 day period; amount consumed per drinking day; number of binges; marital status; employment status; rearrests; other social and psychological factors; and retention rate for the various treatments.

The results of this study were significant. In terms of retention rate, AA fared by far the worst of any of the treatment groups. The group assigned to AA had a 68% dropout rate; the insight group had a 42% dropout rate; lay-RBT had a 40% dropout rate; and pro-RBT had a 46% dropout rate.

As for the number of rearrests for drunkenness during treatment, all treatment groups did significantly better than the control group, with the professionally led insight group performing better than the other treatment groups.

As for economic results, in terms of employment, AA fared the worst of all groups; and in regard to employment-seeking, AA and the control group did worst, while the insight group did the best.

In terms of drinking behavior, all treatment groups reported significantly decreased drinking at the outcome assessment: pro-RBT, 80% of participants; lay-RBT, 100%; insight, 92%; AA, 67%; whereas only 50% of the control group reported decreased drinking. And, "at outcome, there were no significant differences in drinking behavior between [the lay-RBT, AA, and control] groups with regard to the number reporting abstinence" (p. 104).

In regard to bingeing behavior, "The mean number of reported binges was significantly greater ($p = .004$) for the AA group (2.37 in past 3 months) in contrast to both the control (0.56) and lay-RBT group (0.26). In this analysis, AA was [over 4] times [more] likely to binge than the control [group] and nine times more likely than the lay-RBT [group]. The AA average was 2.4 binges in the last 3 months since outcome" (p. 105).

All of this led the study's authors to conclude:

Although AA plays an extremely important part [in] a community's response to alcoholism in terms of education and treatment, it seems to have a definite but delimited "place in the sun." . . . AA seems to have definite limitations of social class, ideology, flexibility of adopting new techniques, and the type of personality it appeals to. Our study suggests further confirmation of this in our severe dropout rate from this form of treatment. It is probable, as Ditman et al.'s (1967) work suggests and ours confirms, that *AA is just not effective as a coerced treatment with municipal court offenders.*

(Brandsma et al., 1980, p. 84, emphasis added)

Finally, it's important to point out that the increase in bingeing behavior among those exposed to AA in this study militates against coercing DUI offenders into AA attendance. One very possible reason for the increase in bingeing is the emphasis in AA upon inevitable loss of control after even one drink, as codified in the AA slogan, "one drink, one drunk." (As we saw in Chapter 1, this assertion is not true, except to the extent that drinkers believe it to be true.) What likely happens is that for those exposed to AA, this inevitable-loss-of-control belief becomes a self-fulfilling prophecy. So, when a true-believing AA member slips and has a drink, or even eats a rum ball or ingests a bit of mouthwash containing alcohol, he or she could be provoked to embark on a full-bore binge. Given this, one can't help but be alarmed at the common practice of coercing DUI defendants into AA attendance and 12-step treatment.

AA's Triennial Surveys

While these are the only two controlled studies with random assignment of subjects ever conducted on AA's effectiveness, there is one other source of information worthy of our attention: the AA monograph, *Comments on AA's Triennial Surveys.*[2] AA has surveyed its members every three years since 1977 (with the exception of a four-year gap between 1992 and 1996). These are large surveys of several thousand AA members, and they measure such variables as length of membership, age distribution, male-female ratio, employment categories, the ways in which members were introduced to AA, and length of abstinence. AA normally uses the results in its promotional

---

2. This document was apparently produced for internal use only, as it is crudely produced (typewritten, photocopied sheets bound with a staple in one corner), is not part of AA's conference-approved literature, and has never been offered to the public; one of us (C.B.) obtained a copy by requesting it in 1991 from AA World Services, and other researchers obtained copies at about the same time.

"Alcoholics Anonymous [insert year] Membership Survey" brochures, but following the 1989 survey, AA undertook a statistical analysis of the previous five surveys. The results were published in the *Comments on A.A.'s Triennial Surveys* monograph.

As regards new member dropout rate, all five surveys were in close agreement. Averaging their results, the *Comments* document graphs the "% of those coming to AA within the first year that have remained the indicated number of months." At one month, the "% of those . . . that have remained" is 19%; at 3 months, 10%; and at 12 months, 5% (Alcoholics Anonymous, n.d., p. 12, Figure C-1).[3] This gives AA a 5% success rate at the one-year point if success is simply defined as continuing AA membership (in what is supposed to be a program for life).

But even this 5% success rate is questionable if AA's success in dealing with alcohol problems is defined as the very modest level of one-year's continuous abstinence, because, as anyone who has spent much time in AA can attest, far from all AA members are abstinent. AA's self-reported rate of recovery (as derived from membership retention) is far from impressive; in fact, it appears to be no better than the rate of spontaneous remission, which has been estimated at anywhere from 1% to 33% per year of those with alcohol problems (Prugh, 1986, p. 24). One survey of the spontaneous remission literature estimates its prevalence at 3.7% to 7.4% per year (Smart, 1975/76, p. 284). If this is true, AA's recovery rate of 5% or less could well be *lower* than the rate of spontaneous remission.[4]

This is most curious when one considers the nature of the disease of alcoholism (in reality, a *behavioral* problem). Given such a disease, one would expect a powerful placebo effect (from participation in AA), which in itself would substantially raise the rate of recovery in AA above that of spontaneous remission. But the placebo effect, judging from the available evidence, simply doesn't exist here. There

---

3. Curiously, on the preceding page (Alcoholics Anonymous, n.d., p. 11), the document states, "[Figure C-1] strongly suggests that about half those who come to A.A. are gone within three months." The most likely explanation of this inconsistency is that the author(s) of the document were comparing the numbers remaining after one month and after three months.

4. Of course, one could argue that at least some of the 95% who drop out of AA in any given year will achieve a year's abstinence; but to ascribe this to their exposure to AA, a program which they (almost certainly and overwhelmingly) dislike, disagree with, and do not follow, seems overly generous to AA. One could well argue that those who drop out of AA and achieve abstinence do so *in spite of,* not because of, AA—which told them that their only alternatives to lifelong AA attendance were "jails, institutions, or death."

seem two likely explanations for this: 1) There are so many coerced persons participating in AA, who very often dislike and actively resist AA's program, that AA's success (and concomitant membership retention) rate is skewed sharply downward; 2) AA is actively harmful. This is definitely possible, given AA's "powerless" and "one drink, one drunk" dogmas; and the evidence on binge drinking supplied by the Brandsma et al. study certainly seems to suggest this interpretation.

The authors of AA's *Comments* document, remarking on the low AA retention rate revealed by their research, note: "Individuals [in AA] may rebel against this result as contradicting our time-honored statement that 'half get sober right away, another 25% eventually make it,' etc. That statement applied to observations made at an earlier time, and there is no reason to doubt that changes in society and in A.A. since that time could create a different circumstance today. Like other findings of the survey, this may be a challenge to the membership to 'change the things we can'" (p. 13).

One change that some AA members[5] could make, if they wanted to, would be to stop participating in the mass coercion of individuals into AA. While that certainly would not immediately end coercion into AA, it would likely cause a noticeable decrease in that practice —and it would go a long way toward restoring AA's good name as a voluntary organization.

Ultimately, eliminating coercion into AA would almost certainly improve AA's current dismal effectiveness rate. At the very least, if AA returned to being a voluntaristic organization, it seems likely that its success rate would increase because of the placebo effect and member motivation, or readiness to change.

The Efficacy of 12-Step and Other Traditional Alcoholism Treatments

Amazingly—given its predominance in the $10-billion-a-year treatment field—there have been relatively few controlled studies (or long-term follow-up [longitudinal] studies of people with treated and untreated alcohol problems) involving 12-step treatment. Most studies, however, have found that 12-step treatment is ineffective as a means of combating alcohol abuse and alcohol dependence—the

---

5. These include AA members working in employee assistance programs, those in the court and penal systems, those working in professional diversion programs (for doctors, nurses, etc.), and those working as professional or paraprofessional treatment personnel who participate in coercive interventions.

findings have been, overall, that it is probably no better than no treatment at all.

The Vaillant Study

The two most important studies of 12-step treatment effectiveness are the massive NIAAA NLAES retrospective study (see Chapter 1) and a long-term longitudinal study of treated and untreated alcoholics by George Vaillant and other Harvard University researchers. The Vaillant study is probably the single best piece of evidence on 12-step treatment. It had several components, including a long-term longitudinal study of a group of "100 alcohol-dependent men and women followed for eight years after being admitted to a clinic for detoxification" (Vaillant, 1995, p. 2). (This clinic was the Cambridge and Somerville Program for Alcohol Rehabilitation, CASPAR, a 12-step inpatient/outpatient program, for which Dr. Vaillant worked as a psychiatric consultant.) Vaillant compared the outcomes of these 100 patients with those of alcoholic members of two comparison groups, subjects of two long-term longitudinal studies begun by other Harvard researchers: a group of 456 "Core City" Boston men, who had been followed since they were school boys; and a group of 204 former Harvard students, who had been followed since their college days. Vaillant also compared the outcomes of the 100 CASPAR patients with those of treated alcoholics in other studies, and with the outcomes shown in studies of untreated alcoholics.

Vaillant's results were that the 12-step hospital treatment he helped to provide was utterly ineffective, as judged in comparison with studies of untreated alcoholics. As Vaillant remarked, "Not only had we failed to alter the natural history of alcoholism, but our death rate of three percent a year was appalling" (Vaillant, 1995, p. 352). He continued, "our results were no better than the natural history of the disorder."

Vaillant is a strong supporter of Alcoholics Anonymous. (He is currently a member of AA's General Service Board.) While reporting these "appalling" results, Dr. Vaillant commented, "if we have not cured all the alcoholics who were detoxified over 8 years ago, the likelihood of members of the Clinic sample attending AA has been significantly increased" (pp. 357–358). But did Vaillant really find that AA is that helpful? Actually, greater attendance at AA by the alcoholics he helped to treat did not enhance their treatment outcomes relative to untreated groups. Furthermore, in the Core City group which was followed for 50 years, 48 men among the alcohol abusers achieved what Vaillant termed "stable abstinence." Of these, about a quarter (27%) relied on AA (defined by having at least 30 AA visits by the age of 48—that is, well less than a year's attendance). In other words, even among those seeking abstinence, the large majority in Vaillant's untreated sample succeeded without AA.[6]

The National Longitudinal Alcoholism Epidemiological Survey

The results of the NIAAA's National Longitudinal Alcoholism Epidemiological Survey are as unsupportive of 12-step treatment as the Vaillant study. As mentioned in Chapter 1, the NLAES study was of 43,000 adult respondents. These included "4,585 adults with prior *DSM-IV* alcohol dependence," who were separately analyzed by Deborah Dawson (1996) in an article published in *Alcoholism: Clinical and Experimental Research.* All of these individuals were serious alcohol abusers, persons who would be termed alcoholics in common parlance. All of them had been alcohol *dependent,* not mere alcohol *abusers.* (Substance abuse and substance dependence are separate *DSM-IV* diagnoses.)

As to treatment, "Individuals were counted as having received alcohol treatment if they reported ever having gone to any of 24 different treatment sources . . . These sources included 12-step programs and others ranging from inpatient wards in general or psychiatric hospitals to halfway houses, employee assistance programs, and various types of doctors and health providers" (p. 773). Since over 90% of all treatment in the United States is 12-step treatment (Roman & Blum, 1997, p. 24), it's fair to regard the treated individuals reported in the NLAES study as 12-step-treated individuals, although it should also be noted that the inclusion of those who have

---

6. Of course, some of this group succeeded by reducing or controlling their drinking. But Vaillant is highly distrustful of this outcome, and spends much of the book attacking it (mentioning one of us, S.P., by name while doing so). However, Vaillant does not reassure readers of his objectivity in this regard. Among other things, all of Vaillant's case studies describe either the (minority) of those who resolved their alcohol abuse by abstaining, or else those who failed because they did not attend AA. (Those who didn't attend AA actually comprised the large majority of subjects who successfully resolved an alcohol problem.) As for controlled drinking, "abstinence as a goal of treatment" occupies 15 lines in Vaillant's index, while controlled drinking does not even appear in the index. Furthermore, while defining "abstinence" as including up to a week's binge drinking in a year (and drinking less than once a month!), Vaillant rules out as controlled drinkers those who showed any sign of a drinking binge.

attended "12-step programs" (read AA) muddies the waters a bit as regards the effectiveness of formal treatment.

Overall, the NLAES found that a third of treated and a quarter (26%) of untreated subjects were abusing or dependent on alcohol in the past year. Of those whose alcohol dependence appeared within the last five years, 70 percent who received treatment were drinking alcoholically in the past year. At 20 or more years since the onset of dependence, 90% of once-dependent individuals who had neither been formally treated nor had participated in 12-step groups were either abstinent or drinking without abuse or dependence, compared with 80% of the treated individuals who were no longer alcoholic. These are remarkable results. They indicate that *more treated than untreated alcoholics are subjecting themselves to alcohol abuse or dependence.*

These results should not be over interpreted, because the treated alcoholics in the NLAES reported a greater degree of alcohol dependence on average than the untreated alcoholics and, according to the NIAAA's Bridget Grant (1996), also reported more drug problems. On the other hand, all of the untreated subjects were diagnosed with alcohol dependence. The conclusion that alcoholics (alcohol-dependent persons) who enter treatment are less likely to achieve remission than untreated alcoholics in the United States, although the populations are not identical, certainly puts a crimp in the claims made by treatment advocates of the value of extending treatment into the lives of more Americans.

Meta-Analyses of Alcoholism Treatment

William Miller and his colleagues at the University of New Mexico have conducted an ongoing meta-analysis of controlled (or clinical) studies of alcoholism treatment (Miller et al., 1995). (A meta-analysis is a statistical method of combining results of disparate research studies. In order to be included in Miller at al.'s analysis, a research study had to compare among matched or randomly assigned alcoholics the results of one type of treatment for alcoholism to another type or to no treatment at all.) Miller et al. reported that 13 treatment types had "too little basis" to support conclusions about their efficacy, while 30 treatment types had sufficient basis to support such conclusions. Treatments were assigned scores based on their combined degree of superiority (or inferiority) to other therapies.

The results of the 211 studies included in the analysis support the conclusion that 12-step inpatient treatment is ineffective. Miller et al. listed 10 studies of "milieu therapy," largely residential or inpatient treatment. Of the 10 studies, seven indicate that milieu therapy is ineffective in dealing with alcohol problems. Other standard approaches fare equally badly. "Unspecified 'standard' treatment" was reported ineffective in all three studies in which it was tested, and "general alcoholism counseling" was found ineffective in 14 out of 15 studies (p. 18).

Of the 30 types of treatment on the Miller et al. list, milieu therapy came in at 20th place on their "cumulative evidence scale"; unspecified standard treatment came in at 22nd place; and general alcoholism counseling came in at 29th place—putting all of these therapies below, among others, "aversion therapy, nausea," "aversion therapy, electrical," and lithium therapy (p. 18).

Two components of standard 12-step therapy, confrontational counseling and educational lectures/films, were studied as separate therapies, and both fared dismally: confrontational counseling came in at 26th place, and educational lectures/films came in dead last.

It's also worth noting that of the 30 therapies listed, only psychotherapy (which came in at 28th place on the cumulative evidence score) was more expensive than milieu therapy, and that unspecified "standard" treatment and general alcoholism counseling were tied as being the fourth most costly treatments.[7]

Two other meta-analyses have confirmed these results (Finney & Monahan, 1996; Holder et al., 1991). They both showed that expensive, commonly used treatments, such as "milieu therapy" and "general alcoholism counseling" (in the U.S., read 12-step inpatient and outpatient treatment), were among the least effective; and they also showed that almost all of the therapies consistently supported in studies as effective, such as the community reinforcement approach, marital therapy, and social skills training, were low cost or medium-low cost. This is hardly surprising given that all three of these surveys

---

7. In contrast, the five most effective therapies listed were: 1) brief intervention; 2) social skills training; 3) motivational enhancement; 4) community reinforcement approach; and 5) behavior contracting. All of these therapies are cognitive-behavioral treatments, and all are in the very low- to moderately low-cost categories, with brief intervention and motivational enhancement tied as the second cheapest forms of therapy of all 30 listed. In discussing this, Miller et al. noted: "We were pleased to see that a number of treatment methods were consistently supported by controlled scientific research. On the other hand, we were dismayed to realize that virtually none of these treatment methods was in common use within alcohol treatment programs in the United States" (Hester & Miller, 1995, p. xi). Miller et al. (p. 13) later noted, "A significant negative correlation ($r = -.385$) was found between the strength of efficacy evidence for modalities and their cost; that is, the more expensive the treatment method, the less the scientific evidence documenting its efficacy."

were exhaustive and that they thus evaluated essentially the same materials—virtually all available generalizable studies of treatment effectiveness.

The Edwards et al. Study / Brief Interventions

One graphic demonstration of the lack of efficacy of expensive treatment appeared in a 1977 study by Edwards et al. These investigators studied "100 men who were married or in a continuing cohabitation (common law marriage), consecutive attenders at the outpatient Alcoholism Family Clinic" (p. 1005). After completing an initial assessment, the men in the "advice" group (and their wives) were given a single counseling session in which they "were told that responsibility for attainment of the stated goals [abstinence, employment, and marital improvement] lay in their own hands" (p. 1006), but that the clinic would make monthly follow-up calls to check progress. The treatment group was introduced to AA and was then given a year of outpatient treatment, including psychiatric and social worker appointments. At the end of one year, there were no significant differences between the two groups on any of the outcome measures. As measured by separate reports from both the subjects and their wives, those in the advice group fared slightly better on some outcome measures, and slightly worse on others, than the treatment group. But there were no significant differences. That is, a year's worth of treatment produced results no better than those from a single advice session.

A number of studies have found that startlingly mild therapeutic interventions comparable to Edwards et al. produce results as good as—or better than—standard therapies. Indeed, this is the basis for the finding in Miller et al. (1995) that so-called brief interventions rate as the most effective alcoholism treatment according to controlled research. In such interventions, a client's drinking is often assessed in an ordinary health care environment, usually by a general practitioner or other nonspecialist health care worker. The health care worker points out heavy or problematic drinking, discusses it with the person, and they then set mutually agreeable drinking-reduction goals. Progress is then checked during periodic follow-ups. In this remarkably straightforward procedure, very simple and inexpensive techniques suffice to improve the drinking behavior of most alcohol abusers. Nothing could be further from the elaborate 12-step spiritual approach that is embedded in virtually every alcoholism treatment program in the United States.

12-Step Drug Treatment

Given that 12-step drug and alcohol treatment are virtually inter-changeable, and in a great many cases are administered in the same facilities by the same personnel, it's reasonable to conclude that their results should be similarly dismal. (As mentioned above, the *National Treatment Center Study Summary Report* states that only 2.4% of the treatment facilities surveyed offered segregated alcohol and drug treatment.)

To the best of our knowledge, there have been no controlled studies of 12-step drug treatment with random assignment of subjects and no-treatment control groups. The best studies available are two studies from the early 1990s of 12-step outpatient treatment in com-parison to community reinforcement approach, or CRA (Higgins et al., 1991; Higgins et al., 1993), and one study of 12-step outpatient treatment versus cognitive-behavioral relapse prevention treatment (Wells et al., 1994).

The community reinforcement approach is a behavioral program that organizes an individual's environment to reinforce sobriety rather than relying on personal commitment or any kind of spiritual or internal resolution of the problem. (For example, the Higgins et al. CRA studies tied work and financial rewards to continued abstinence from cocaine.) Such cognitive-behavioral therapy intro-duces and reinforces new ways of thinking and approaches to problem-solving so that addicts learn alternative ways of coping with stress and insecurity other than turning to drugs or alcohol. This type of therapy relies on practical skills, and does not teach drug users that they are addicts with a life-long disease.

The Higgins Studies

In the first study (Higgins et al., 1991), 13 consecutively admitted cocaine-dependent patients at an outpatient treatment facility were offered behavioral treatment, the main feature of which was the community reinforcement approach. All 13 accepted. An additional 15 consecutively admitted cocaine-dependent patients were offered standard 12-step outpatient treatment (described in Chapter 1); 12 of the 15 accepted. The only major differences between the two groups were that the behavioral group had been using far more cocaine than the 12-step clients (an average of 10.2 grams for the behavioral clients versus 3.7 grams for the 12-step clients during the "most recent peak use" week), and that 69% of the clients assigned to the behavioral group were intravenous users compared with 16% of those assigned to the 12-step group (p. 1221).

Despite the greater severity of the problems of the clients in the behavioral group, their results were far better than those of the 12-step clients. Eleven (85%) of the 13 clients in the behavioral group completed the full 12 weeks of treatment, whereas only five (42%) of the 12 clients in the 12-step group completed treatment. In addition, ten of the clients in the behavioral group achieved four weeks of cocaine abstinence; six achieved eight weeks; and three achieved 12 weeks. In contrast, only three of the 12-step clients achieved four weeks of cocaine abstinence, and none achieved eight weeks, let alone 12 weeks. These results were confirmed by urinalysis.

The second study (Higgins et al., 1993), which featured a larger sample, random selection of subjects, and a longer study period (24 weeks versus 12 weeks in the original study), confirmed the first study's results. In the behavioral group, 11 of the 19 clients (58%) completed all 24 weeks of treatment, while in the 12-step group only two of the 19 clients (11%) completed 24 weeks of treatment. Only one of the behavioral clients, but eight of the 12-step clients, dropped out of the study after only one therapy session. And 74% of the behavioral clients managed to abstain from cocaine for at least four weeks; 68% abstained for eight weeks; and 42% abstained continuously for 16 weeks. The comparable figures for the 12-step group were 16% for four weeks; 11% for eight weeks; and 5% (one client) for 16 weeks.

The Wells Study

The third study of 12-step drug treatment versus cognitive-behavioral drug treatment involved 110 cocaine-abuse clients alternately assigned to 12-step outpatient therapy or cognitive-behavioral outpatient relapse prevention therapy (Wells et al., 1994). Treatment lasted for 24 weeks and consisted of 17 two-hour therapy sessions for both groups. There were no statistically significant differences between the 12-step and relapse prevention clients at intake, although the relapse prevention patients were using cocaine, alcohol, and marijuana somewhat more often than the 12-step patients at that point—on average, slightly over 25% more often, as measured in days used per month.

Results were measured in the number of drug-using days per 30 days at 12 weeks and six months following the start of treatment. In regard to cocaine use, the 12-step clients had been using cocaine an average of 4.4 days per month at intake. This dropped to 1.3 days per month at the 12-week measure, but climbed back to 1.9 days per month at the six-month measure. The same pattern was seen in alcohol use by 12-step clients, who drank an average of 7.7 days per month at intake, dropped to 5.0 days per month at the 12-week measure, but climbed back to 7.2 days per month at the six-month measure. Note that such subjects succeeded neither at abstaining entirely nor at limiting their alcohol use, that they did not succeed at abstaining from cocaine, and that their use of the drug was rebounding at the six-month measure.

In contrast, the relapse prevention clients showed a steady drop in cocaine use, and only a slight rebound in alcohol use. Cocaine use fell steadily from 5.5 days per month at intake, to 2.3 days per month at the 12-week measure, to 1.6 days at the six-month measure. Drinking averaged 9.9 days per month at intake, dropped to 7.9 days per month at the 12-week measure, and then increased slightly to 8.4 days per month at the six-month measure.

Only with marijuana was there a continual decline in use by the 12-step clients: from 4.8 days per month at intake, to 3.2 at 12 weeks, to 3.0 at six months. The relapse prevention clients showed a similar, though slighter, decrease: from 5.9 days per month at intake, to 5.0 at 12 weeks, to 4.8 at six months.

Primarily because of the statistically significant ($p > .04$) increase in the amount of alcohol consumed by the 12-step clients between the 12-week and six-month measure, Wells et al. (p. 14) concluded, "With its emphasis on anticipating and coping with future high-risk situations, relapse prevention [treatment] would be expected to be superior [to 12-step treatment] in helping clients maintain reductions in drug usage over time."

Use by 12-step clients of alcohol and cocaine were similar—they both showed an initial steep decline, followed by a steep increase between the 12-week and six-month measures. In contrast, the relapse prevention clients showed only a very slight increase in alcohol use between the 12-week and six-month measures, and a large decrease in cocaine use in the same period. Finally, the relapse prevention clients showed a continual decrease in cocaine use across all three measures; while they were using cocaine on 25% more days per month than the 12-step clients at intake, by the end of the study they were using cocaine on 13% *fewer* days than the 12-step clients.

The Texas Prison Study

A number of research studies have claimed that exposing inmates to treatment (or, often, coercing them into treatment) reduces recidivism (returning to crime) and relapse (returning to addiction/alcoholism) rates.[8] Thus, the requirement of treatment in prisons and even the substitution of treatment for imprisonment (for example, through sentencing by drug courts) have become mantras for drug policy reformers and treatment providers. Yet, one of the most careful studies of the effects of treatment on inmates and probationers (those given treatment in place of imprisonment), a comparative study conducted over three years in the Texas penal system, yielded a less positive—and in some respects, opposite—result.

That study was released by Texas' Criminal Justice Policy Committee (Eisenberg, 1999). (The nature of the treatment used was not described in any detail, but it almost certainly was 12-step treatment.) This report covered four programs involving 1654 prisoners who had undergone treatment while in prison, and 1673 probationers who had undergone treatment while on probation.

The recidivism rate three years after treatment was exactly the same for those prisoners who had undergone treatment as for those in the no-treatment comparison groups (drawn from the same population): one program had a 42% recidivism rate for both treated and comparison groups, while the other program had a 37% recidivism rate for both the treated and comparison groups. The results with probationers were even more discouraging. Three years after treatment, treated probationers in one program had a 38% imprisonment rate, while members of the no-treatment comparison group had a 35% imprisonment rate; and in the other program, the treated probationers had a 44% imprisonment rate compared with only a 35% imprisonment rate for the comparison group.

When contemplating that other studies have yielded more positive results, the chief investigator in this study observed:

---

8. The most oft-cited example is a mathematical modeling study by Rydell et al. (1997) indicating that treatment is more cost-effective for cocaine users than imprisonment. We agree that imprisonment for drug use and/or drug abuse is a ridiculous and self-defeating policy, but to rate the effectiveness of treatment in comparison with a nonsensical policy is meaningless.

Outcome evaluations for programs in other states have focused primarily on reporting the outcomes of offenders completing the program and not on all program participants. . . . For example, an evaluation of a California therapeutic community program for prisoners reported that 25% of offenders completing the program were arrested in one year versus 67% of the comparison group arrested. When the recidivism rate of offenders not completing the program is included, the recidivism rate of all program participants is 53%.

(Eisenberg, 1999, p. 12)

In many cases, optimistic claims about treatment are based only on those who complete treatment—which is another way of evaluating only the best-prognosis patients. Much of the optimism about programs treating convicted felons is based on such poor science. After all, what does it mean that, in an expensive, large-scale treatment program in one of our largest states, treatment—at best—did no good?

Many probationers and prisoners who drop out of treatment programs must find those programs particularly objectionable, given the dire consequences they face (imprisonment or continued imprisonment) for failing to complete these programs.

Dropout Rates

The typically high dropout rate of 12-step treatment programs is a telling indication of their lack of effectiveness. Twelve-step treatment programs often make grossly exaggerated claims about their effectiveness, with some citing success rates as high as 75%, 85%, or even 95%. A brief look at dropout rates from such programs gives lie to such claims. SAMHSA's 1992–1997 TEDS report states that, overall, only 47% of patients complete treatment (and another 12% are transferred to other programs—with no indication of whether they complete that treatment) (SAMHSA, 1999). Thus, the overall completion rate in American treatment is, at best, under 60%, and could be under 50%. Remembering that the 12-step approach is utilized in 93% of American treatment facilities, according to the *National Treatment Center Study Summary Report*, it's fair to take these percentages as the percentages for 12-step treatment.

In the group subjected to the most direct coercion, marijuana clients, 52% of whom are directly coerced by the criminal justice system and only 18% of whom are individually referred, one finds a similar pattern: only 48% complete treatment, with another 11%

being transferred to other programs. That so many clients (many, undoubtedly, under threat of jail or prison time) leave these programs is a good indication of how objectionable they find 12-step treatment.

Why should dropout rates be taken into account when calculating the effectiveness of treatment programs? Consider two hypothetical alcohol-abuse treatment programs, "A" and "B." Both admit 100 comparable clients, and both show recovery rates of 80% for those who complete treatment. Based on this, are both programs equally successful? If the dropout rate for "A" was only 50% and the dropout rate for "B" was 70%, and the recovery rate in both programs was 80% for those who completed treatment, "A" would yield 40 recovered clients, or almost twice as many as "B," which would yield only 24 recovered clients. Obviously, the two programs are far from equally successful.

But 12-step advocates typically ignore the sky-high dropout rates in 12-step treatment programs, dismissing dropouts with cliches such as "the program works if you work the program" (implying that "the program" *always* "works," and that when it doesn't the fault is *always* the client's). This, of course, misses the point, as dropouts *must* be included when calculating effectiveness of treatment.

The "Best" Evidence of the Efficacy of 12-Step Treatment

There are no scientific studies featuring random assignment of subjects and no-treatment control groups that indicate that 12-step groups or 12-step treatment are effective means of dealing with addiction problems. In the absence of such studies, 12-step advocates have repeatedly cited uncontrolled, ungeneralizable studies as if they were generalizable, and they have latched onto three studies with comparison groups (but without no-treatment control groups) as evidence (or even "proof") of the efficacy of AA and 12-step treatment. One 12-step advocate, George Vaillant (1995, p. 360), provides a good example of the hyperbole common to such apologetics: "The recent randomized trial by Walsh and colleagues (1991) has put all negative findings about the limitations of hospital treatment for alcohol abuse in question." What exactly is Vaillant referring to?

The Walsh Study

Walsh et al. (1991) was a study of 227 alcoholic industrial workers in New England, who were coerced by their employer into either 12-step inpatient treatment or AA, or were given a "choice" of treatment options—although the authors note that "the staff or the employee assistance program sometimes encouraged them" to enter either 12-step inpatient treatment or AA. As a result, of the 71 workers in the choice group, 62 (87%) entered either 12-step inpatient treatment or AA. Of the remaining nine subjects, three chose psychotherapy, and six chose no treatment at all. The researchers lumped them in with the 62 workers who had chosen some form of 12-step program. Thus, this study not only didn't have a no-treatment control group, it didn't even have a non-12-step comparison group.

The subjects were followed for 24 months, and the major outcome results studied were "job outcome" (i.e., how many from each group were fired), drinking outcome, and "other drugs and group outcomes." Overall, the inpatient group did better than the AA or choice groups, though it should be noted that "better" here is in comparison with rather poor outcomes.

In terms of job outcome, there were "no significant differences among the groups." Overall, 14% of clients were fired during the study's two-year period (p. 778). As for drinking outcomes, there were no significant differences between the groups in regard to four important measures, "mean number of daily drinks, number of drinking days per month, binges, and serious symptoms," although the inpatient group did significantly better than either the AA or choice groups in regard to continuous abstention: 37% for the inpatient group; 17% for the choice group; and 16% for the AA group.

The inpatient group also did better than either the AA or choice groups in regard to (re)hospitalization: 42% of the randomly assigned subjects were hospitalized for additional treatment: 23% of the hospital group, 38% of the choice group, and 63% of the AA group over the two-year period.[9]

---

9. Note the word "additional." These findings mean that of the group that had already been forced into a hospital, about a quarter needed to be hospitalized *a second time*, with its extremely high costs. All of those in the AA group who were subsequently hospitalized (63%!) were experiencing their first hospital episode. It is not possible to know how many of the 38% of the choice group who received additional treatment in a hospital were among the 40% who chose hospitalization in the first place.

As for drug outcomes, "of the cocaine-using subjects in the hospital and choice groups, less than 30 percent underwent additional inpatient treatment, as compared with 63 percent of the cocaine users randomly assigned to AA alone" (p. 779).

Overall, these outcomes can only be described as miserable, especially considering that being coerced into treatment under threat of job loss is a powerful wake-up call—which in itself should have jolted some workers into making significant changes—and considering the very high cost of the treatment employed. The average cost of treatment for the compulsory AA group came to $8840 over the two-year study; the average cost for the choice group was $14,400 for those who chose initial inpatient treatment, and $8800 for those who didn't; and the average cost for the compulsory inpatient group was $10,040.

Due to the nature of this study (comparing only 12-step approaches), any generalized conclusions derived from it about the effectiveness of 12-step treatment should be approached with great caution. What would be truly telling would be a similar trial, but one involving a no-treatment control group and comparisons with low-cost behavioral treatments, such as motivational enhancement, social skills training, and the community reinforcement approach. Nonetheless, what may be most overwhelming in the results of this study is the poor performance of the AA-alone group. This group had the highest (re)hospitalization rate and the lowest rate of never becoming intoxicated (although it shared the lowest abstinence rate with the few "choice" subjects, many of whom of course selected AA).

Project MATCH

The second commonly cited "proof" of the effectiveness of 12-step treatment is Project MATCH (1997). When this $35-million, NIAAA-funded study was released in 1997, treatment supporters claimed variously that it demonstrated the validity of 12-step treatment, that all of the tested forms of treatment work equally well, or even that 12-step treatment is superior to other forms of treatment.[10] In reality, it showed none of these things.

---

10. Enoch Gordis, director of the NIAAA, said that while the MATCH findings "challenge the notion that patient-treatment matching is necessary for alcoholism treatment, the good news is that treatment works" (Bower, 1997); and Margaret Mattson (1997), a principal NIAAA MATCH coordinator, declared, "The results indicate that the Twelve Step model . . . is beneficial."

Project MATCH compared three forms of outpatient and aftercare treatment: motivational enhancement; cognitive behavioral coping skills therapy; and "12-step facilitation" therapy. All three forms of treatment were delivered in one-on-one counseling sessions, though the number of scheduled sessions was only four for motivational enhancement, compared with 12 for the other two forms of therapy. Post-treatment assessment was carried out over a period of 12 months following the end of formal treatment.

The significant findings of Project MATCH were that patients in all three groups experienced remarkably similar improvement, as measured by the number of drinking days per month and the incidence of bingeing. The only significant difference between the groups was that 12-step-treated clients with less severe psychological problems had more abstinent days than similar clients in the other two groups. But this one positive difference was not one of those predicted by the researchers. Of 21 predicted differences in outcomes, depending upon the match between a patient's characteristics and the type of treatment received, *none* of the hypotheses generated by this distinguished group of alcoholism researchers (comprising the leading alcoholism treatment scientists in the United States) was substantiated. What then did Project MATCH show?

On average, the alcoholics in this study reduced their drinking days from 25 to fewer than 6 per month, and from 15 to 3 drinks on each drinking occasion (Connors, 1998). Clearly, these are dramatic results, but were they the result of treatment or of other factors?

Project MATCH was so over designed that it seems likely that *any* form of treatment used in it would have shown similar results. All clients in Project MATCH were volunteers, and their volunteer status in itself shows a fairly high degree of motivation, a very important biasing factor, contrasting them with the majority of treatment enrollees in the U.S. (see Chapter 1). In addition, subjects with simultaneous drug dependencies were not accepted, even though patients with both drug and alcohol problems are the most common admittees to substance abuse treatment (SAMHSA, 1999) and show lower remission rates than alcohol-only clients (Grant, 1996). During the screening process approximately 10% of potential clients opted out of the study for reasons such as "the inconvenient location of the study or transportation problems." More than half of the remaining potential clients were eliminated from the study for reasons such as "failure to complete the assessment battery, residential instability, [and] legal or probation problems." These disqualifications ensured that only the most well-adjusted clients would participate, thus introducing another positive biasing factor: social and emotional stability. In other words, as far as alcohol-abuse clients go, Project MATCH was dealing with those most likely to succeed in *any* program; of 4,481 potential participants who went through initial screening, only 1,726 became study participants.

Client expectations were another positive biasing factor. The clients knew that they were taking part in a special study, and the manner in which sessions were conducted undoubtedly led to high expectations. The study entailed "compliance enhancement procedures (i.e., calling clients between sessions, sending reminder notes and having collateral contacts)" (p. 23). The most skilled professionals and researchers in the United States first wrote manuals detailing each type of treatment. Supervisors and counselors were then trained using the manuals as reference. Every one-to-one therapy session was videotaped, and supervisors monitored a quarter of the sessions.

This degree of training and supervision makes treatment in Project MATCH entirely unlike standard treatment administered in the U.S. The difference between the forms of treatment employed in Project MATCH and actual treatment in the U.S. was undoubtedly most pronounced in the study's 12-step facilitation therapy. In the real world, 12-step treatment is predominantly *group* treatment, and individual therapy and group sessions are normally administered by paraprofessionals with limited professional training (usually AA/NA members with the title Certified Alcoholism Counselor). Furthermore, the trained therapists administering 12-step facilitation in Project MATCH would have been unlikely to engage in the highly directive, even abusive, behavior that is commonplace in 12-step programs, where drinkers are confronted with their deficiencies and forced to confess that they are alcoholics.

The high number of follow-ups with patients (for the purpose of assessment) actually may have been the most confounding factor of all in Project MATCH. Several studies have found that follow-ups are critical determinants of treatment outcomes—that is, rather than telling people what to do, checking to see how they are doing on a regular basis is the key to helping them reduce their drinking. Indeed, this is the key to brief interventions, where a minimal intervention is secondary to regular follow-ups with patients. In line with such findings, the briefest of the treatments in Project MATCH —motivational enhancement (ME)—produced results identical with those of the other treatments. ME had only four scheduled sessions as compared to the 12 sessions scheduled for the 12-step and social skills treatments (although patients on average attended only about two-thirds of these). The researchers thus noted that subjects in the ME groups actually spent more time in follow-up assessments (five hours) than they did in the treatment being assessed!

Given all of these biasing factors, it was hardly surprising that all forms of treatment showed remarkably similar, and positive, outcomes. Indeed, it seems possible that almost *any* form of treatment might have shown similar results. The study's authors recognized —after the fact—this possibility, when they noted: "Compliance enhancement procedures . . . and the greater attention of individual treatment may have produced a level of overall compliance that made it difficult for differences between treatments to emerge." They continued, "The overall effect of being a part of Project MATCH, with its extensive assessment, attractive treatments and aggressive follow-up, may have minimized naturally occurring variability among treatment modalities and may, in part, account for the favorable treatment outcomes." We'll never know for sure, though, because, as the researchers put it, "the efficacy of the three treatments cannot be demonstrated directly since the trial did not include a no-treatment control group" (Project MATCH, 1997, pp. 23–24).

Even accepting the findings of Project MATCH as valid, the conclusion emerges that 12-step treatment should *not* be the preferred form of treatment for alcohol-dependent and alcohol-abusing individuals. Because all three forms of treatment studied in Project MATCH showed very similar results, it stands to reason that the most cost-effective treatment should be the preferred treatment. And that preferred treatment would be motivational enhancement, which produced the same results as 12-step treatment with half or fewer treatment sessions.

In the end, what Project MATCH actually demonstrated was that with extremely well-designed and controlled treatment (unlike that delivered virtually anywhere in the U.S. today), even very alcoholic patients can reduce their drinking substantially. As the motivational enhancement results showed, such improvement does not require extensive time in treatment—a couple of hours may be sufficient. In Project MATCH, such treatment produced excellent results at a fraction of the time and cost required by standard treatment programs.

The Ouimette Study

The third study commonly cited by 12-step advocates as evidence of efficacy was conducted by Ouimette et al. (1997) with participants in Veterans Administration substance abuse programs. This large study surveyed 3699 patients in 15 VA hospitals who had participated in either 21- or 28-day inpatient treatment, and divided them by treatment type: 12-step, mixed 12-step/cognitive-behavioral, and cognitive-behavioral. The programs were classified according to descriptions provided by program directors and staff members. Results were measured using 11 variables, such as daily alcohol consumption, abstinence, remission, employment status, housing status, and arrests, and were derived primarily from self-report an average of 13.2 months after the patients left the programs.

The results were surprising:

> Although 12-step patients were somewhat more likely to be abstinent at the 1-year follow-up, 12-step, C-B, and combined 12-step–C-B treatment programs were equally effective in reducing substance use and improving most other areas of functioning. The finding of equal effectiveness was consistent over several treatment subgroups: Patients attending the "purest" 12-step and C-B programs, and patients who received the 'full dose' of treatment. Also, patients with only substance abuse diagnoses, those with concomitant psychiatric diagnoses, and patients who were mandated to treatment showed similar improvement at the 1-year follow-up, regardless of type of treatment received.
>
> (Ouimette et al., 1997, p. 230)

A few pages later the authors note:

> [A]nalyses examining the main effects of treatment type were performed on the subset of patients who received the 'full dose' of 12-step, C-B, and mixed treatment. Results were the same as in the complete sample.
>
> (Ouimette et al., 1997, p. 236)

This statement is highly provocative. It makes one wonder about the results for those who dropped out—were these very different from the results of those who went all the way through treatment? Unfortunately, there is no way to examine this. The authors—who analyzed the results for several different subgroups—did not analyze the results for treatment dropouts (P.C. Ouimette, personal communication to C.B., September 22, 1999).

There were other loose ends in this study, especially the presence of factors that tended to bias its results in favor of 12-step treatment. The most important of these biasing factors is that in calculating their results, the authors disregarded the difference in follow-up rates between the 12-step and C-B groups. Fully 85% of the C-B patients participated in the follow-up self-report, while only 78% of the 12-step patients did so, a statistically significant difference (p>.001). Given that failure to participate in follow-up studies is often an indication of a bad outcome, and that 12-step devotees would *want* to report favorable outcomes (probably more so than C-B patients, who wouldn't have religious zeal as a motivator), this omission could well have biased the results in favor of 12-step treatment.

Other aspects of the study also seemingly biased the results in favor of 12-step treatment. One is that, in calculating their results, the researchers refused to classify any patient as remitted who had smoked as little as a single joint in the more than a year between treatment and follow-up. Given the extremely heavy emphasis on abstinence from alcohol and illicit drugs (but not tobacco) in 12-step treatment, and this study's reported higher abstinence (but not overall improvement) rate among those who underwent 12-step treatment, it seems very likely that more otherwise-remitted C-B patients than 12-step patients were classified as continuing substance abusers in this study's conclusions because of marijuana use, no matter how infrequent.

In addition to these factors potentially biasing results in favor of the 12-step treatment, there were additional problems with this study's methodology that impede drawing *any* firm conclusions from it. The programs studied were *not* "pure" 12-step or C-B programs; all contained significant elements of both approaches. It is also relevant that "[s]taff in all three program types did not differ on psychosocial model beliefs, probably reflecting the emphasis on social and environmental change in all programs" (p. 232). This is an essentially cognitive-behavioral emphasis (in contrast to the 12-step emphasis, which reduces alcoholism to an *individual* disease, the cure for which is *individual*—turning one's will and life "over to the care of God"), and at least suggests that any success that the 12-step VA treatment showed might have been the result of its inclusion of cognitive-behavioral components.

As with other research, "all programs expected aftercare participation and provided referrals to both outpatient treatment and community-based self-help organizations" (p. 232). But the authors give no details on how many patients participated in aftercare, nor how long, nor what type. Since it seems likely that a fair number did participate in such care, this makes it extremely difficult to determine whether any effects shown were the result of the 21- or 28-day treatment (or patient effects) or the possible year-plus of aftercare.

Finally, the Ouimette et al. study's population was very distinctive. It was composed entirely of military veterans; it was entirely male; blacks were greatly over represented (49%); hispanics (3%) and anglos (46%) were greatly under represented; only 24% of its subjects were employed; only 19% were married; and subjects were older than average (43). It seems very likely that militarily trained subjects would respond better to the regimented, religious approach embodied in the 12 steps than average. This may have been a population best suited to the 12 steps (in which case, the absence of superior results from this type of therapy suggests that even for this group alternative approaches are at least equally effective). Would a youthful, middle-class, college population respond similarly well to the 12 steps?

We should also note that the Ouimette et al. study did not have a no-treatment control group, which means—as the authors conclude — "the possibility exists that these three treatment programs produce patient outcomes similar to those that naturally occur with no treatment" (p. 239).

Some Thoughts On 12-Step Treatment Effectiveness

Normally, in scientific discourse on the treatment of diseases, the burden of proof falls on those proposing a treatment. That is, those who assert that a treatment is effective are obliged to provide convincing evidence of its efficacy before it passes beyond clinical studies, let alone is administered on a mass scale. Yet those who promote the disease concept of alcoholism and 12-step treatment have never provided such proof, and they ignore the preponderant conclusion of the available generalizable scientific studies that 12-step groups and 12-step treatment are ineffective (or are neither the most effective nor the most cost-effective) means of dealing with addiction problems. That they ignore the available scientific studies and offer virtually no evidence beyond anecdotal claims and uncontrolled studies, yet continue to trumpet 12-step groups and 12-step treatment as the best, if not the *only*, means of dealing with addiction problems, is a telling sign that their advocacy of the $10 billion dollar-a-year, frequently coercive 12-step industry is not a matter of standard medical evaluation. Rather, their support for this approach is most likely a matter of religious belief and/or of financial interest.

Is Abstinence Necessary?

In addition to the questions of whether standard substance abuse treatment works, of whether standard treatment is superior to minimal or no treatment, and of whether forcing people into treatment against their will is justified (if it can be) by successful outcomes, a related question is whether substance abusers must be required to abstain from all recreational substance use. Over 1,000,000 Americans are coerced into treatment annually, and probably nearly all are required to abstain from alcohol entirely during—and often after—treatment under threat of probation or parole violation, prosecution, loss of employment, loss of professional certification, loss of child custody, or loss of organ transplant candidacy, among other penalties. This adherence to abstinence is routinely enforced by mandatory urinalysis (or, at least, the threat of it).

Why should anyone be forced to submit to such indignities and to suffer such drastic penalties for taking so much as a single drink? The answer lies in 12-step alcohol treatment ideology and its influence on public policy. It has become an article of faith in the American alcoholism treatment industry that abstinence is the only acceptable treatment goal. Indeed, in a survey of treatment providers, 75% of those who responded stated that "nonabstinence was not an acceptable goal for patients in their program," and of the remaining 25%, "70% reported moderate drinking as appropriate for only 1–25% of their clients." In addition, of those who accepted moderate drinking (in any form) as a goal, only one-fifth (that is, 5% of the total) worked in inpatient facilities (Rosenberg & Davis, 1994). That the requirement of abstinence is almost total in such treatment programs is clear in the *National Treatment Center Study Summary Report.* In addition to reporting that 93% of treatment facilities (and over 95% of inpatient facilities) utilize the 12-step approach, this report found that "nearly all the programs (98.6%) said they advocated abstinence from alcohol for all their alcohol and/or drug dependent patients" (Roman & Blum, 1997, p. 24). This rejection of moderate drinking as a goal is attributable to two closely interrelated belief systems: AA ideology and its offspring, the disease concept of alcoholism, both of which posit that alcoholics can never learn to drink safely, and that if they attempt it they will only get worse.

But what is the evidence regarding moderate (or "controlled") drinking by alcoholics? Do they really suffer inevitable disaster if they take so much as a single drink?

One widely publicized study provides evidence that a significant number of problem drinkers can and do return to nonproblem drinking rather than turn to abstinence. That study is Project MATCH. Even though virtually all subjects were diagnosed alcohol dependent, and all three forms of treatment in Project MATCH had abstinence goals, significant numbers of individuals in both the outpatient and aftercare groups (of all three forms of treatment) resumed "regular drinking" (as opposed to "heavy drinking") during the 12-month follow-up period: this included 35% of outpatient clients and 25% of aftercare clients (Project MATCH, 1997, p. 14).[11] This is perhaps the most significant finding of Project MATCH.

Other studies have confirmed that a great many alcoholics (and not only problem drinkers or alcohol abusers, but those classified as alcohol dependent) resolve their alcohol problems through moderation rather than abstinence. The NLAES (Dawson, 1996) provides a particularly important demonstration of this fact, because this extremely large (n=4,585) national survey of ever-alcohol-dependent individuals found that reduced drinking is the most common way in which people overcome alcoholism. NLAES showed that at 10 to 20 years since onset of dependence, fully 30% of those who had been treated and 64% of those who had never been treated were drinking without abuse or dependence, and that at 20 or more years since the onset of dependence, 24% of the treated individuals and 60% of the untreated individuals were drinking without abuse or dependence.[12] Of all NLAES subjects, more than half (58%) of untreated and fully half of all alcoholics, whether treated or untreated, were able to drink without achieving a *DSM-IV* diagnosis. This means that a high percentage of individuals who undergo 12-step abstinence treatment end

---

11. In Project MATCH, relapse was defined as three consecutive days of drinking 6 or more drinks per day for men, and 4 or more drinks per women over the same period.

12. The reason for the decrease in the percentage of those drinking without abuse or dependence is that the older individuals get, the more likely they are to abstain from alcohol. The percentage of treated individuals showing "alcohol abuse or dependence" fell from 26% in the 10-to-20-year bracket to 20% in the 20-years-or-more bracket; and the comparable percentages in the never-treated group were even more dramatic: in that group, the percentage with alcohol abuse or dependence fell from 20% to 10%. At the same time, the percentages of those abstaining rose from 44% to 55% in the treated group, and 16% to 30% in the untreated group. To put it another way, the longer since the onset of dependence, the more likely individuals are either to abstain or to drink moderately. This provides further confirmation that the supposed inevitable progression of the disease of alcoholism has no basis in reality.

up drinking moderately *despite* the disease-concept indoctrination they receive during treatment, and that moderate drinking is the *standard* outcome for formerly alcohol-dependent individuals who never undergo treatment.

Other studies confirm this finding. Reports that at least some formerly alcohol-dependent individuals resolve their problems through moderation have appeared in scholarly journals since at least 1962 (Davies, 1962).[13] For example, in 1976 the first Rand Report (Armor et al., 1976) reported that of treated alcoholics, 12% were drinking normally 6 months after treatment and 22% were drinking normally 18 months after treatment. A follow-up study (Polich et al., 1981) reported that a similar percentage were drinking moderately four years after treatment. A 1985 study of treated alcoholics reported that 20 years after treatment 15% of those responding were drinking moderately (O'Connor & Daly, 1985). And a 1986 study of treated, formerly alcohol-dependent persons indicated that 16 years after treatment, 20% of the surviving subjects were drinking moderately— whereas only 15% were abstaining (McCabe, 1986).

More recent studies have confirmed that a high number of formerly alcohol-dependent persons resolve their problems through moderate drinking. A 10-year study of treated alcoholics reported that in the year prior to the 10-year follow-up, 24% of the subjects were drinking moderately (Finney & Moos, 1991, pp. 48–49), and that over the years there was even "a small increase in the number of persons reporting social or moderate drinking," rather than an increased danger of moderate drinkers falling off the wagon. Two sizable 1996 surveys of Canadians (of, respectively, 11,634 and 1,034 respondents) reported that "most individuals (77.5% and 77.7% respectively) who

---

13. Definitions of normal or moderate drinking vary tremendously from study to study, which explains in part why the reported percentages of individuals who recover via moderation rather than abstinence vary so much from study to study. The Project MATCH "survival analysis" criteria were very liberal in comparison to those of other studies, some of which would qualify an individual who drank six or seven beers on one single day out of the year as relapsed. The Sobell et al. (1996) study (quoted below) falls close to this extreme. It defines "allowable drinking" as "1) usual drinking of three drinks or fewer for men and two drinks or fewer for women; 2) no more than 2 days of five to seven drinks in the last year . . .; and 3) a maximum number of drinks consumed on any one occasion in the past year of seven." Under these criteria, a great many normal social drinkers would be defined as alcohol abusers. Indeed, NLAES reports that "past year consumption estimates . . . for persons who had never been diagnosed with alcohol dependence [were an] average daily intake of .6 oz of ethanol, 14.7 days of drinking 5+ drinks, and 3.7 occasions of intoxication" (Dawson, 1996, pp. 773–774) .

had recovered from an alcohol problem for 1 year or more did so without help or treatment. Sizable percentages (38% and 63%) also reported drinking moderately after resolving their problems" (Sobell et al., 1996, p. 966).

Over the years, these and other studies have confirmed the general finding that moderate drinking is a common means of resolving drinking problems, including alcohol dependence. Those who resolve their problems in this manner include a surprisingly large number of treated alcoholics who have been indoctrinated into the belief that they *cannot*—under pain of an eventual, horrible death— ever drink again. At the same time, the resumption of non-problematic drinking is far more common among untreated alcoholic and problem drinkers; in NLAES, the much greater likelihood of continued drinking that does not meet *DSM-IV* criteria for alcohol abuse accounts for the superiority in outcomes favoring those alcoholics who do not enter treatment.

All of these studies—but especially the long-term studies, such as NLAES, McCabe, and Finney and Moos—provide powerful evidence that abstinence is not the only way to beat an alcohol problem, and that the disease concept of alcoholism, with its loss-of-control beliefs and claims of inevitable progression of alcohol problems, is simply unfounded assertion. Thus, it seems grossly unfair—in fact, a crime— that individuals are routinely coerced into total abstinence and suffer drastic consequences if they take so much as one drink, in the complete absence of scientific evidence that total abstinence is necessary.

A number of studies have compared the results of controlled drinking and abstinence goals in treatment. These studies have generally found results to be comparable (and particularly when alcoholics are allowed to select their treatment). One of the first studies of traditional abstinence treatment versus controlled drinking treatment (Pomerleau et al., 1978) reported a 72% improvement rate in the controlled drinking group at the nine-month follow-up, versus only a 50% improvement rate in the abstinence group. A longer-term study of individuals assigned to either behavioral abstinence treatment or behavioral controlled-drinking treatment (Sanchez-Craig et al., 1984) showed no significant differences in rates of improvement throughout the two years of the study. An even longer-term study (Rychtarik et al., 1987) showed no differences between those given abstinence treatment and those given controlled-drinking treatment at follow-ups five to six years after treatment, with about equal numbers in both treatment groups abstinent or drinking moderately.

Furthermore, the opportunity to select and pursue a treatment goal—whether abstinence or controlled drinking—enhances the likelihood of success. This predictable outcome would be anticipated in any other field than alcoholism and substance abuse, where the abstinence fixation has been in place for decades. Again, the seemingly remarkable results of NLAES, that more untreated alcohol-dependent individuals overcome alcoholism than treated individuals, could be largely the result of the opportunity untreated individuals have, once they become serious about resolving an alcohol problem, of selecting a realistic goal which they believe they can attain.

Studies specifically measuring the effects of goal-choice upon outcome provide no support to those who endorse coerced abstinence. One of the first such studies (Booth et al., 1984) reported on a behavioral residential program in the United Kingdom in which patients were given the choice of an abstinence goal, a moderation goal, or, because of medical conditions, were assigned an abstinence goal. There were no significant differences between the groups voluntarily choosing either abstinence or moderation at the 12-month follow-up. The only significant difference was that the assigned-abstinence group did considerably worse than either of the voluntary-goal groups.

A slightly longer-term (two-year) study (Elal-Lawrence et al., 1986) showed that abstinence, successful moderation, or relapse were unconnected to patients' initial choice of treatment goals. Nonetheless, alcoholics' success at either outcome was related to their belief systems and previous experiences, rather than to the severity of their alcohol dependence (whereas treatment specialists and researchers have generally claimed that more severely alcoholic individuals have no choice but to abstain). This result was clarified in Orford and Keddie's (1986) finding that alcoholics' *persuasion* that controlled drinking or abstinence is possible is more critical for achieving either of these goals than is their level of alcohol dependence.

Graber and Miller (1988), on the other hand, showed that there were differences—but not statistically significant ones—between groups given the choice of abstinence or controlled-drinking treatment three-and-a-half years after treatment. In this study, the number of those achieving abstinence was equal in both groups, while the number of "asymptomatic" or "improved" drinkers was higher in the abstinence-goal group. Indeed, in the abstinence group, 75% of those who had improved were drinking, not abstinent; *all* of the apparently greater improvement in the abstinence-goal group was attributable to the number of abstinence subjects who were still drinking—either nondestructively, or less destructively than before treatment—and not from the small number who had achieved abstinence.

A 1992 study by Booth et al. confirmed the results of Booth et al.'s first study. In the second study, there was again no difference in outcome between those choosing abstinence treatment and those choosing controlled-drinking treatment. There was a slight shift from moderation to abstinence goals—initially, 60% chose an abstinence goal, rising to 64% by the end of the study—but the investigators reported no difference in overall outcomes for the two groups.

A 12-month study of "chronic alcoholics" given the choice between behavioral abstinence or controlled-drinking treatment (Hodgins et al., 1997) again showed the typical pattern of clients moving from moderation to abstinence goals during treatment. In this study, 44% of clients chose an abstinence goal at intake, but by the fourth treatment session almost half of the moderation-goal clients had switched their goal to abstinence. The authors reported, "Goal at initial assessment was not significantly related to consumption at follow-up generally, except for the number of intoxicated days. Those with an initial goal of abstinence reported fewer intoxicated days at follow-up" (p. 251). They also reported that their data "did not reveal a relationship between goal choice and outcome in terms of employment (days worked), social stability, and participation in leisure and social activities at the 3, 6, and 12-month follow-ups." While 88% of those who chose an abstinence goal showed at least improved status at the 12-month follow-up, a significant percentage of those who chose a moderation goal also improved—69% at the 12-month follow-up.

During the course of many of these studies, patients shifted their choice of goals—often from moderation to abstinence; those who *chose* abstinence after an initial moderation goal often had good outcomes. Miller (1991) labeled this approach to abstinence through a process of personal searching and the development of a realization that abstinence is best for the individual "warm turkey" (as opposed to "cold turkey").

In summary, studies of assigned-abstinence versus moderation-goal treatment, and of client choice in treatment, indicate that there is often little connection between initial goal and eventual outcome. Other studies show advantages in motivation and outcome from allowing subjects to choose their own treatment goals. In any case, the research consistently indicates that a substantial number of former alcohol abusers and alcohol-dependent persons resolve their problems through moderation rather than abstinence. It also indicates that there is simply no justification in a large majority of cases for coercing anyone into total abstinence; and the evidence also indicates that the often-barbaric penalties inflicted upon persons who have as little as one drink are unjustified.

DUI Studies

DUI studies are not a good measure of alcohol-abuse treatment effectiveness for several reasons. In the first place, at least half of those coerced into participating in treatment as a result of DUI charges do not meet "diagnostic criteria for alcohol abuse or alcoholism" (NHTSA, 1996, p. 1). Most drunk drivers are, in fact, better characterized as antisocial or criminally oriented individuals who have extensive arrest records for offenses other than DUI, both before and after their DUI convictions (Argeriou et al., 1985).

Given the non-alcoholic nature of most of the individuals subjected to DUI-induced treatment, it is reasonable to expect that any observed changes in their behavior are the result of factors other than efficacy of treatment for a problem—alcohol abuse or dependence —from which they do not suffer. In addition, almost all DUI studies measure outcome in rearrest or accident rates—that is, outcomes in DUI studies are at best an indirect measure of treatment efficacy.

Even where efficacy in reducing DUI recidivism is shown, this does not demonstrate that the individuals in question are drinking less, merely that they are driving less often under the influence of alcohol or are simply being more careful and are being caught less often. In fact, rather than indicating treatment efficacy, these results speak to the "harm reduction" approach. That is, rather than helping people overcome a disease or disorder, punishment (sometimes in the form of treatment) generally works by prodding people to resolve to avoid harmful behaviors, while they continue to drink.

There have been a number of studies on the effects of treatment and alcohol education in reducing DUI recidivism and accident rates as compared with normal judicial sanctions. The bulk of this research shows that suspension or revocation of a driver's license is more effective than treatment in dealing with driving-under-the-influence offenders (see, for example, Hagen, 1980; Salzberg & Klingberg, 1983). In a major quasi-controlled comparison, four California counties in which an alcohol rehabilitation treatment program was implemented were compared to four counties where simple licensure actions were imposed. The major difference was that DUI convicts had fewer crashes in the licensure action counties. However, although license revocations or suspensions were more effective than treatment, this advantage arose primarily because drivers were more careful, and not because they were rehabilitated, or even drove less while intoxicated (Perrine & Sadler, 1987). "Neither rehabilitation nor sanctions had much effect on rearrests for DWI" (USDHHS, 1990, p. 248). Here, as elsewhere, the emperor (AA/12-step treatment) wears no clothes. For information regarding DUI studies useful to individuals facing 12-step coercion for both DUI and non-DUI charges, see Nichols (1990), Ross (1992), and USDHHS (1990).

One important piece of information for those charged with or convicted of driving under the influence is that most such individuals are not alcohol dependent or even alcohol abusers—a number are social drinkers who made a mistake and were caught at it and others are dangerous drinkers rather than alcohol-dependent drinkers. A deputy director in the National Highway Traffic Safety Administration states that, "During any given 1-year period, approximately 20 percent of licensed drivers drive while intoxicated" (Nichols, 1990, p. 45). Compare this with the 7.4% of the population who are either alcohol abusers or alcohol dependent, as estimated by the Department of Health and Human Services (USDHHS, 1997, p. 21), and it immediately becomes apparent that a majority of those who drive under the influence are not alcoholics.

Yet, in most areas of the U.S., a large majority, if not all, of those convicted of DUI or placed in DUI pretrial diversion programs are forced as a condition of probation (or deferred prosecution) to participate in AA or 12-step treatment (Brodsky & Peele, 1991; Weisner, 1990). Clearly, there is no legitimate rationale for coercing non-alcoholics into alcoholism treatment—especially given the demonstrated lack of efficacy of such treatment in reducing DUI recidivism.

What Works?

America's present, religiously based alcohol-abuse treatment system is a dismal failure. It is extremely expensive, massively coercive, apparently no more effective than the rate of spontaneous remission, and has blocked the implementation of more effective alternatives (see Brodsky & Peele, 1991; Bufe, 1998; Peele et al., 1991). But no matter how depressing the current situation may seem, there is at least some good news: effective, inexpensive treatments exist—although they are not widely used.

The three extant meta-analyses of treatment effectiveness (Finney & Monahan, 1996; Holder et al., 1991; Miller et al., 1995), all of which reviewed the available controlled studies of treatment effectiveness (roughly 200 in all three analyses), reached similar conclusions about which treatments work and which ones don't. Interestingly, all three treatments that showed good evidence of efficacy in all three meta-analyses were cognitive/behavioral approaches. Here are brief descriptions of these treatments, as well as descriptions of two additional well-supported therapies.

Community Reinforcement Approach (CRA). This is the single best-supported therapy. It's a moderately low-cost form of outpatient treatment; it was devised and first tested over a quarter-century ago; the first controlled study of its efficacy appeared in 1973; every study of its efficacy—six, so far—has shown extremely encouraging results; and it is not in use as a regular form of treatment at a single one of the 15,000 alcoholism treatment centers in the United States (though, at this writing, there is an ongoing efficacy study in Albuquerque).

The basic premise of the community reinforcement approach—most often a one-on-one therapy, although it can be used in group settings—is that alcohol abuse does not occur in a vacuum, that it is highly influenced by marital, family, social, and economic factors (the exact opposite of the AA/12-step premise that alcoholism [or drug addiction] is a purely *individual* disease that exists independently of social conditions). CRA attempts to help the client improve his or her life in all of these areas, in addition to giving up drinking (or using drugs). Thus, a CRA program will typically include the following components: 1) communications skills training; 2) problem-solving training; 3) help finding employment; 4) social counseling (that is, encouraging the client to develop nondrinking relationships); 5) recreational counseling (that is, encouraging or helping the client to find rewarding nondrinking activities); and 6) marital therapy. Other treatment components are sometimes used—for example, disulfiram (Antabuse), drink-refusal training, or rewarding the client materially for abstinence—but these six components form the core of the CRA approach.

Social Skills Training. This form of group therapy is another very well supported approach. The basic premise of social skills training is that alcohol/drug-abuse clients lack basic skills in dealing with work, family, other interpersonal relationships, and their own emotions. Thus, they benefit from training in areas such as communications skills (including giving and receiving criticism, listening and conversational skills), conflict resolution, drink-refusal, assertiveness, and expressing feelings.

Behavioral Marital/Family Therapy. This is essentially standard marital counseling, but with an emphasis on altering behaviors related to drinking, such as helping the non-alcohol-abusing spouse abandon futile nagging about drinking and instead begin to reward sober behavior. The remainder of the therapy involves couples counseling, the goal being to repair alcohol abuse-caused damage to the relationship, as well as dealing with non-alcohol-caused problems.

There are a number of other forms of therapy with reasonably good indications of efficacy, but the above are highly supported across all three meta-analyses cited. Other therapies with indications of efficacy include behavior contracting, brief intervention, disulfiram, and motivational enhancement.[14]

Brief Intervention / Motivational Enhancement. Brief intervention was the highest scoring (i.e., most effective-rated) treatment in the Miller et al. (1995) meta-analysis, while motivational enhancement was ranked as the third most effective form of treatment. At the same time, they were also among the most inexpensive therapies, with only "self-help manual" being lower in cost.

Brief intervention shares elements with motivational enhancement (one of the treatments tested by Project MATCH) in that the patient and the therapist create a mutually agreed-upon goal. The first step in creating this goal is often an objective assessment of the person's drinking habits, or a comparison of his or her drinking levels with community standards, or else a comparison with optimum levels of drinking for health purposes. In brief intervention, the goal is usually reduced drinking; in motivational enhancement, it is either reduced drinking or total abstinence. The key is to allow patients to select a goal that is consistent with their own values and that they thus "own" as an expression of their genuine desires.

In a brief-intervention session, the health-care worker simply sums up the goal: "So, we agree you will reduce your drinking from 42 drinks a week to 20, no more than four on a given night." Motivational enhancement is a bit more subtle: the therapist nudges without directing, by responding to the patient's own values and

14. For a detailed description of the above-described forms of therapy (and several others) see Hester and Miller's *Handbook of Alcoholism Treatment Approaches* (1995).

desire for change. The dialogue in a motivational-enhancement session might go like this:

THERAPIST: What is most important to you?
PATIENT: Getting ahead in life. Getting a mate.
T. What kind of job would you like? What training would that take?
P. [Describes.]
T. Describe the kind of mate you want. How would you have to act, where would you have to go, to meet and deal with a person like that?
P. [Describes.]
T. How are you doing at achieving this?
P. Not very well.
T. What leads to these problems?
P. When I drink, I can't concentrate on work. Drinking turns off the kind of person I want to go out with.
T. Can you think of any way to improve your chances of succeeding at work or with that kind of mate?

Here we see that the goal of therapy is to draw the connection between what people genuinely want—their own goals—and the institution of helpful behaviors, or the elimination of behaviors that interfere with achieving their goals. In brief intervention, in addition, drinkers know that they and their helper will be regularly assessing progress toward the agreed-upon goals in systematic but non-judgmental meetings—a central element, as we saw in the highly praised results of Project MATCH. (To examine these nondirective approaches, see Horvath, *Sex, Drugs, Gambling and Chocolate: A Workbook for Overcoming Addictions;* Miller & Rollnick, *Motivational Interviewing: Preparing People to Change Addictive Behavior,* and Peele et al., *The Truth About Addiction and Recovery.*)

Summary

One finding shines through all of these complicated results: the most beneficial outcomes to drug and alcohol problems occur with minimal treatments, or else depend primarily on the characteristics and motivation of the patient, rather than on any specific treatment. Not only is 12-step treatment unjustified, but hardly any formal treatment seems to be necessary if drug and alcohol abusers become properly involved in defining and directing their own efforts toward change. That is, they'll likely succeed if they want to change, and if they have support in their efforts to change.

3

12-Step Groups as Religious Organizations

by Charles Bufe

Narcotics Anonymous, Cocaine Anonymous, Marijuana Anonymous, 12-step drug and alcohol treatment programs, and all other 12-step groups are, in terms of ideology, carbon copies of Alcoholics Anonymous. For that reason, I'll simply use "AA" in place of "AA, NA, CA, MA, and 12-step drug and alcohol treatment programs" in the following discussion.

Because the key factor in determining the constitutionality of coerced 12-step participation is the religious nature of 12-step programs, it's first necessary to define the term religion. So, before deciding whether AA and other 12-step groups are religious organizations, let's first consider definitions of religion from three widely known American dictionaries. (To conserve space, I've included only the primary and secondary definitions of "religion" from the *Webster's Unabridged* and *Random House* dictionaries.)

religion, n. 1. concern over what exists beyond the visible world, differentiated from philosophy in that it operates through faith or intuition rather than reason, and generally including the idea of the existence of a single being, a group of beings, an eternal principle or a transcendent spiritual entity that has created the world, that governs it, that controls its destinies, or that intervenes occasionally in the natural course of its history, as well as the idea that ritual, prayer, spiritual exercises, certain principles of everyday conduct, etc., are expedient, due, or spiritually rewarding, or arise naturally out of an inner need as a human response to the belief in such a being, principle, etc. 2. a specific fundamental set of beliefs and practices generally agreed upon by a number of persons or sects: *the Christian religion.*
—*The Random House Dictionary of the English Language*

religion, n. 1. The service and adoration of God or a god as expressed in forms of worship. 2. One of the systems of faith and worship. 3. The profession or practice of religious beliefs; religious observances, collectively. 4. Devotion or fidelity; conscientiousness. 5. An awareness or conviction of the existence of a supreme being, arousing reverence, love, gratitude, the will to obey and serve, and the like.
—*Webster's Collegiate Dictionary*

religion, n. 1. a set of beliefs concerning the cause, nature, and purpose of the universe, esp. when considered as the creation of a superhuman agency or agencies, usually involving devotional and ritual observances, and often containing a moral code governing the conduct of human affairs. 2. a specific fundamental set of beliefs and practices generally agreed upon by a number of persons or sects: *the Christian religion; the Buddhist religion.*
—*Webster's Unabridged Dictionary*

These definitions vary considerably, but they have several things in common, the most important being belief in God. All three of them mention this (or a synonym for it) in their primary definitions of the term "religion." The other most important defining criteria are faith, ritual, and commonly held beliefs, all of which are mentioned by all three dictionaries, though not necessarily in their primary definitions. It's also important to note that under the above definitions not all of these things need be present to qualify a person, organization, or ideology as religious. Belief in God is enough. It's the primary determining factor; all of the others are subsidiary and flow from it.[1]

To put the matter in schematic form, religion—according to these dictionary definitions—primarily consists of:

1) Belief in God (or gods)
2) Faith
3) Ritual
4) Commonly held beliefs

Under these defining criteria, especially the first and most important, AA and all other 12-step groups are undeniably religious in nature. Their history, ideology, and practices leave no doubt on this point. A brief look at dictionary definitions of "religious," the adjectival form of "religion," reinforces this conclusion. (Again, to conserve space, only the primary and secondary definitions are included here.)

---

1. The definitions quoted here are similar to those found in other commonly used dictionaries (e.g., *Webster's New World College Dictionary* [3rd Ed.] and *Webster's Ninth New Collegiate Dictionary*), which likewise emphasize deistic belief.

religious, adj. 1. of, pertaining to, or concerned with religion: *a religious holiday.* 2. imbued with or exhibiting religion; pious; devout; godly: *a religious man.*
—*The Random House Dictionary of the English Language*

religious, adj. 1. Manifesting devotion to, or the influence of, religion; godly. 2. Belonging to, or followed by, an order of religious; as the *religious* life.
—*Webster's Collegiate Dictionary*

religious, adj. 1.of, pertaining to, or concerned with religion: *a religious holiday.* 2. imbued with or exhibiting religion; pious; devout; godly: *a religious man.*
—*Webster's Unabridged Dictionary*

At the risk of belaboring the obvious, all of the primary and secondary definitions here indicate that "religious" basically means "having to do with religion." Note also that all of these definitions emphasize the importance of deistic belief to religion by including the term "godly" in either their first or second meanings.

Thus, even a cursory glance at AA's official, conference-approved literature, with its repeated mentions of God, the importance of belief in God, and its exhortations to pray to God—not to mention AA meetings, with their public prayers, witnessing, collections, and confessions—provides convincing proof that Alcoholics Anonymous is a religious organization.

Religious Elements in AA's Practices

AA's religiosity is immediately apparent to almost anyone who attends an AA meeting. Many newcomers are struck by the revival-like atmosphere of 12-step meetings (including this writer, who, at his first AA meeting in 1983, in a church basement, half expected the congregants to begin speaking in tongues).

A typical AA meeting[2] begins with a prayer, the Serenity Prayer. *As Bill Sees It* (Wilson, 1967), a prayer book-like piece of official (conference-approved) AA literature, complete with a ribbon hanging from the top of its spine, notes: "In 1941, a news clipping was called to our attention by a New York member. In an obituary notice from a local paper, there appeared these words: 'God grant us the

---

2. Meeting formats vary considerably, but many of the elements I describe here, especially the opening and closing prayers, public confession, and collection of donations, occur at almost all meetings; and, in addition to these elements, public witnessing occurs at virtually all "speaker meetings."

serenity to accept the things we cannot change, the courage to change the things we can, and the wisdom to know the difference.' Never had we seen so much A.A. in so few words. With amazing speed the Serenity Prayer came into general use" (Wilson, 1967, p. 108). Another similar account by AA co-founder Bill Wilson (also in conference-approved literature) of the adoption of this prayer notes: "with amazing speed the Serenity Prayer came into general use and took its place alongside our two other favorites, the Lord's Prayer and the Prayer of St. Francis" (Wilson, 1957, p. 196).

Thus AA meetings normally open with a prayer to God, directly meeting two of the four criteria of religious activity (belief in God and ritual [public prayer]), and indirectly meeting at least one of the other two (faith—that God *can* "grant" "serenity," "courage," and "wisdom"). One could also argue that this prayer meets the fourth defining criterion of religion as well: given "the amazing speed [with which] the Serenity Prayer came into *general* use" (emphasis added), it seems reasonable to conclude that the concepts it outlines constitute commonly held beliefs.

Following the Serenity Prayer, members normally introduce themselves in ritualized fashion: "Hi, I'm Bill. I'm an alcoholic," "I'm Ed. I'm an alcoholic," "I'm John, alcoholic," until everyone has identified him or herself using the key term, "alcoholic." The meeting secretary will then ask if there are any out-of-towners at the meeting and, if so, to please identify themselves. Next, he or she will ask if any of the members has a birthday (an anniversary of months or years of sobriety).[3] If anyone does, he or she will often participate in another ritual—being awarded a "sobriety chip." Next, often, the secretary will make any AA-related announcements.

What happens after this varies considerably, depending on the type of meeting. At speaker meetings, a speaker will rise and address the meeting for anywhere from 15 minutes to over an hour. Such addresses often fall into the following pattern: the speaker will begin with a lurid and prolonged description of his drinking behavior, and how it led to his downfall. He'll then describe the shame and hopelessness he felt as a drinking alcoholic, and how as a last resort he went to an AA meeting. He'll then say how he was put off by "the

---

3. As used in AA, "sobriety" and "birthday" do not have the same meanings that they do in standard English. AA, like many other religious groups (and cults), uses special jargon and assigns special meanings to standard terms. In AA, "sobriety" means, always, "absolute abstinence," and, very often (depending on the term's user), also "working a good program"—that is, working the steps and turning one's life and will over to God. "Birthday" signifies the day one stopped drinking.

God stuff" at the meeting, but that the people there "had something [he] wanted," so he kept coming back. Before long, he overcame his doubts, and since turning his life over to AA's "Higher Power," his life has been transformed. Following such presentations, the secretary will normally throw the meeting open to questions and comments, and pass the hat.

Another typical type of AA meeting is the discussion meeting. Such meetings can either be open to any topic raised by members or, often, are on topics suggested by the meeting secretary. Topics can range anywhere from day-to-day ways of staying sober to one's relationship with God. Still another typical meeting is the "step meeting," the purpose of which is to discuss the 12 steps, AA's central (and, as we'll see, very religious) tenets.

At almost all meetings, at a set time the secretary will normally close the meeting. At most, members rise, hold hands, say the Lord's Prayer, and end with the chant, "Keep coming back! It works!"

The above descriptions come from my attendance at scores of AA meetings in San Francisco in the mid and late 1980s. Judging from meeting descriptions in AA's official literature, meetings have changed little since AA's early days. Clarence S., founder of AA in Cleveland, briefly describes early meetings in Akron (AA's birthplace): "The leader would open with a prayer, then read Scripture. Then he would spend 20 to 30 minutes giving witness—that is, telling about his past life. Then it would open for witness from the floor" (Alcoholics Anonymous, 1980, pp. 139–140). Another early member recalls that "the meeting closed with the Lord's Prayer" (p. 141).

The official biography of AA's co-founder, "Dr. Bob" Smith, describes a discussion meeting in Akron in the 1940s: "When the time came, the speaker would go up front, wait for quiet, and introduce himself. He opened with a prayer of his own choosing, then gave a five-minute 'lead.' Usually it would be on a specific subject—a passage from *The Upper Room* [a Methodist periodical] or a verse from the Bible. Then he asked other members to make short comments" (Alcoholics Anonymous, 1980, p. 220). Smith's official biography later notes: "The widow of an oldtimer remembered Dr. Bob standing up at the meeting with 'the Good Book under his arm' and recalled that he used to say the answers were there if you looked for them. . . . Dr. Bob donated that Bible to the King School Group [his "home" group], where it still rests on the podium at each meeting" (pp. 227–228).

Clarence S. also describes early meetings in Cleveland (the place where the name "Alcoholics Anonymous" was first used, rather than

"Oxford Group"): "We opened with an audible prayer. The speaker, who was chosen four weeks in advance, spoke for 45 minutes, and we closed with the Lord's Prayer" (Alcoholics Anonymous, 1980, p. 261).

Thus, AA meetings—at least in terms of structure and content—seem to have changed remarkably little over the past six decades. AA meetings normally begin and end with a prayer to God, often include readings from an "inspired" text (formerly the Bible, now, usually, the Big Book) and their central sections normally deal with either redemption via a Higher Power (speaker meetings) or with the proper ways to work AA's religious program (step meetings). Given these facts, it's easy to see—through history, philosophy, tradition, and current practice—that AA meetings are religious in nature. In fact, appeal-level courts have carried out analyses quite similar to those in this chapter and have found that both internally (in terms of its historical documents and the wording of its "sacraments"; cf. *Griffin v. Coughlin*, 1996), and externally (in terms of its practices, such as prayers and witnessing at meetings; cf. *Warner v. Orange County*, 1999) that AA is indisputably religious.

Religious Elements in AA's Program and Literature

The 12 steps are the backbone of the AA program. A majority of Alcoholics Anonymous members regard them in the same reverent manner that fundamentalist Christians regard the Ten Commandments. This is no accident, considering the overtly religious nature of the steps and how they are presented: they were drawn directly from the teachings of the Oxford Groups, the evangelical Christian movement to which AA's co-founders, Bill Wilson and Dr. Bob Smith, belonged, and of which AA was a part until the late 1930s; and in the Big Book (*Alcoholics Anonymous*—AA's fundamental text) (Wilson, 1939, 1976) the 12 steps are presented as the means by which to directly access God's help. In Chapter 5, titled "How It Works," the Big Book's author, AA co-founder Bill Wilson, comments immediately before listing the steps:

> Remember that we deal with alcohol—cunning, baffling, powerful! Without help it is too much for us. But there is One who has all power—that One is God. May you find Him now!
>
> Half measures availed us nothing. We stood at the turning point. We asked His protection and care with complete abandon.
>
> Here are the steps we took, which are suggested as a program of recovery.
>
> (Wilson, 1939, 1976, pp. 58–59)

Please note the capitalization. Please also note that God's help is presented here as *necessary* to overcoming an alcohol problem. ("Without help it is too much for us. But there is One who has all power—that one is God.")

The 12 steps themselves are just as religious as Wilson's introduction to them:

1. We admitted we were powerless over alcohol—that our lives had become unmanageable.
2. Came to believe that a Power greater than ourselves could restore us to sanity.
3. Made a decision to turn our will and our lives over to the care of God *as we understood Him.*
4. Made a searching and fearless moral inventory of ourselves.
5. Admitted to God, to ourselves, and to another human being the exact nature of our wrongs.
6. Were entirely ready to have God remove all these defects of character.
7. Humbly asked Him to remove our shortcomings.
8. Made a list of all persons we had harmed, and became willing to make amends to them all.
9. Made direct amends to such people wherever possible, except when to do so would injure them or others.
10. Continued to take personal inventory and when we were wrong promptly admitted it.
11. Sought through prayer and meditation to improve our conscious contact with God *as we understood Him,* praying only for knowledge of His will for us and the power to carry that out.
12. Having had a spiritual awakening as the result of these steps, we tried to carry this message to alcoholics, and to practice these principles in all our affairs.

(Wilson, 1939, 1976, pp. 59–60)

There are several things worthy of note in these steps. The first is that these are *not* a set of sequential steps to help individuals overcome alcohol problems. Alcohol is mentioned only in the first step, which strongly implies that individuals cannot overcome alcohol problems on their own. The remainder of the steps implore alcoholics to abandon attempts at self-help in favor of engaging in religious activities and turning their problems over to God.

God or a synonymous term is mentioned in fully half of the 12 steps (steps 2, 3, 5, 6, 7, 11). Despite the qualifying phrase, "as we understood Him," the God referred to in the steps is most decidedly a conventional patriarchal God as conceived in Judeo-Christianity. (Note the capitalized masculine pronouns, "Him" and "His.") Many members of AA will deny this, and will insist that the "Power greater than ourselves" mentioned in step 2 can be anything that an individual chooses—a doorknob, a lightbulb, a bedpan, or even AA itself (G.O.D.—Group Of Drunks). AA co-founder Bill Wilson himself used this line of argument: "You can, if you wish, make A.A. itself your 'higher power'" (Wilson, 1953, p. 27).

But the very next step gives lie to this contention: how can individuals turn their "will [sic] and lives over to the care of God" if God is a doorknob? This concept of God reduces AA's program to gibberish. Because of the qualities and powers AA ascribes to it, AA's God cannot be anything other than a conventional, patriarchal God.

In order for the AA 12-step program to make sense, the God mentioned in the steps must be a God intimately concerned with the lives of individuals, a God concerned with "our wrongs," a God that will direct lives and remove "shortcomings" and "defects of character" if only "humbly asked." No doorknob can do this. And while in a totalitarian society it might be possible for an individual to turn his "will and li[fe]" over to AA (as G.O.D.) and to have AA run all aspects of his life, this is not a possibility in a relatively open society. It's also exceedingly difficult to see how AA (as G.O.D.) could remove "shortcomings" or "defects of character," and the concept of an individual praying to AA (as G.O.D.) (step 11) is simply grotesque.

There's no getting around it: the God presented in the 12 steps —the bedrock of AA—is a patriarchal, all-powerful deity, vitally concerned with, and intervening in, the lives of its supplicants. In short, it's the God of patriarchal religions.

This holds true for the other Anonymous groups as well. The 12 steps of—in all likelihood—all such groups are essentially identical to those of AA, differing in only the use of single terms in the first and twelfth steps.[4] For instance, Narcotics Anonymous (after AA, the largest of the 12-step groups) uses "our addiction" in place of

---

4. It's likely that no one really knows how many 12-step Anonymous groups exist, and estimates range up into the hundreds. So, it's impossible to state flatly that the 12 steps are essentially identical in all 12-step groups. What is indisputably true is that the steps in all of the largest 12-step groups (including NA, CA, and MA) are essentially identical to those of AA, differing only in the use of single terms in the first and twelfth steps.

"alcohol" in the first step, and "addicts" rather than "alcoholics" in the twelfth step; other than that, NA's 12 steps are identical to AA's. To cite another example, Sexaholics Anonymous—yes, this group really exists—substitutes "lust" for "alcohol" in the first step and "sexaholics" for "alcoholics" in the twelfth step; all of the other steps are exactly the same as AA's. Thus the programs of NA and other 12-step groups are just as religious as AA's program. To emphasize that its program is identical to AA's, *Narcotics Anonymous,* NA's "Basic Text" (the NA equivalent of the Big Book), plainly states, "We follow a program borrowed from Alcoholics Anonymous" (NA, 1982, p. 11).

There are other religious elements in the steps. Step 2 ("Came to believe that a Power greater than ourselves could restore us to sanity") is an expression of another defining criterion of religiosity: faith. Steps 4 and 5 ("Made a searching and fearless moral inventory of ourselves," "Admitted to God, to ourselves, and to another human being the exact nature of our wrongs") are a description of a common religious ritual: confession. Step 11 ("Sought through prayer and meditation to improve our conscious contact with God *as we understood Him,* praying only for knowledge of His will for us and the power to carry that out") is a direct invocation of still another common religious ritual: prayer; and step 7 ("Humbly asked Him to remove our shortcomings") also strongly implies prayer, but doesn't use the term directly.

As if to emphasize the religiosity of step 7, Wilson, in his discussion of how to "work" the steps, comments:

> Are we now ready to let God remove from us all the things which we have admitted [in steps 4 and 5] are objectionable? Can He now take them all—every one? If we still cling to something we will not let go, we ask God to help us be willing.
>
> When ready, we say something like this: "My Creator, I am now willing that you should have all of the good and bad. I pray that you now remove from me every single defect of character which stands in the way of my usefulness to you and my fellows. Grant me strength, as I go out from here, to do your bidding. Amen." We have then completed Step Seven.
>
> (Wilson, 1939, 1976, p. 76)

Thus, according to AA co-founder Wilson, one should "work" the seventh step through *prayer.* He makes a similar recommendation regarding the tenth step:

Every day is a day when we must carry the vision of God's will into all of our activities. "How can I best serve Thee—Thy will (not mine) be done." These are thoughts which must go with us constantly.

(Wilson, 1939, 1976, p. 85)

In his discussion of step 11, Wilson describes the purpose of the 12 steps: divine guidance, coming into "conscious contact with God," and relying upon divine "inspiration":

In thinking about our day we may face indecision. We may not be able to determine which course to take. Here we ask God for inspiration, an intuitive thought or a decision. We relax and take it easy. We don't struggle. We are often surprised how the right answers come after we have tried this for a while. What used to be the hunch or the occasional inspiration gradually becomes a working part of the mind. Being still inexperienced and having just made conscious contact with God, it is not probable that we are going to be inspired at all times. We might pay for this presumption in all sorts of absurd actions and ideas. Nevertheless, we find that our thinking will, as time passes, be more and more on the plane of inspiration. We come to rely upon it.

(pp. 86–87)

As we'll see later in more detail, none of the concepts codified in the 12 steps originated with AA's co-founders or early members. Rather, they came directly from the Protestant evangelical group (Oxford Group Movement) of which AA was a part for its first several years, and to which both AA co-founders belonged when they met in 1935.

Going beyond the steps, religious elements abound in the Big Book. It devotes an entire chapter (Chapter 4, "We Agnostics") to attacking atheists and agnostics as being "prejudice[d]" or crazy, and to presenting belief in God as the only way to restore "sanity." In that chapter Wilson comments, "To one who feels he is an atheist or agnostic such an experience seems impossible, but to continue as he is means disaster . . . To be doomed to an alcoholic death or to live on a spiritual basis are not always easy alternatives to face" (Wilson, 1939, 1976, p. 44). He next comments, "But [the "new man's"] face falls when we speak of spiritual matters, especially when we mention God, for we have re-opened a subject which our man thought he had neatly evaded or entirely ignored" (p. 45). He goes on, "We found that as soon as we were able to lay aside prejudice and express even a willingness to believe in a Power greater than ourselves, we commenced to get results" (p. 46), and he concludes, "God restored us all to our right minds. . . . When we drew near to Him He disclosed Himself to us!" (p. 57). Thus in AA, if one rejects deistic belief, one is by definition insane, "prejudice[d]" and "doomed to an alcoholic death." (See also step 2, in which God is credited with "restor[ing] us to sanity.")

The Big Book is also saturated with religious terms. Author Vince Fox took the first 20 pages of preliminary matter plus the 164 pages of actual text (excluding the personal stories) and found 174 references to "God and God-associated words" (God, God's, godly, God-given, etc.). He also found another 62 "personal pronouns relative to God, with first letter capitalized" (He, His, Him, etc.) (Fox, 1993, p. 51). When one adds other synonyms for "God" (Maker, Father, Creator, Higher Power, Power greater than ourselves, etc.—all with initial capitalization), the number of "God and God-associated words" in the Big Book rises to in excess of 250. In addition to those hundreds of godly references, Fox also reports that the Big Book contains 11 biblical references—and all this in a short text typeset in a space-wasting format.

A pro-AA researcher's figures agree with those of Fox: "The name 'God,' spelled with a capital 'G,' appears at least 132 times through page 164 of the Big Book; and pronouns for God, such as 'He', 'Him', 'His', etc., are mentioned eighty times" (Stewart C., 1986, pp. 115–116, as cited by Dick B., 1992, p. 97).

It's also relevant that Bill Wilson believed that he was under divine guidance when he wrote the 12 steps. Wilson's wife Lois states:

> How could he bring the program alive so that those at a distance, reading the book, could apply it to themselves and perhaps get well? He had to be very explicit. The six Oxford Group principles that the Fellowship had been using were not enough. He must broaden and deepen their implications. He relaxed and asked for guidance. When he finished writing and reread what he had put down, he was quite pleased. Twelve principles had developed—the Twelve Steps.
>
> (L. Wilson, 1979, p. 113) (Note the capitalization.)

(Not incidentally, anyone who accepts that Bill Wilson was divinely guided when he wrote the 12 steps must necessarily grant those steps the status of revealed wisdom. This places Wilson on the level of the Old Testament prophets, and the Big Book on the level of scripture.)

Another indication that Wilson and his fellow AAs believed that he was divinely inspired is found in AA's official Wilson biography, *Pass

It On (Alcoholics Anonymous, 1984), where Wilson (or a fellow AA in his company, though it was probably Wilson) is quoted as follows in replying to a suggestion that Wilson make changes in the Big Book: "Why [change it]? What is the matter with it? It is perfect"(p. 204). One doubts that Bill Wilson was so egotistical as to think that he, as a "powerless" individual, could write a "perfect" work; he undoubtedly believed that he was under God's direction when he wrote the book. Many current AA members almost certainly believe that Wilson did indeed have divine help. In the mid 1990s, one service worker in AA's General Service Office stated: "I consider the Big Book as an inspired text, written by Bill under the guidance of the spirit" (quoted in Delbanco & Delbanco, 1995, p. 51).

AA's second most important text, *Twelve Steps and Twelve Traditions* (known colloquially as the "Twelve and Twelve"), the second book published by AA, and also written by Bill Wilson (Wilson, 1953), is a guide to "working" the 12 steps and to following the 12 traditions, AA's organizational principles. Its very title emphasizes the centrality of the 12 steps to Alcoholics Anonymous.

Twelve Steps and Twelve Traditions amply confirms that the 12 steps are indeed religious principles (as defined by the dictionary criteria listed above). One indication that this is so is that *Twelve Steps and Twelve Traditions* is every bit as soaked in religious terminology as the Big Book. As an example, a quick reading reveals that the nine pages devoted to the discussion of step 2 contain at least 30 references to God, synonyms for it, or capitalized masculine pronouns referring to it. Wilson's actual statements are even more revealing.

In his discussion of step 2, Wilson notes: "we had to look for our lost faith. It was in A.A. that we rediscovered it. So can you" (Wilson, 1953, p. 29). This presents the achievement of "faith"—one of the defining criteria of religion—as a central purpose of AA.

In discussing step 3, Wilson underlines the religiosity of the steps by commenting: ". . . it is only by action that we can cut away the self-will which has always blocked the entry of God—or, if you like, a Higher Power—into our lives. . . . Therefore our problem now becomes just how and by what specific means shall we be able to let Him in" (p. 34). He continues: "That is just where the remaining Steps of the A.A. program come in. Nothing short of continuous action upon these as a way of life can bring the much desired result" (p. 40). Wilson then makes an extremely revealing statement: "Our whole trouble had been the misuse of willpower. We had tried to bombard our problems with it instead of attempting to bring it into agreement with God's intention for us. To make this increasingly possible is the purpose of A.A.'s Twelve Steps, and Step Three opens the door" (p. 40).

These three statements emphasize the centrality of deistic belief in AA, and that the purpose of AA's 12 steps includes the induction of such belief, but goes beyond it: the purpose of the 12 steps, as indicated here by Wilson, is not only to lead individuals to belief, but to have them turn their wills and lives over to the God to which the steps lead them.

Wilson ends his discussion of step 3 with the recommendation, "In all times of emotional disturbance or indecision, we can pause, ask for quiet, and in the stillness simply say [the Serenity Prayer]" (p. 41). This is a recommendation to engage in still another activity that's a defining criterion of religion: ritual (prayer).

In his discussion of step 4, making "a searching and fearless moral inventory," Wilson makes an extraordinary suggestion: that one's inventory of moral "defects" be based on "a universally recognized list of major human failings—the Seven Deadly Sins [!] of pride, greed, lust, anger, gluttony, envy, and sloth" (p. 48). Contrary to Wilson's assertion, these are not "a universally recognized list of major human failings." Rather, they are a specifically *Christian* list of sins coming straight out of the Church of the Middle Ages.[5] To point out the obvious, many atheists and agnostics would consider every single one of these "universally recognized . . . failings" as far less loathsome than cruelty—which Wilson does not list as a universally recognized character defect—and almost certainly as no worse than hypocrisy and sanctimoniousness. In his discussion of "moral [another religious term] failings," Wilson sticks to his specifically medieval Christian list of defects—thus pointing out the Christian origins and orientation of AA's 12-step program.

As for step 5, the ritual of confession, Wilson notes: "Many an A.A., once agnostic or atheist, tells us that it was during this stage of Step

---

5. The Seven Deadly Sins originated with the early Greek Christian theologian, Evagrius of Pontus, who listed eight such sins. Their number was reduced to seven by Pope Gregory the Great in the 6th century, and they were later treated by Thomas Aquinas in his *Summa Theologica.* They were very much a part of religious consciousness as well as a major part of common culture in ultra-religious medieval Europe (which, of course, was virtually 100% Christian); and they played the part of subject matter in such well known plays as *Everyman* (author unknown) and *Dr. Faustus,* by Christopher Marlowe. They also received mention in Chaucer's *The Canterbury Tales,* and were the subject of Hieronymus Bosch's famous painting, "The Seven Deadly Sins." Thus, it would be fairer to classify them as "a universally recognized list of Christian sins" than "a universally recognized list of major human failings." There's no escaping their Christian origins and context.

Five that he first actually felt the presence of God. And even those who had faith already often become conscious of God as they never were before" (p. 62). Among other things, this statement strongly implies that one of the effects of working step 5 is the production of faith in God—an unambiguously religious effect.

Commenting on step 6, Wilson states: "Of course, the often disputed question of whether God can—and will, under certain conditions—remove defects of character will be answered with a prompt affirmative by almost any A.A. member. To him, this proposition will be no theory at all; it will be just about the largest fact in his life" (p. 63). This statement implies deistic belief, faith that God can "remove defects of character," and, importantly, unanimity of belief—the fourth defining criterion of religion.

Going on to step 7, Wilson states: "As long as we placed self-reliance first, a genuine reliance upon a Higher Power was out of the question" (p. 72). He later continues, "Refusing to place God first, we had deprived ourselves of His help. But now the words 'Of myself I am nothing, the Father doeth the works' began to carry bright promise and meaning" (p. 75). This statement again underlines the centrality of deistic belief in AA, and the centrality of suppression of self and suppression of self-direction that AA's particular type of deistic belief involves.

Regarding step 8, Wilson concludes: "It is the beginning of the end of isolation from our fellows and from God" (p. 82). Yet again, this emphasizes that the primary focus of the steps is deistic belief.

In discussing step 10, Wilson comments: "we are today sober only by the grace of God and . . . any success we may be having is far more His success than ours" (p. 92). This is a very direct statement about the centrality of deistic belief in AA, and the belief that AA's God plays a directing role in the lives of AA members.

Wilson begins his comments on step 11 with the statement: "Prayer and meditation are our principal means of conscious contact with God" (p. 96). This is a direct statement of the importance of both deistic belief and religious ritual in AA; and note the term "our," which implies uniformity of practice. To emphasize the importance of prayer in AA, Wilson continues: "Those of us who have come to make regular use of prayer would no more do without it than we would refuse air, food, or sunshine" (p. 97). Indeed, the entire discussion of step 11 in the "Twelve and Twelve" is a paean to the power and wonders of prayer.

In his discussion of step 12, Wilson makes another extraordinarily revealing statement:

So, practicing these Steps, we had a spiritual awakening about which finally there was no question. Looking at those who were only beginning and still doubted themselves, the rest of us were able to see the change setting in. From great numbers of such experiences, we could predict that the doubter who still claimed that he hadn't got the "spiritual angle," and who still considered his well-loved A.A. group the higher power, would presently love God and call Him by name.

(Wilson, 1953, p. 109)

This reveals that not only are AA's 12 steps religious in nature, but that their goal is *religious indoctrination.*[6] This also reveals that AA's "Power greater than ourselves" (from step 2) is a component in a bait-and-switch tactic leading to belief in a conventional, patriarchal God.

In this statement, Wilson is positively gloating about the effectiveness of AA's indoctrination process in changing religious beliefs. This is really the last word about the purpose and effects of AA's 12 steps.

AA's Religious Origins

Because the purpose of this chapter is merely to demonstrate that AA is a religious organization, the discussion here of AA's origins as part of the Protestant evangelical group, the Oxford Group Movement (OGM—later Moral Re-Armament, MRA), will be somewhat brief. It's enough here to show that AA's central beliefs and practices are religious in nature, and that they came directly from the religious group of which AA was originally a part.[7]

---

6. For a thorough, step-by-step description of AA's indoctrination process, see Ken Ragge's *The Real AA: Behind the Myth of 12-Step Recovery* (1998).

7. Those interested in more detailed accounts of AA's religious roots should consult the works of historian Dick B., especially *Design for Living: The Oxford Group's Contribution to Early A.A.* (1992) and *The Good Book and the Big Book* (2nd Ed.) (1997), as well as the writings of Gaetano Salamone published by Rational Recovery, particularly *Religious and Spiritual Origins of the 12-Step Recovery Movement* (1997). Both of these authors trace the central concepts of the Oxford Group Movement—concepts appropriated by AA, and which form the heart of its program—back to biblical and early Protestant sources. Those interested in a detailed overview of Oxford Group Movement ideology and activities around the time of AA's founding, and of AA's relationship to the Oxford Group Movement, should consult *Alcoholics Anonymous: Cult or Cure?* (2nd Ed.), Chapters 2–5 (Bufe, 1998). Those with Internet access can find Dick B.'s web site at http://www.dickb.com/index.shtml; and they can find Rational Recovery's web site at http://www.rational.org.

There are two common misconceptions about AA's origins: 1) that AA sprang into being as an independent entity with the meeting of its two co-founders, Bill Wilson and Bob Smith, in 1935; and 2) that the ideas expressed in the 12 steps were conceived and formulated independently by Bill Wilson. Both of these beliefs are entirely wrong. For the first several years of its existence AA was a part of the Oxford Group Movement; and the concepts codified in the 12 steps came entirely from the Oxford Groups—there is not a single original idea in them.

As for what the Oxford Group Movement (now Moral Re-Armament) is, the Rev. Sherwood Day noted in an OGM pamphlet, *The Principles of the Oxford Group Movement*, that "the principles of 'The Oxford Group' are the principles of the Bible" (cited by Dick B., 1992, p. 6). More recently, T. Willard Hunter, a long-time OGM member, ordained minister, and close associate of OGM founder Frank Buchman in the 1940s and 1950s, stated: "The Oxford Group was initiated by an American, Frank N.D. Buchman, as a life-changing Christian movement" (Hunter, n.d., p. 1). Lois Wilson (AA co-founder Bill Wilson's wife) defined the OGM as "an international evangelical movement" (L. Wilson, 1979, p. 92).

When AA's co-founders met in Akron, Ohio in May 1935, they were both members of that international evangelical movement. It had been founded approximately 15 years earlier by Lutheran minister Frank Nathan David Buchman, who had originally called it "A First Century Christian Fellowship." Throughout the 1920s, its focus was campus missionary activities. In the late 1920s, Buchman, who had moved to England, began to call his crusade the Oxford Group Movement—though its ties to the town of Oxford and Oxford University were tenuous.

By the early 1930s, the focus of the Oxford Group Movement had shifted from campus evangelism to mass evangelism aimed at the middle and upper classes, with some OGM events drawing over 10,000 participants. During this period, both Bill Wilson (a former Wall Street insider) and Bob Smith (a Dartmouth-educated surgeon) became members. Smith, a very religious man, had joined approximately two-and-a-half years prior to his meeting with Wilson, and had been active in the local Oxford Group in Akron. Wilson was introduced to the Oxford Group Movement in the fall of 1934 by a former drinking buddy, Ebby Thatcher, who credited the Oxford Groups with helping him to stop drinking (temporarily, as it turned out).

Wilson later recalled the Oxford Group message that Thatcher brought to him: "You admit you are licked; you get honest with yourself; you talk it out with somebody else; you make restitution to the people you have harmed; you try to give of yourself without stint, with no demand for reward; and you pray to whatever God you think there is, even as an experiment" (Wilson, 1957, pp. 62–63). This list is very similar to the list of OGM principles Lois Wilson compiled: "The Oxford Group precepts were in substance: surrender your life to God; take a moral inventory; confess your sins to God and another human being; make restitution; give of yourself to others with no demand for return; pray to God for help to carry out these principles" (L. Wilson, 1979, p. 92). One can easily see here the formula later codified in the 12 steps.

Shortly after Ebby's visit, Wilson entered the drying-out facility, Towns Hospital, where he had his "spiritual awakening" (under the influence of morphine, belladonna, and other drugs).[8] Following that awakening, he plunged himself into OGM work.

He later recalled:

> Confession, restitution, and direct guidance of God underlined every conversation. They [OGM members] were talking about morality and spirituality, about God-centeredness versus self-centeredness. . . . Their aim was world conversion. Everybody, as they put it, needed changing. . . . Agreeing with James in the New Testament, they thought people ought to confess their sins "one to another." . . . Not only were things to be confessed, something was to be done about them. This usually took the form of what they called restitution, the restoration of good personal relationships by making amends for harms done.
>
> They were most ardent, too, in their practice of meditation and prayer . . . They felt that when people commenced to adhere to these high moral standards, then God could enter and direct their lives. Under these conditions, every individual could receive specific guidance, which could inspire every decision and act of living, great or small.
>
> (Alcoholics Anonymous, 1984, pp. 127–128)

Wilson—convinced that the OGM principles outlined by Ebby Thatcher were his gateway to salvation—began attending OGM meetings at the Rev. Sam Shoemaker's Calvary Episcopal Church. (Shoemaker was then the leading OGM figure in the United States, and Wilson would eventually become close friends with him.) At the same time, Dr. Bob Smith was attending Oxford Group meetings in Akron, Ohio, and still drinking heavily.

---

8. For details of Wilson's spiritual awakening under the belladonna cure, see *A.A. The Way It Began*, by Bill Pittman (1988), pp. 163–169.

They met in May 1935, when Wilson was in Akron on a business trip. They had a lot in common: serious alcohol abuse problems, conservative politics, upper-middle-class backgrounds, membership in the Oxford Group Movement, and faith that the principles of the Oxford Group Movement were the means of salvation—as regards alcohol and all other human problems. Given that one of the OGM principles was that one must "carry the message" to other "sinners," it was natural that Wilson and Smith teamed up to save other alcoholics through converting them to Oxford Group beliefs. Thus what was to become AA was born in June 1935, when Smith quit drinking and he and Wilson plunged into carrying the Oxford Group message to other alcoholics.

Smith and Wilson spent the summer of that year attempting to save alcoholics in Akron, and upon Wilson's return to New York at the end of summer, both men continued to "carry the message" to alcoholics in their respective cities. For the next two years what was to become AA operated as part of the Oxford Group Movement in New York, as it did for the next four years in Akron. Commenting on the direction in those years of what came to be AA, Wilson's worshipful biographer, Robert Thomsen, comments: "They [Smith and Wilson] tried to base everything they did, every step they took toward formulating their program, on Oxford Group principles" (Thomsen, 1975, p. 239).

As we've already seen, meetings at this time opened and closed with prayers, often featured scripture reading, and usually included a speaker "giving witness." Prayer was quite prominent in meetings during this period, and at the Akron meetings potential members were required to get down on their knees and "surrender" to God before joining the group (Alcoholics Anonymous, 1980, pp. 85, 88–89, 101). Another indication of the importance of prayer to what was to become AA is the original wording of the Big Book's step 7: "Humbly *on our knees* asked Him to remove these shortcomings— holding nothing back" (Alcoholics Anonymous, 1984, p. 198, emphasis added). *Pass It On*, AA's official Wilson biography, notes: "In both Akron and New York, early members followed the Oxford Group practice of kneeling together in prayer" (p. 191).

The reasons that AA eventually split off from the Oxford Group Movement had virtually nothing to do with differences over principles. Rather, the reasons for the split were either 1) personality conflicts; 2) social-status concerns; or 3) purely pragmatic matters. When AA split off from the Oxford Group Movement in New York in 1937, it was primarily because of personality conflicts between Bill Wilson and members of the Oxford Group at Calvary Episcopal

Church, who felt that Wilson was "not maximum," because he'd started holding OGM meetings for alcoholics only at his and Lois' house (L. Wilson, 1979, p. 103). The nonalcoholic Oxford Groupers also felt that Wilson's work with alcoholics was "narrow and divisive" (Alcoholics Anonymous, 1984, p. 169). For their part, the alcoholic OGM members felt that the other Groupers didn't understand them.

The reasons for the split from the OGM in Akron (and Cleveland) were similar; there was no conflict with the OGM over principles. The wife of Bill D., AA's third member, recalls: "It was all Oxford Group then [mid and late 1930s] . . . We were all members" (Alcoholics Anonymous, 1980, p. 88). During the entire time before the split with the OGM, Dr. Bob was quite dedicated to the Oxford Group's Christian principles: "When he stopped drinking, people asked, 'What's this not-drinking-liquor club you've got over there?' 'A Christian fellowship,' he'd reply" (p. 118). One early member of Akron AA recalls: "We were Oxford Groupers until we physically moved out" (of the locale of the OGM's Akron meetings) (p. 157).

One of the reasons that the split occurred in Ohio was that there were social tensions in the Akron Oxford Group similar to those in New York:

> Bill [D.] noted that the Oxford Group's practice of "checking" (one member's judging the authenticity of divine guidance that another claimed to have received) gave alcoholics the feeling that the O.G. leaders were ganging up on them. He also cited a technique of making people feel unwanted or uncomfortable until they agreed with some particular O.G. point of view.[9]
> (Alcoholics Anonymous, 1980, p. 157)

But there were other factors at work in Akron (and Cleveland) in 1939. Some "Oxford Groupers felt that participation by alcoholics lowered their own prestige," and—because of well-justified fear of public drunkenness and subsequent ridicule—"the alcoholics were becoming more insistent on anonymity at the public level—a principle that clashed with Buchman's program of advertising the 'change' in people's directions as a way of attracting others to his organization" (pp. 158–159).

As well, many of the alcoholic members of the OGM were worried that continued OGM affiliation would drive away Roman Catholic

---

9. Those who voice disagreement with almost any aspect of AA dogma will face such pressure at most AA meetings; and similar—though often more intense—social pressure is now a standard part of 12-step treatment.

alcoholics, or result in their being banned from joining by the Catholic hierarchy:

> By early 1939, Clarence S. had developed into a spark-plug for the Cleveland A.A. contingent. He and Dorothy were bringing men down every week to the [OGM] meeting at T. Henry's [in Akron]. Many of them were Catholic. Clarence remembered telling them that the Oxford Group meetings wouldn't interfere with their religion. "However, the testimony given by members at the meetings seemed like open confession to them, and this was something they were not allowed to practice," according to Clarence. "Furthermore, the idea of receiving guidance didn't sit well. And to top it off, they [the Oxford Groupers] were using the wrong Bible [the King James version, rather than the Catholic-approved Douay version]."

> (Alcoholics Anonymous, 1980, p. 162)

As a result of these problems, the Cleveland group began calling itself Alcoholics Anonymous, after the recently published Big Book, in May 1939, and the Akron group later began doing the same.

The New York group—no longer a part of the Oxford Group Movement, but still adhering to OGM principles—was also having problems reconciling its principles and practices with those of potential Catholic members, and was quite worried that Catholics would be barred from joining. The result of these worries was that when Bill Wilson wrote the Big Book he adhered to OGM principles almost to the letter, codified the central OGM principles as the heart of AA's program (the 12 steps)—and pointedly failed to give the Oxford Groups a single word of credit in the entire book. He also pointedly included no specifically Protestant references in the book; rather, he relied upon nondenominational religious terminology ("God," "Father," "Creator," etc.). After he finished writing it, he even submitted the manuscript to the Catholic Committee on Publications of the Archdiocese of New York and "quickly accepted . . . some minor changes" the Committee recommended (Alcoholics Anonymous, 1984, p. 201).

Before ending this discussion of AA's religious background, it is fitting to return to the OGM principles that were codified in the 12 steps. Commenting on an early draft of the Big Book's famous steps, AA's official Wilson biography, *Pass It On*, notes:

Oxford Group ideas prevail in these original six steps, as listed by Bill:
"1. We admitted that we were licked, that we were powerless over alcohol.
"2. We made a moral inventory of our defects or sins.
"3. We confessed or shared our shortcomings with another person in confidence.
"4. We made restitution to all those we had harmed by our drinking.
"5. We tried to help other alcoholics, with no thought of reward in money or prestige.
"6. We prayed to whatever God we thought there was for power to practice these precepts."

(Alcoholics Anonymous, 1984, p. 197)

Wilson shortly expanded these six steps to the present twelve. Because the principles in these six steps almost completely overlap those of the 12 steps, it's fair to say that the above passage in *Pass It On* is a direct admission in AA's conference-approved literature that AA's 12-step program comes straight from the Oxford Group Movement.

In later years, when fears of Catholic reaction had faded, Bill Wilson and AA explicitly credited the Oxford Group Movement as the source of the concepts codified in the 12 steps:

The Twelve Steps of A.A. simply represented an attempt to state in more detail, breadth, and depth, what we had been taught—primarily by you [former OGM American leader, Sam Shoemaker]. Without this, there could have been nothing—nothing at all.

(Dick B., 1992, p. 10, citing a 1963 Wilson letter to Shoemaker)

Likewise:

Where did early AA's . . . learn about moral inventory, amends for harm done, turning our wills and lives over to God? Where did we learn about meditation and prayer and all the rest of it? . . . straight from Dr. Bob's and my own early association with the Oxford Groups, as they were then led in America by that Episcopal rector, Dr. Samuel Shoemaker.

(Wilson, 1988, p. 198)

In *Alcoholics Anonymous Comes of Age*, Wilson again credits Shoemaker and the Oxford Groups with providing AA's central principles:

. . . Many a channel had been used by Providence to create Alcoholics Anonymous. And none had been more vitally needed than the one opened through Sam Shoemaker and his Oxford Group associates . . . the early A.A. got its ideas of self-examination, acknowledgment of character defects, restitution for harm done, and working with others straight from the Oxford Groups and directly from Sam Shoemaker, their former leader in America, and from nowhere else. . . . A.A. owes a debt of timeless gratitude for all that God sent us through Sam and his friends in the days of A.A.'s infancy.

(Wilson, 1957, pp. 39–40)

Thus AA kept the substance of the Oxford Group Movement's religious program while, for purely pragmatic reasons, changing the label and softening some terms. Wilson later explained the pronounced AA tendency toward euphemism in this way: "These ideas had to be fed with teaspoons rather than by buckets" (Wilson, 1957, p. 75). (The "spiritual, not religious" claim is a good example of this.)

To put all this in better perspective, let's take a look at exactly which steps correspond to which OGM principles. The Buchmanite principles of *personal powerlessness* and the necessity of *divine guidance* are embodied in steps 1, 2, 3, 6, 7, and 11; the principle of *confession* is embodied in steps 4, 5, and 10; the principle of *restitution* to those one has harmed is embodied in steps 8 and 9; and the principle of *continuance*,[10] of continuing to practice the other OGM principles and to carry the message to other "defeated" persons ("alcoholics," in the steps), is embodied in steps 10 and 12.

To spell out some of these correspondences in more detail: AA inherited the Oxford Group belief that human beings in themselves

---

10. This is one of the Oxford Group Movement's "Five Cs": Confidence, Conviction, Confession, Conversion, Continuance. They formed the basis of the OGM's indoctrination process, in which the potential convert first gained *confidence* in the "soul surgeon," then arrived at *conviction* of his own sinfulness, followed by *confession* of his sins, which led to *conversion* to OGM beliefs, followed by *continuance* of OGM practices in daily life (prayer, "quiet time" [meditation in which God supposedly tells the "listener" what to do], Bible reading, attending OGM meetings, witnessing [often in the form of public confession], carrying the message to others, etc.). For a full description of this process, see the OGM manual, *Soul Surgery*, by H.A. Walter (1932).

There are striking parallels to the Oxford Group's Five Cs in AA's indoctrination process: first, the newcomer arrives at *confidence* in AA through being repeatedly told (in the mass media, during treatment, and at meetings) that AA really works and is the only way to beat an alcohol problem; he then arrives at *conviction* that he is powerless over alcohol; he then engages in public *confession* of that powerlessness at every AA meeting he attends ("Hi, I'm Joe. I'm an alcoholic."), and also confesses his own sinfulness to God and his sponsor ("another human being") (steps 4 and 5); this leads to *conversion* to the AA belief system (see Wilson, 1953, p. 109); and this in turn leads to *continuance* in practicing the other AA principles (step 10) and in "carry[ing] this message" to other alcoholics (step 12).

are powerless and that only submission to God's will is sufficient to solve human problems. (AA lists only the problem of alcohol, though the underlying belief is identical; the third step, in which one turns one's "will and . . . li[fe] over to the care of God," makes this obvious.) It also inherited the belief that God will guide anyone who "listens." An additional Oxford Group legacy is the belief that it is necessary for human beings to confess their "wrongs" (in AA) or "sins" (in the Oxford Groups); furthermore, both groups employ(ed) both private and public confessions. The Oxford Groups emphasized private confessions from "sinners" to individual "soul surgeons," and public confessions at "houseparties," while AA emphasizes private confessions from "pigeons" (newcomers being indoctrinated into the AA program) to "sponsors" (experienced members responsible for indoctrinating individual newcomers), and public confessions at AA meetings.

Another ideological correspondence between AA and the Oxford Groups can be found in their attitude toward recruitment of those who have doubts about their programs. The Oxford Groups en-couraged doubters, including agnostics, to pray and to practice "quiet times," acting "as if" they believed in God. The assumption was that God would make himself known to the supplicant, God having a plan for every human life and being ready to reveal it to anyone who would listen. In AA, the approach to doubters and the assumptions under-lying that approach are identical to those of the Oxford Groups. AA even has a prescriptive slogan for newcomers harboring doubts: "Fake it until you make it."

The result of all this is indoctrination—religious indoctrination into the divinely guided "A.A. way of life." As Bill Wilson himself noted, "Some A.A.s say, 'I don't need religion, because A.A. is my religion'" (Wilson, 1988, p. 178). Another of his comments sheds more light on what that religion is:

> Nearly every A.A. member comes to believe in and depend upon a higher Power which most of us call God. In A.A. practically no full recovery from alcoholism has been possible without this all-important faith. God, *as we understand Him*, is the foundation upon which our fellowship rests.
>
> (Wilson, 1957, p. 253)

Recall also Wilson's comments about the effects of working the steps:

> So, practicing these Steps, we had a spiritual awakening about which finally there was no question. Looking at those who were only beginning and still doubted themselves, the rest of us were able to see the change setting in. From great numbers of such experiences, we could predict that the doubter who still claimed that he hadn't got the 'spiritual angle,' and who still considered his well-loved A.A. group the higher power, would presently love God and call Him by name.

> (Wilson, 1953, p. 109)

Finally, the Oxford Group Movement (now Moral Re-Armament, MRA) has recently and inadvertently confirmed that the 12 steps have nothing specifically to do with alcoholism or addictions of any kind, but are, rather, a set of universal religious principles designed to lead to a "God-controlled" life—what AA calls the "the A.A. way of life." In *It Started Right There: AA & MRA*, MRA writer T. Willard Hunter states: "These [12 steps] are the life-changing procedures pioneered by Frank Buchman, developed by Sam Shoemaker, and codified for AA by Bill Wilson. They are here adjusted in only two places . . . for application to the universal human condition."

These remarks immediately precede a fill-in-the-blanks, *generic* 12 steps (Hunter, n.d., pp. 10–11).[11, 12]

Summary

It is fitting to end this discussion of AA's religious origins and religious orientation with consideration of the 12 steps, for when those steps were published in the Big Book, AA's ideology (its "program") was set in stone. (Anyone familiar with AA will understand how extremely remote the possibility is of any change—let alone any substantive change—in its program, given the procedural difficulties involved in making changes, and given the reverence in which most AA members hold the steps, Big Book, and Bill Wilson.)

---

11. The blanks are only in steps 1 and 12; all of the other steps are exactly the same as AA's steps.

12. Thus, MRA has brought the process full circle by putting AA's codification of OGM/MRA principles into an MRA publication. The primary difference between how AA originally borrowed MRA's principles and MRA's borrowing of AA's codification of those principles is that MRA *credited* AA.

Prior to the publication of the Big Book, what was to become AA was part of the Oxford Group Movement, adhered to OGM beliefs, and participated in OGM practices, such as prayer, Bible reading, and public confession at meetings. As we've seen, when Bill Wilson wrote the 12 steps, he merely codified the OGM's central beliefs—there is not a single original concept in the steps—while giving no credit whatsoever to the Oxford Groups or their founder and leader, Frank Buchman. When AA broke away from the Oxford Group Movement in 1939—for reasons having essentially *nothing to do* with differences over ideology—it retained the central OGM principles as the core of the AA program. It also retained a great many OGM practices, such as prayer, both private and public confession, public witnessing, reading from an "inspired" text at meetings (now the Big Book rather than the Bible), and "carrying this message."[13] Thus one could well argue that the AA of today not only is clearly a religious group, but for all practical purposes *is* the Oxford Group Movement targeted at a single group (alcoholics) and marketed under a different brand name.

Repeated assertion that "AA is spiritual, not religious" cannot alter this reality.

---

13. Striking similarities between AA and the OGM abound in areas beyond ideology and religious practices. For example, both groups have (or had, in the case of the OGM—as MRA, it continues to exist, but only as a shadow of its former self) a fondness for slogans, and both are very anti-intellectual. To express this anti-intellectualism in slogan form, the Oxford Groups had the axiom, "Doubt stifles and makes abortive our attempt to act upon God's Guidance," while AA has the slogans, "Your best thinking got you here," "Utilize, don't analyze," "Let go and let God," and "Keep It Simple, Stupid." For a detailed discussion of the many similarities between AA and the OGM, see *Alcoholics Anonymous: Cult or Cure?* (2nd Ed.), Chapter 4, "The Oxford Groups & AA: Similarities & Differences" (Bufe, 1998, pp. 57–63).

4

The Courts and Coerced 12- Step Attendance

by Stanton Peele

Four higher courts have evaluated cases in which corrections departments/institutions or conditions of probation have required attendance at Alcoholics Anonymous, Narcotics Anonymous, or therapy based on AA's 12 steps. In these cases, failure to comply entailed serious penalties (return to prison, loss of parole opportunities, or major benefits such as family visits). All of these cases have been decided since 1996. Uniformly, the courts have ruled that mandated 12-step attendance violates the First Amendment of the U.S. Constitution. The Bill of Rights begins with the statement that "Congress shall make no law respecting the establishment of religion or prohibiting the free exercise thereof. . . ." The first part of this statement is called the "Establishment Clause" and has been interpreted by the U.S. Supreme Court to mean that no government body can require or encourage religious observance of any type. (This is also known as the separation of church and state.) Two Federal circuit courts (the appeals courts just below the U.S. Supreme Court) and two state high courts (Tennessee and New York) have found that prisons or courts violate this clause when they require that inmates or probationers undergo 12 step therapy or participate in 12-step support groups.

The 12 Steps

The 12 steps, written by AA co-founder Bill Wilson, are a fundamental part of the AA recovery program. These 12 steps now form the basis of most alcohol and drug treatment in the U.S., and are central to Establishment Clause cases involving mandated treatment. (They are used in 93% of alcoholism treatment programs, according to Roman and Blum, 1997). For a thorough discussion of the religious nature of the 12 steps, see Chapter 3. The 12 steps (this is the Narcotics Anonymous version) are as follows:

1. We admitted that we were powerless over our addiction, that our lives had become unmanageable.
2. We came to believe that a power greater than ourselves could restore us to sanity.
3. We made a decision to turn our will and our lives over to the care of God as we understood Him.
4. We made a searching and fearless moral inventory of ourselves.
5. We admitted to God, to ourselves, and to another human being the exact nature of our wrongs.
6. We were entirely ready to have God remove all these defects of character.
7. We humbly asked Him to remove our shortcomings.
8. We made a list of all persons we had harmed, and became willing to make amends to them all.
9. We made direct amends to such people wherever possible, except when to do so would injure them or others.
10. We continued to take personal inventory, and when we were wrong promptly admitted it.
11. We sought through prayer and meditation to improve our conscious contact with God, as we understood Him, praying only for knowledge of His will for us, and the power to carry that out.
12. Having had a spiritual awakening as a result of those steps, we tried to carry this message to addicts and to practice these principles in all our affairs.

Resolved and Unresolved Issues

Decisions Affecting State Actions and 12-Step Programs

The 12 steps are religious/Christian. Although 12-step advocates, prison administrators, and lower courts have argued, based on the third step's phrase, "God as we understood Him," that AA's 12 steps are universal and do not refer to a particular religion, all higher court rulings have held that both the internal content of the 12 steps and the accompanying rituals of 12-step groups, such as regular prayers, imply a traditional religious concept of God. Moreover, in their submissions in such cases, Jewish advocacy groups have argued that the 12 steps are specifically Christian in nature.

Coercion means being subjected to serious penalties for not attending 12-step therapies for which there are no alternatives. Coercion is determined to exist when an inmate, defendant, or probationer cannot realistically reject AA without suffering adverse consequences. Coercion has not been found to occur when courts and prisons offer nontheistic alternative therapy options along with the choice of 12-step treatment.

The Supreme Court has not ruled on the 12 steps. Despite these higher court rulings, the U.S. Supreme Court has not yet ruled on whether compelling people to participate in AA and other 12-step programs violates the First Amendment. On the one hand, this means that the Supreme Court may someday either uphold or reverse circuit and state supreme court rulings. On the other hand, the Supreme Court in December of 1996 declined to hear an appeal of *Griffin v. Coughlin*, and in November of 1997 declined to hear an appeal of *Warner v. Orange County Department of Probation*, leaving those decisions intact—meaning that any Supreme Court ruling on this subject is likely at least several years off.

Private Employers and 12-Step Programs

The extent to which private organizations may require 12-step treatment has not yet been limited in line with the "Free Exercise Clause." Private employers and other nongovernmental organizations have greater freedom to require that employees undergo 12-step treatment, since the Establishment Clause refers only to governmental actions. But the second clause of the portion of the First Amendment dealing with freedom of religion, called the "Free Exercise Clause," means that all Americans can personally choose to observe or not to observe any religion. Title 9 of federal law, for example, forbids religious tests for employment. Thus, private organizations may not require people to be religious or to follow a specific religion. However, to date, no court has ruled against an employer's forcing an employee to attend AA or 12-step therapy.

Employers can fire employees for simple use or intoxication, even off duty. Employers generally have wide latitude in terminating employees. Thus, showing up to work drunk, even once, or any use of illegal drugs, is sufficient for discharge. In such circumstances, employers can present employees with the choice of AA attendance or being fired, since employers are completely within their legal rights to fire employees rather than allow participation in some alternative program. Even being charged with an off-duty drug or DUI offense may trigger the employer's right to terminate an employee.

Especially sensitive jobs. Groups that are especially likely to be subjected to compulsory treatment on penalty of loss of license are health professionals (doctors and nurses) and transport workers. Individuals in these categories are deemed to be in especially sensitive positions due to the effect of their physical and emotional condition on public safety, according to the Federal Rehabilitation Act of 1973 and the Americans with Disabilities Act (ADA). This was the basis of the Supreme Court's decision in *Skinner v. Railway Labor Executives* (1989) permitting drug testing of railroad employees following accidents (see Husak & Peele, 1998).

A Georgia Superior Court (*Masters v. Talbott*, 1999) has now found a prominent treatment provider liable for forcing treatment on a physician on the basis of an inaccurate diagnosis of alcohol dependence, and for the damages he suffered from loss of employment (see Chapter 6). But this decision was not based on either informed consent or violation of the First Amendment due to the religious nature of the treatment program and required AA meetings. Nor was the suit directed at the employer or licensing body for requiring or compelling the treatment; rather, it was directed at the treatment provider for misdiagnosis and coercion.

U.S. Court Rulings Against Mandated AA/12-Step Program Participation

Griffin v. Coughlin (1996)

New York's highest court, the Court of Appeals, prohibited (in a 5-2 decision) the Corrections Department from making a prisoner's participation in the Family Reunion Program conditional on his attendance in the prison's Alcohol and Substance Abuse Treatment (ASAT) Program. The court ruled that such participation violated the

Establishment Clause. This ban would apply to any compulsion to participate in "a curriculum which adopts in major part the religious-oriented practices and precepts of Alcoholics Anonymous." The decision emphasized the "proven effectiveness of the A.A. approach to alcoholism or drug addiction rehabilitation" and the acceptability of "a noncoercive use of A.A.'s 12-step regimen as part of an alternative prisoner drug and alcohol abuse treatment effort . . . , providing it offered a secular alternative to the A.A. component." The American Jewish Congress filed a friend-of-the-court brief in support of the inmate's claims.

Facts

In 1991, David Griffin, an inmate in the New York State penal system, had qualified for the Family Reunion Program. However, because he had used heroin from 1955 to 1968, his participation in the family program was conditioned on his participation in the ASAT Program at the facility. Griffin, who was on record as an atheist, objected to the 12-step program on the grounds of the Establishment Clause (the requirement of a separation between church and state), but his objection was denied.

The Corrections Department argued that ASAT's major emphasis was participation in AA and NA, which "have proven to be the most effective method for preventing relapse of the recovering alcoholic or chemical substance abuser" and were the "'state of the art' major component of any addiction program. Pointing to A.A. literature, respondents averred that the references to God actually mean some 'higher power as the individual may understand such higher power,' not as the concept would be known by 'organized religions.'"

Lower Courts

"The Supreme Court [NY's trial court] dismissed the petition without affording petitioner a hearing to develop a record of the facts underlying his complaint. The Appellate Division" found (211 AD2d 187), citing AA's Big Book and 12 steps, "that, despite the repeated references to 'God' in the Twelve Steps and Twelve Traditions, A.A. does not 'demand' adherence to any particular faith but to 'spirituality' and 'open-mindedness.' The court also found quite significant that A.A. allows participants to select their own conception of God, as shown by the reference in Step 3 to 'God as we understood Him.'"

Court's Analysis

The court agreed that the ASAT program was built fundamentally on AA's 12 steps. The New York Court of Appeals then conducted the most thorough judicial review on record of the religious nature of AA and its philosophy and practices.

"Concededly, there are passages in A.A. literature, relied upon heavily by respondents, the Appellate Division and the dissent here, which, in stressing the openness and inclusiveness of the A.A. movement, eschew any intent to impose a particular sectarian set of beliefs or a particular concept of God upon participants. However, a fair reading of the fundamental A.A. doctrinal writings discloses that their dominant theme is unequivocally religious, certainly in the broad definitional sense as 'manifesting faithful devotion to an acknowledged ultimate reality or deity' (Webster's 9th New Collegiate Dictionary 995 [9th ed 1990]). Indeed, the A.A. basic literature most reasonably would be characterized as reflecting the traditional elements common to most theistic religions."

In addition to the 12 steps, "the 12 Traditions include a profession of belief that 'there is one ultimate authority—a loving God as He may express Himself in our group conscience.' While A.A. literature declares an openness and tolerance for each participant's personal vision of God . . . , the writings demonstrably express an aspiration that each member of the movement will ultimately commit to a belief in the existence of a Supreme Being of independent higher reality than humankind. Thus, in the A.A. Big Book . . . , Chapter 1, 'Bill's Story,' describes the spiritual transformation of one of the co-founders of A.A., in which he finally achieved salvation from his alcoholism: by 'enter[ing] upon a new relationship with my Creator. . . . I must turn in all things to the Father of Light who presides over us all.' In Chapter 4, entitled 'We Agnostics,' the theme is unambiguously proselytizing of unenlightened, self-centered atheists." Reviewing the corpus of AA, the court noted that "followers are urged to accept the existence of God as a Supreme Being, Creator, Father of Light and Spirit of the Universe. In 'working' the 12 steps, participants become actively involved in seeking such a God through prayer, confessing wrongs and asking for removal of shortcomings. These expressions and practices constitute, as a matter of law, religious exercise for Establishment Clause purposes, no less than the non-denominational prayer in *Engel v. Vitale* (370 US 421) [school prayer]."

The Court spent considerable time contesting the minority

opinion in this decision, which discounted the religious roots and bases of AA: "In an effort to downplay the religiosity of the foregoing A.A. tenets, the dissent suggests, without verification from actual source materials, that the unequivocally proselytizing themes of early A.A. texts have implicitly been superseded by later more secular A.A. writings into which A.A. doctrine has evolved . . . . Even if the dissent's disavowal of A.A.'s religiosity is found not compelling, the dissenters suggest that the A.A. component of the ASAT Program (1) is essentially insignificant or 'attenuated,' albeit requiring at least weekly attendance at A.A. operated group meetings for 26 weeks and constant working of the Twelve Steps in all other parts of the ASAT curriculum; and (2) is readily severable from the predominantly secular ASAT Program (Dissent, Slip Opn, at 22), although the ASAT Program Manual itself states that participation in the A.A. group meetings is 'essential to the fulfillment of program goals.' These alternative arguments are therefore also unpersuasive."

Even if the religious principles of AA were somehow separable from ASAT's therapeutic program, "the A.A. volunteers who are invited to conduct the prison self-help group meetings of inmates in the ASAT Program, where the 12 steps are worked, can reasonably be expected to be wholeheartedly imbued with and committed to the religious precepts predominating in the A.A. basic texts. . . . Exactly that result was proved at trial before the United States District Court in *Warner v. Orange County Dept of Probation* (870 F Supp 69 [SDNY]). . . . In *O'Connor v. State of California* (855 F Supp 303, 306 [D Cal]), virtually identical findings were made on the religiously-oriented conduct of A.A. meetings, attendance at which had been imposed as an alternate condition of probation."

"The Appellate Division committed a second error by disregarding application of the second prong of the three-part test (the purpose-effect-entanglement test) for primary Establishment Clause analysis articulated in *Lemon v. Kurtzman* (403 US 602). . . . State-coerced adherence to a religious sect is not necessary to prove an Establishment Clause violation under any portion of the Lemon test. Specifically, under the second prong of the Lemon test, State action is invalid if its 'primary effect' is to advance or promote religion (*Lemon v. Kurtzman*, 403 US, at 612). . . . 'Our cases simply do not support the notion that a law found to have a primary effect to promote some legitimate end under the State's police power is immune from further examination to ascertain whether it also has the direct and immediate effect of advancing religion' (*Committees for Public Education and Religious Liberty v. Nyquist*, 413 US 756, 783 n 39).

A violation also is established if the State action's 'inevitable effect is to aid and advance' religion (id., at 793)."

"That inmates who choose not to follow the 12 steps through the ASAT program thereby lose important benefits clearly violates U.S. Supreme Court outlined restrictions since, in the words of constitutional law scholar Laurence Tribe (Tribe, American Constitutional Law [2d ed], at 1173), the prison has 'apparently employed the machinery of the state to gather an [involuntary] audience for religion.'"

The court concluded that the "dissent's criticisms of our holding . . . misread(s) our decision in persistently characterizing it as hostilely 'root[ed] in a proposition' that A.A. itself and its religious practices and precepts are constitutionally 'objectionable'. . . . To the contrary, we have repeatedly indicated throughout the decision that the decisive factor in our analysis was not the incorporation of A.A. doctrine and practices into the ASAT Program, but the facility's application of coercive pressure to participate in an exclusive inmate drug and alcohol treatment program having that component. Rather than condemning A.A. and its practices we specifically acknowledged A.A.'s 'proven effectiveness.' Our decree specifically prohibits only the coercive aspects of conditioning petitioner's eligibility for the Family Reunion Program on attendance in the ASAT Program as presently constituted."

Kerr v. Farrey (1996)

The United States Court of Appeals For the Seventh Circuit (Wisconsin, Illinois, and Indiana), reversing a district court decision, unanimously held "that the state . . . impermissibly coerced inmates to participate in a religious program, thus violating the Establishment Clause." In this case, an inmate was threatened with being sent to a higher security prison and with rejection of his parole applications for refusing to attend Narcotics Anonymous meetings.

Facts

James Kerr, an inmate at Oakhill Correctional Institution in Wisconsin, was required to attend Narcotics Anonymous meetings or face negative consequences. NA was the only substance abuse program offered in the prison. Kerr contended that he "didn't have a choice in the matter; that attendance was mandatory; that if [he] didn't go, [he] would most likely be shipped off to a medium (i.e., higher security) prison, and denied the hope of parole," and that other negative inferences stemming from his refusal might appear in his prison record.

Kerr pointed out that the Oakhill NA meetings began with a prayer invoking the Lord and that the NA "Basic Text" book (like AA's Big Book) contained innumerable references to spirituality and God. Kerr "objected to dragging God's name into 'this messy business of addictions,'" while finding that NA's view of God conflicted with his beliefs about free will. Thus, he claimed, NA attendance violated both the Establishment and Free Exercise clauses of the First Amendment. Prison Warden Catherine Farrey claimed that inmates were required only to observe NA meetings and that, moreover, the concept of a "higher being" invoked by NA "was viewed as a very personal matter and could range from a religious concept of God to the non-religious concept of individual willpower."

Lower Court

The district court held that the NA requirement "neither advanced nor inhibited religion, and that there was no state entanglement 'in terms of economic support.'" The court also held that the NA requirement did not "impermissibly burden" Kerr's religious freedom.

Court's Analysis

The Court of Appeals wrote: "The Supreme Court put it this way in the leading case of *Everson v. Board of Education*, 330 U.S. 1, 15-16 (1947): [t]he 'establishment of religion' clause of the First Amendment means at least this: Neither a state nor the Federal Government can set up a church. Neither can pass laws which aid one religion, aid all religions, or prefer one religion over another. Neither can force nor influence a person to go to or to remain away from church against his will or force him to profess a belief or disbelief in any religion. No person can be punished for entertaining or professing religious beliefs or disbeliefs, for church attendance or non-attendance."

The Supreme Court has long debated the Establishment Clause. In cases "dealing with government efforts to 'coerce anyone to support or participate in religion or its exercise,'" having as their essence "that the state is somehow forcing a person who does not subscribe to the religious tenets at issue to support them or to participate in observing them," the Court has ruled squarely against the religious rule or regulation. These include the Court's school prayer cases, in which the Court "struck down the practice of beginning the school day with a prayer, scripture readings, or the Lord's Prayer, where some students (or their families) did not subscribe to the religious beliefs expressed therein. See *Engel v. Vitale*, 370 U.S. 421 (1962) (official prayer); *School District of Abington Township v. Schempp*, 374 U.S. 203 (1963) (Bible reading and Lord's Prayer). . . . The fact that the prayers and morning exercise sessions were technically voluntary did not dispel the inherently coercive nature of the setting for impressionable children, compelled by law to attend the school."

"The second group of cases has inspired more controversy within the Supreme Court itself. These are the cases in which existing religious groups seek some benefit from the state," such as using publicly funded transportation for parochial school students. *Lemon v. Kurtzman* 403 U.S. 602 (1971) is the seminal case of this sort, in which states provided financial aid to parochial schools. Also in this category are use of public spaces by religious groups or for religious displays. This type of case has produced the three part "Lemon test," which asks; 1) whether the statute has a secular legislative purpose; 2) whether its principal or primary effect is one that neither advances nor inhibits religion; and 3) whether it avoids excessive entanglement with religion. 403 U.S. at 612-13.

"In our view, when a plaintiff claims that the state is coercing him or her to subscribe to religion generally, or to a particular religion, only three points are crucial: first, has the state acted; second, does the action amount to coercion; and third, is the object of the coercion religious or secular? In Kerr's case, the first two criteria are satisfied easily. There is no question that the prison authorities act for the State of Wisconsin in these circumstances. The fact that NA ran the treatment program is of no moment, since it is clear that the prison officials required inmates to attend NA meetings (at the very least, to observe). On the record as it comes to us, it is also undisputed that Kerr was subject to significant penalties if he refused to attend the NA [meetings] . . . . The final element requires somewhat more discussion."

Is AA religious? "The district court thought that the NA program escaped the 'religious' label because the twelve steps used phrases like 'God, as we understood Him,' and because the warden indicated that the concept of God could include the non-religious idea of willpower within the individual." The Seventh Circuit rejected this interpretation, since "a straightforward reading of the twelve steps shows clearly that the steps are based on the monotheistic idea of a single God or Supreme Being. . . . Kerr alleged, furthermore, that the meetings were permeated with explicit religious content. This was therefore not a case . . . where the only religious note was struck by the insertion of the words 'under God' in the Pledge of Allegiance. . . . [Thus] the program runs afoul of the prohibition against the state's favoring religion in general over non-religion." The Court further noted that, unlike in *O'Connor v. California*, 855 F. Supp. 303 (C.D. Cal. 1994), where the court found no violation of the Establishment Clause, Oakdale offered no alternatives to NA or AA.

Qualified immunity of officials. The prison officials involved in the case could have been liable for depriving Kerr of his rights, despite the limited immunity from such liability granted to public officials in some cases, if they should have been aware that their actions were illegal. The Seventh Circuit concluded that the prison officials qualified for immunity in this case because they could reasonably not have known about recent decisions forbidding coercion into 12-step programs. However, one could infer that it would be harder for other officials to qualify for such limited immunity in the future.

Free exercise claim. The Seventh Circuit rejected Kerr's claim that NA attendance "impeded his ability to practice his own personal religion" since the argument he presented in his appeal that NA opposed his belief in free will did not represent a sufficient development of this issue.

Practical Result

James Kerr received no monetary damages (due to the immunity found to hold for prison officials) and had long since been released from prison. He was entitled to expungement of any references in his records to adverse consequences he suffered from his objections to NA. Assistant Warden Jeff Wydeven said he had not read the court's ruling but said he could not imagine "what changes, if any, might have to be made in the Oakhill treatment programs to comply with the ruling" (Rinard, 1996).

Aftermath—Brainwashing Claim

Kerr attempted to tackle the immunity issue again in order to gain a damages award by accusing the prison drug rehabilitation programs administered by the Wisconsin prison system of brainwashing, which he claimed constituted cruel and unusual punishment, in violation of the Eighth Amendment. The specific parts of the program that comprised brainwashing were its attacks on "criminal thinking." Kerr noted the following elements of this approach to changing inmates' attitudes:

1) He was required to write and then read publicly to the program group confessions of his alleged "criminal thinking errors."
2) He was required to write an autobiography which was then used against him by the social workers running the program.
3) He and others in the program were required to inform on each other five times a day about violating rules.
4) The social workers in the program used intimidation by screaming at Mr. Kerr at length.
5) Mr. Kerr was punished for a "criminal thinking error" by being required to scrub walls with a toothbrush for hours.

The Federal District Court for Eastern Wisconsin ruled that the defendants were immune from liability and that action was barred by Prison Litigation Reform Act (PLRA), *Kerr v. Puckett*, F. Supp. 354 (E.D. Wisconsin 1997), and the decision was upheld by the United States Court of Appeals for the Seventh Circuit. *Kerr v. Puckett*, 138 F.3d 321 (7th Cir. 1998). The Circuit Court indicated that this type of approach was common to AA, boot camp, and other rehabilitative programs. The Court ruled that "states are free to approach matters otherwise, and to seek rehabilitation even if that entails programs that prisoners find unpleasant" (meaning that the program did not constitute cruel and unusual punishment). The Court was particularly unsympathetic to Kerr's aversion to AA and similar programs in this decision: "Many prisoners, of whom Kerr apparently was one, leap at the chance to get out early by participating in substance-abuse-control programs. They learn that there is no gain without pain. Imprisonment is not a kind way to produce either rehabilitation or specific deterrence; 'tough love' may be the best medicine."

Warner v. Orange County Department of Probation (1999)

The United States Court of Appeals for the Second Circuit affirmed 2-1 a district court ruling that recommending an inmate plaintiff's participation in Alcoholics Anonymous as a condition of probation violated the Establishment Clause. 95 F.3d 202 (2nd Cir.

1996). The plaintiff received nominal monetary damages (one dollar). A dissenting judge stated that the Free Exercise Clause was a better basis for Warner's cause, and warned of the great possibilities for finding liability created by a decision that mandatory AA sentences without alternatives violate the Constitution.

Facts

Robert Warner pled guilty to driving drunk and without a license, his third alcohol-related driving violation in little more than a year. A municipal judge ordered the Orange County (NY) Department of Probation (OCDP) to prepare a presentence report, which included the conditions that the probationer "totally abstain from the use of intoxicating beverages," avoid "establishment[s] where the primary business is the sale or consumption of alcohol," and "attend Alcoholics Anonymous at the direction of [his] probation officer." The judge sentenced Warner to three years of probation with these conditions. After almost two years of attendance, Warner objected as an atheist to the AA meetings. His probation officer decided that Warner lacked sufficient commitment to the program and ordered continued AA attendance, and even greater AA involvement, on Warner's part. Group prayer was common at the meetings Warner attended. Warner filed a claim that requiring him to attend AA meetings forced him to participate in religious activity in violation of the First Amendment's Establishment Clause, and that OCDP was responsible because it recommended participation in AA to the sentencing court as a condition of probation. OCDP argued that: 1) "the determination of probation conditions is solely the responsibility of the sentencing judge"; 2) OCDP "is protected from any damages judgment by a quasi-judicial absolute immunity"; and 3) requiring Warner to attend AA did not violate the Establishment Clause.

Lower Court

The federal district court of Southern New York found that the 12 steps as stated "involved a substantial religious component" and that OCDP was responsible for Warner's attendance at AA. The religious component in AA was amplified by meetings that began with a religious invocation and always ended with a Christian prayer. The district court found that the program "placed a heavy emphasis on spirituality and prayer, in both conception and in practice."

Court's Analysis

OCDP's responsibility. The Court of Appeals wrote that in order to establish OCDP's liability, "Warner must first demonstrate that his injury resulted from a custom or policy of Orange County, as opposed to an isolated instance of conduct. The OCDP's recommendation that Warner be required to participate in A.A. therapy was unquestionably made pursuant to a general policy. This was one of six standard special conditions, set forth on a form captioned 'Additional Conditions of Probation Pertaining to Alcohol,' which OCDP routinely submitted to sentencing judges in alcohol cases." The general rule of tort (civil) responsibility is that actors "be held liable for 'those consequences attributable to reasonably foreseeable intervening forces, including the acts of third parties.'" Moreover, the court noted, a probation official is supposedly a neutral advisor on whose objective opinion the trial judge will usually rely, "particularly . . . when the recommendation deals with a provider of therapy since Judges are unlikely to possess particularized information about the relative characteristics and merits of different providers of therapy."

Warner's consent. "Warner—following the advice of his attorney—sampled A.A. sessions prior to sentence and made no objection to their religious content at the time of sentence . . . ." But "it was not clear that Warner was aware at the time that the religious content gave him any legal basis to object. . . . Furthermore, even if aware of his rights, he might well have been afraid to annoy the sentencing judge by objecting to the standard recommendation of the probation department. In short, for several reasons, it was entirely foreseeable at the time probation made its recommendation that Warner might not object. For the same reasons and others, Warner's conduct did not constitute consent." That Warner would foreseeably not object to his sentence is a novel approach to overcoming the defense that Warner's failure to object initially to a probationary recommendation constituted consent.

OCDP's immunity. The circuit court upheld OCDP's liability. "OCDP, when it formulated its policy of recommending A.A., was aware of the program's Twelve Steps and of their deeply religious character. Accordingly, there can be no question as to the reasonable foreseeability of the religious nature of the program OCDP was recommending for Warner. . . ." OCDP did not gain the immunity associated with prosecutors and court officers (such as judges) involved in the judicial process. Municipalities (including counties) do not enjoy immunity from suits.

AA and the Establishment Clause. "The Supreme Court has repeatedly made clear that 'at a minimum, the Constitution guarantees that government may not coerce anyone to support or participate in religion or its exercise. . .' *Lee v. Weisman*, 112 S. Ct. 2649, 2655 (1992) (quoting *Lynch v. Donnelly*, 465 U.S. 668, 678 (1984)). . . . The A.A. program to which Warner was exposed had a substantial religious component. Participants were told to pray to God for help in overcoming their affliction. Meetings opened and closed with group prayer. The trial judge reasonably found that it 'placed a heavy emphasis on spirituality and prayer, in both conception and in practice.' We have no doubt that the meetings Warner attended were intensely religious events. . . .

"There can be no doubt, furthermore, that Warner was coerced into participating in these religious exercises by virtue of his probation sentence. Neither the probation recommendation, nor the court's sentence, offered Warner any choice among therapy programs. The probation department's policy, its recommendation, and its printed form all directly recommended A.A. therapy to the sentencing judge, without suggesting that the probationer might have any option to select another therapy program, free of religious content. Once sentenced, Warner had little choice but to attend the A.A. sessions. If Warner had failed to attend A.A., he would have been subject to imprisonment for violation of probation. (references omitted) Had Warner been offered a reasonable choice of therapy providers, so that he was not compelled by the state's judicial power to enter a religious program, the considerations would be altogether different." (*Griffin v. Coughlin* cited without full citation in the original, see above.)

"Orange County argues that even if Warner was forced to attend the meetings, he was not required to participate in the religious exercises that took place. The County argues that, as a mature adult, Warner was less susceptible to such pressure than the children who were required to stand in respectful silence during a school prayer. . . . We do not find Orange County's argument convincing. Although it is true Warner was more mature, his exposure was more coercive than the school prayer in Lee. The plaintiff in Lee was subjected only to a brief two minutes of prayer on a single occasion. Warner, in contrast, was required to participate in a long-term program of group therapy that repeatedly turned to religion as the basis of motivation. . . . Warner was also paired with another member of A.A. as a method of enhancing his indoctrination into the group's approach to recovery from alcoholism. Most importantly, failure to cooperate could lead to incarceration. . . . [That] Warner managed to avoid indoctrination despite the pressure he faced does not make the County's program any less coercive, nor nullify the County's liability.

"The County argues further that the non-sectarian nature of the A.A. experience immunizes its use of religious symbolism and practices from Establishment Clause scrutiny. The argument is at the very least factually misleading, for the evidence showed that every meeting included at least one explicitly Christian prayer. Furthermore, the claim that non-sectarian religious exercise falls outside the First Amendment's scrutiny has been repeatedly rejected by the Supreme Court," notwithstanding the Supreme Court's acceptance of religious prayers to begin legislative sessions.

Judge R.K. Winter's dissent. "My dissent is based on two of the available grounds. First, Warner waived his claim . . . . Second, the invocation of the Establishment Clause, rather than the Free Exercise Clause, puts into play a principle that portends changes in our penal system that are not required, in my view, by the Constitution."

1) Consent. "This lawsuit is an instance of remarkable gall. Warner voluntarily selected and began attendance at A.A. meetings on the advice of counsel in order to impress the sentencing court with his determination to overcome his alcoholism. Now he complains that a subsequent recommendation of a probation officer that he attend such meetings entitles him to monetary damages." Instead, according to Judge Winter, this constitutes voluntary acceptance of the sentenced therapy and a waiver of any claims.

2) AA and the Establishment Clause. The dissent emphasized that OCDP's action violated the Free Exercise Clause rather than the Establishment Clause. To find the latter, Judge Winter opined, "would endanger any number of ubiquitous penal programs that are, in my view, clearly permissible," such as prison chaplains or sentences to community services (like soup kitchens) which may involve prayers. "None of the programs described above violate the Establishment Clause in my view" according to the three-part test in *Lemon*, because "each has a secular purpose in that they all further rehabilitation in one way or another. None have as a principal or primary effect the advancement or inhibition of religion. Any such effect is incidental.

Finally, they do not lead to excessive entanglement of the government in religion," since prison religious programs are commonplace. "I . . . see no difference between the penal programs described above and Warner's sentence so far as the Establishment Clause—in contrast to the Free Exercise Clause—is concerned. . . . [Nonetheless] I do not view compulsory activity with a substantial religious component as a valid penal measure, at least where equally effective secular rehabilitative programs are available . . . . [but rather] [c]ompulsory attendance at religious ceremonies as part of a penal sentence surely raises serious issues under the Free Exercise Clause and might well require the provision of a choice between secular and sectarian programs. . . . This is a decision with important ramifications. . . . At a practical level, my colleagues' decision exposes every probation authority in this circuit to suits for damages and attorney's fees in virtually every case in which a recommendation of attendance at A.A. meetings has been made and accepted within the statute of limitations period, if no available alternative was offered and such recommendations were commonly made."

Rehearing of Appeal

After the original Second Circuit decision in 1996, U.S. Senator Orrin Hatch of Utah called the ruling one of the worst instances of "judicial activism" by Clinton judicial appointees. In May 1997, the original appeals panel amended its opinion. 115 F.3d 1068 (2nd Cir. 1997). It continued to uphold the original trial ruling, but also vacated that opinion to remand the case for additional fact-finding in regards to the issue of waiver (did Warner's failure to raise the issue of AA attendance at his original probation hearing waive his right to do so later?). In June 1997, the original trial judge ruled that Warner's failure to object to the imposition of AA attendance did not comprise a waiver. 968 F.Supp. 917 (S.D. NY 1997). In April 1999, the same 2-1 majority on the Second Circuit appeals panel that did so originally upheld this ruling, but reiterated the award of nominal damages on the grounds that they did not want to penalize a public agency that was trying to "require an alcoholic to deal with his addiction." 173 F.3d 120 (2nd Cir. 1999).

Following the initial decision, the attorney for New York's Orange County, Richard B. Golden, noted, "There are alternatives out there. Do the probation officials think they are satisfactory? Absolutely not." For Golden, the issue is one of national importance. "Throughout New York state and, I believe, throughout the country, it is a standard condition that probationers in DWI cases attend AA. There is no other suitable alternative that comes anywhere close to the effectiveness of AA" (Murray, 1996).

Orange County applied for certiorari—that is, appealed to the U.S. Supreme Court—on June 30, 1999. In November 1999, the Supreme Court denied certiorari.

Evans v. Tennessee Board of Paroles (1997)

The Supreme Court of Tennessee, responding to petitions from two inmates regarding their failed parole hearings, found unanimously that the trial court erred in dismissing one of the inmates' —Anthony Evans'—claim for injunctive relief as to the Board's requirement that he participate in Alcoholics Anonymous. The court remanded the case to the trial court to determine whether AA was religious in nature, while citing case evidence that this was indeed the case.

Facts

Two Tennessee inmates claimed that the parole board, in rejecting parole for each, had not conducted open hearings as required by law, while claiming that one (Arnold) was illegitimately required to continue in a sex offender treatment program and the other (Evans) in AA. The court rejected both inmates' claims that their parole decisions required a public hearing. Also, noting that parole was a privilege and not a right, the court denied Arnold's claim that he not be required to continue in the sex offenders' program. But the court held that the trial court erred in dismissing Evans' claim for injunctive relief against the Board's requirement that he continue to participate in AA.

Evans contended that AA was a religious program and that the Board of Paroles' requirement that he continue in the program violated the Establishment Clause. Evans noted that the Tennessee Department of Correction administered a single alcohol program centered around AA's 12 steps. Evans cited the emphasis in the 12 steps on reliance on a higher power—in the third edition of AA's basic text, its Big Book—which he claimed "is used as an all-purpose guide for anyone having difficulty in working the twelve (12) steps." He furthermore pointed to the group prayers at the meetings, which started with the nondenominational Serenity Prayer and closed with the Christian Lord's Prayer.

Lower Courts

The trial court dismissed each petition for failure to state a claim upon which relief could be granted, and the Court of Appeals affirmed the trial court's judgment.

Court's Analysis

The Tennessee Supreme Court noted that, "While the Supreme Court has wrestled with questions of whether a certain policy or practice favors or establishes a religion, there is no debate that a government policy that requires participation in a religious activity violates the Establishment Clause:

> [I]t [is] 'beyond dispute' that the Constitution guarantees that the government may not coerce anyone to support or participate in religion or its exercise. Individuals may disagree in a particular case over other issues, such as whether it is the state who acted, or whether coercion is present, or whether religion or something else is the aim of the coercion. But in general, a coercion-based claim indisputably raises an Establishment Clause question. *Kerr v. Farrey*, 95 F.3d 472, 479 (7th Cir. 1996) (quoting *Lee v. Weisman*, 505 U.S. at 587, 112 S.Ct. at 2655)."

While not granting Evans parole, the court found his request that the Board of Paroles omit consideration of his continued participation in AA in future decisions was a potentially meritorious claim which the trial court had erred in failing to consider. "If, on remand, the trial court finds that the treatment program at issue is a religious one and that there are no alternative secular treatment programs offered, then to require a prisoner to attend or participate in such a treatment program would constitute a violation of the Establishment Clause. Attending or failing to attend such religious meetings can not be considered in a decision whether to grant or deny parole."

Summary[1]

In the highest courts at which the issue has been decided, 12-step treatment programs and groups, including AA, NA, et al., have been determined to be religious activities that the state cannot legally compel individuals to attend. These decisions are based on the First Amendment of the Constitution, and in particular its Establishment Clause barring the state from supporting, and especially from compelling, religious activities. Compulsion in this instance means merely the provision of desired benefits for attending, or the infliction of real penalties for not attending, 12-step groups or treatment. In general, the courts have decided that simply offering a non-religious alternative to 12-step programs removes the onus from offering such programs. Notwithstanding this unanimity, the issue remains unsettled in the sense that the U.S. Supreme Court has not ruled on this issue and has specifically declined to do so by failing to take up the opportunity to review appeals of two of these decisions (*Griffin v. Coughlin* and *Warner v. OCDP*).

More fundamentally, even in states and jurisdictions—even in the very institutions—covered by these decisions, authorities seem reluctant to accept them and to cease forcing individuals (namely probationers and prison inmates) into 12-step groups and treatment programs. So, it's quite hard for inmates and others involved in the penal system to rely on these rulings for protection. Even though inmates are among those with the time to attempt such cases, suing for a remedy for forced participation in a 12-step group is an arduous and time-consuming procedure. Prison inmates must first exhaust so-called administrative remedies—that is, they must first appeal to the institution and corrections system—before resorting to the courts (although they can ask for a restraining order or other injunctive relief). In many instances, inmates will be released from prison before a timely court decision can be obtained. At the same time, there is little direct precedent for resisting 12-step program assignments by private employers.

How, then, is one to use the precedents reviewed in this chapter? For the most part, an individual concerned about these issues—either due to direct involvement or out of a concern for reform—will usually be better off trying to approach those in charge, or those with legal

---

1. Valuable ideas for this section were derived from the *SMART Recovery Coordinator's Manual* (Appendix I), by Steve McCulloch (SMART Recovery, 1996).

responsibilities in the system, with the information in this chapter and book. In many cases, making responsible individuals aware of what the law has to say about the need to provide people with alternatives to 12-step groups rather than to coerce them to attend such groups —as well as making them aware of practical alternatives for meeting legal requirements—should stimulate a willingness to explore change. The alternative, to attempt legally to compel such change, is a last resort.

For example, the author has assisted Rich Dowling, of SMART Recovery, in presenting information about AA alternatives to prison officials in New Jersey and instituting SMART Recovery groups and other treatment alternatives in a number of penal institutions in the state. We have found that most reasonable prison officials and others in the penal system respond to the simple logic that different people respond to different kinds of programs. They see the appeal of the idea that a person's "buying into" a treatment program is critical to their succeeding at it. Providing additional options, when properly presented, simply seems like good business.

In requesting changes to broaden alternatives, remember that you need only point out the legal rulings. If the case concerns you, you can say that the religious element in AA and like programs—that is, asking God or a higher power to assist your sobriety—violates your beliefs or convictions. It is better not to detail your religious beliefs —and, actually, it is a violation of your privacy to be asked to do so. Whether you are Jewish, atheist, agnostic, or Buddhist is your privilege and is not to be questioned. The requirement that your request be honored, strictly speaking, is limited to state agencies, including penal and court agencies, but also government employers such as the military and other federal agencies (e.g., the Federal Aviation Administration).

Even so, those who stand in for the government—including those who report compliance with 12-step attendance requirements to the state, or arguably state medical licensing authorities—are likewise obligated to observe these court rulings. "Whenever a state, formally or informally, delegates to private persons functions that have traditionally been the exclusive prerogatives of the state, those persons become state actors for the limited purpose of performing these functions." *Granberg v. Ashland County,* 590 F.Supp. 1005, 1008 (W.D. Wisc. 1984), citing *Terry v. Adams,* 345 U.S. 461 (1953). Thus, you can argue to a state medical board that it is obligated to follow court rulings applicable to government agencies since, on behalf of the state, it is licensing people to practice medicine.

If any agency refuses to honor your request, ask for its decision in writing. Alternately, or in addition, ask for the exact regulation compelling you to attend a 12-step group. You might say, "If I am obligated to attend one type of meeting, please show me where this requirement is described." At the same time, keep notes identifying your requests, responses to them, and the dates and persons involved —perhaps their exact words—in these rejections. Likewise, note the religious and other elements you find offensive in these programs. Also note penalties or sanctions you experience due to your questioning of the offensive elements. If you should be forced to take legal action, such information can be critically helpful.

In granting qualified immunity to prison officials, the court in *Kerr v. Farrey* ruled that the officials could not reasonably have known of recent decisions indicating that their conduct in compelling people to attend 12-step programs was illegal. This is obviously less true today and cannot be true if the complainant has presented an official or his or her representative with notice of these decisions (as provided, for example, by this book).

You may also reach out to people and groups concerned about these matters, including Rational Recovery and SMART Recovery representatives, for advice about alternatives and how to make use of them. Hiring a lawyer is an expensive proposition. You may seek the assistance of the American Civil Liberties Union (ACLU) or other concerned civil rights attorneys. (When approaching the ACLU, it might be helpful to remind them of the four appeal-level court decisions ruling that coerced 12-step attendance is a violation of the Establishment Clause.) If a civil rights violation can be established, there are provisions in the federal law for payment to be made to attorneys who represent plaintiffs in such cases.

For many civil libertarians (including, one would hope, those who comprise the ACLU), the decisions reviewed in this chapter, although hard won, are fairly pale guarantees of individual rights. For example, as the dissent in *Warner* indicated, why should the state be supporting AA and similar programs, with their religious premises, at all? In this view, providing an alternative nonreligious program would still not rescue the corrections department or related agency from a violation of the Establishment Clause.

Alternately, one could argue, why is it the state's business to sentence people to treatment of any kind? Of course, the penal system has the upper hand in that such sentencing is in lieu of imprisonment or other criminal sanctions which people prefer to avoid. In this case (as has occurred in at least some lower courts), individuals could be asked to design their own plan to avoid drugs, alcohol, or intoxicated misbehavior. Just as a probationer or parolee can be reimprisoned for failure to attend AA, the individual could then be held accountable for his or her own relapse prevention program.

Above all, keep in mind that the state does not have the right to tamper with your inner beliefs and feelings about yourself in relation to the universe. At least up to the present, this has remained the province of the individual, the family, and the church.

5

Informed Consent
Missing In Action in Addiction Treatment

by Stanton Peele and Archie Brodsky

During the past several decades, informed consent has become an established principle of health law as well as clinical ethics, so much so that it has been the subject of a presidential commission (President's Commission, 1982). The requirement that a physician obtain a patient's informed consent to medical treatment (*Canterbury v. Spence*, 1972; *Natanson v. Kline*, 1960) is based on a consensus that individuals have the right to control access to their own bodies and to make informed decisions about their own health and well-being —decisions with which others might disagree—and live or die with the consequences. Moreover, the courts have repeatedly affirmed that a person (even one who is hospitalized for mental illness, if competent) has the right to refuse any and all medical treatment (e.g., *Rogers v. Commissioner of the Department of Mental Health*, 1983), and the right of refusal is recognized to varying degrees in many state statutes and regulations.

Legal Requirements

Although statute and case law concerning the scope and application of informed consent and the right to refuse treatment vary from one jurisdiction to another (cf. the U.S. Supreme Court's declining to promulgate uniform national standards in *Washington v. Harper*, 1990), basic principles are generally consistent (Appelbaum & Gutheil, 1991; Bursztajn et al., 1991; Deaton et al., 1993; Schwartz, 1994). The right to give or withhold informed consent is held by competent adults. Parents or guardians must give informed consent for minors, and a legal guardian must be appointed to give informed consent to treat a person who is adjudged incompetent to consent.

Competence is not a global trait. Separate judicial determinations must be made as to whether a mental disability renders a person incompetent (for example) to manage his or her finances, to make a will, or to stand trial. When it comes to giving informed consent to medical treatment, the requisite elements of competence include an appreciation of the situation and its consequences, together with the capacity to understand relevant information, to process that information rationally, and to communicate one's choices to care providers (Appelbaum, 1997; Appelbaum & Grisso, 1988; Grisso & Appelbaum, 1995).

Besides competence, two other elements are necessary to informed consent: *information* and *voluntariness.* In order to make an informed decision, a person must be informed about the nature of the treatment offered, its risks and benefits (i.e., possible outcomes, including side effects, and their probability of occurrence), and possible alternative treatments. The risks and benefits of no treatment at all must also be considered. The requirement of voluntariness means that consent must be given freely, and cannot be coerced. While physical coercion clearly violates this stipulation, establishing that psychological or emotional coercion has occurred in a given case is a clinico-legal judgment on which expert opinions may differ.

Statutory and judicial exceptions to the informed-consent requirement mainly involve emergencies in which the need to act quickly overrides the need for consent (*Rogers v. Commissioner of the Department of Mental Health,* 1983). The right to informed consent may also be overridden or compromised when others are directly endangered by a person's decisions. It is often on the basis of such supposedly emergency considerations—as determined by the provider, who frequently stretches this concept to the breaking point—that treatment is imposed on drug users and alcoholics.

Ethical Principles

In clinical ethics, the duty to obtain informed consent can be derived from at least four major ethical principles: *beneficence, non-maleficence, autonomy,* and *justice.* Of these four, the principle of respect for autonomy is the most central to informed consent. Today, this principle of autonomy is often associated with, and bolstered by, that of *authenticity.* That is, not only should one be free from external coercion in making health-care decisions, but one should feel free to make decisions that truly express one's inner values and convictions, one's sense of who one is and what one stands for (Bursztajn & Brodsky, 1994; Peele & Brodsky, 1991).

This is a deeper, more active conception of informed consent than that common in years gone by. It means that clinicians support the patient in a process of self-discovery rather than simply give the patient a checklist to sign (Gutheil et al., 1984). At one time, "doing good" and "not doing harm" were typically conceived of in paternalistic terms, whereby the clinician's sense of good versus harm mattered more than the patient's. But such imposition of values would be out of keeping with the social priorities of recent decades.

In terms of addiction treatment, therefore, this modern conception of client-centered care imposes on the provider an obligation to actively encourage the expression of the individual's values. To say that this is rarely the case in drug and alcohol treatment is an understatement. Simply for a provider not to combat and suppress the individual's values would be a great improvement in most treatment settings. Several clinicians have outlined the differences between such a client-centered approach and that typically used in standard drug and alcohol treatment programs (Miller & Rollnick, 1991; Peele et al., 1991).

One such set of contrasts between an approach that respects client choices and the standard 12-step approach is provided on the following page:

Table 1

Differences Between the 12-Step
and
Life Process Approaches to Addiction

12-Step/Disease Model	*Life Process Program*
Your addiction is inbred (genetic, biological)	Your addiction is a way of coping with life experience
You get the same therapy as everyone else	You design a treatment that fits you
You must accept your identity as an addict/alcoholic	You focus on problems and not labels
Your therapy and cure are dictated to you	You arrive at your own goals and therapy plan
Either you are addicted or you aren't	Your addiction will vary depending on your situation
Your addictive symptoms are drummed into you	You identify the negative consequences of the addiction
Any claims you have to being okay are attacked as denial	Positive aspects of your self-image are accepted and amplified

Source: Peele et al. (1991, p. 174).

Clinical Benefits

In addition to its legal and ethical bases, informed consent should be a clinical imperative. A growing body of research shows the predictable result that patients participate more fully in treatment and experience better outcomes when they have the opportunity to choose a form of treatment they believe in. This has repeatedly been shown to hold true in the case of alcohol treatment. In particular, personal values and beliefs have been found to be critical in terms of whether people accept—and succeed at—abstinence or controlled drinking goals.

In terms of a client-centered approach to assessment and treatment, motivational interviewing and brief interventions (which follow similar principles) have been shown to be the most effective treatments overall (Miller et al., 1995). Moreover, since motivational interviewing and brief interventions respect individual choices and in fact build and rely on clients' efforts, these treatments are the most cost effective (by producing the best results at the least cost).[1] Indeed, in the NIAAA's widely heralded Project MATCH (1997), which found all treatments to be equivalently effective under its highly structured research protocol, motivational enhancement had one-third as many scheduled sessions as the other two treatments (12-step facilitation and social skills training). In other words, motivational enhancement produced results as good as the other key therapies with a third the investment in treatment, even given that all therapies were administered under ideal conditions of therapy design and therapist training and supervision (Peele, 1998) (see Chapter 2).

With informed consent, clinicians need to recognize and respect patients' values and beliefs—in particular, how they view the nature of their drinking problems (Heather et al., 1982). Indeed, research shows that an individual's "persuasion" as to what his or her drinking problem is and what outcome is most likely is a better predictor of outcomes viz. controlled drinking and abstinence than are objective measures of the severity of their alcohol dependence (Heather et al.,

---

1. There is some disagreement in meta-analyses about which treatments are the most effective. Miller et al. (1995) list brief interventions as #1 in evidence of effectiveness, and motivational interviewing as #3, both of which are tied as being by far the lowest in cost except for "self-help manual"; Holder et al. (1991) list "brief motivational counseling" as #3 in effectiveness, and Finney & Monahan (1995) give brief motivational counseling—the only formal therapy with minimal cost—a negative evidence of effectiveness score (see Chapter 2).

1983; Elal-Lawrence et al., 1986; Orford & Keddie, 1986). Beyond this, the exercise of autonomy can itself be therapeutic, promoting growth and responsibility (Booth et al., 1992; Miller, 1991; Sanchez-Craig & Lei, 1986; Sobell et al., 1992). By this empirical yardstick as well as on principle, clinicians who want to "do good" (beneficence) and "not do harm" (nonmaleficence) need to respect their patients' values, preferences, and decision-making autonomy.

Remedies

A person who has been denied informed consent can seek administrative and legal remedies. One can report an alleged ethical violation to the state board of licensing or registration and to the national and state professional associations for the profession in question. Before doing so, it is prudent to read the ethics codes of those associations—including, if applicable, those of a medical specialty field, such as psychiatry—to formulate the precise wording of a complaint and to gauge how strongly the profession is likely to respond to such a complaint.

An example is provided in Appendix A of an ethics complaint submitted to the American Society of Addiction Medicine (ASAM, whose Principles of Medical Ethics are listed at its web site, http://www.asam.org). As that analysis shows, prominent members of the ASAM violate its stated ethical standards as a matter of course, without seeming to fear disciplinary action by this professional body. Thus, the best referral may be to the supervising physician's licensing body (usually a state medical board). As a last resort, a highly motivated individual may have to turn to the civil courts for redress. Professional referrals are also not available in the case of psychotherapists who do not belong to any regulated profession. In fact, the overwhelming bulk of assessment and treatment in addiction is conducted by counselors with certificates as addiction or alcoholism counselors (CACs), and referrals to their licensing bodies or governing boards may be of little use.

Under common law, unconsented touching during treatment is a form of battery, an intentional tort. Failure to obtain informed consent is an unintentional or negligent tort (*Canterbury v. Spence*, 1972; *Natanson v. Kline*, 1960). Notwithstanding the sensational cases in which patients are drugged and then violated, only a very small proportion of informed-consent cases reach the criminal courts. In civil law, informed consent is a cause of action separate and distinct from professional malpractice. In practice, however, it is not difficult to persuade a jury to view the absence of informed consent as part of a pattern of substandard care in a given case. Especially with non-routine procedures, properly obtaining informed consent has become part of the "standard of care" against which physicians' actions are measured in malpractice cases, and its denial a deviation from that standard (Bursztajn et al., 1997). Note that, when a case is brought against a physician on a theory of informed consent, the mere failure to obtain required informed consent is sufficient to establish liability. On the other hand, when failure to obtain informed consent is alleged as a deviation from the standard of care in a malpractice action, the same elements must be proved to sustain the claim as in any other malpractice case, i.e., a breach of the physician's duty of care that directly causes damage to the patient.

Standard of care is itself an evolving notion, as the old "community standards" of a locally oriented society have been supplanted by national standards for certified medical specialties (*Restatement of Torts*, 1965; *Robbins v. Footer*, 1977) and, in some cases, by an objective cost-benefit analysis (*Helling v. Carey*, 1974). But informed-consent laws actually came about in *opposition* to professional custom. Court decisions (*Scaria v. St. Paul Fire and Marine Insurance Co.*, 1975; *Zeleznik v. Jewish Chronic Disease Hospital*, 1975) and even state legislation reaffirming professional custom as the standard of care in malpractice cases (*Washington Revised Code*, 1975) have generally upheld the patient's right to informed consent irrespective of customary professional practice.

The 1999 case of G. Douglas Talbott (Chapter 6), past President and a Board Member of ASAM, broke new legal ground in this regard. Talbott and associates were found liable for $1.3 million in actual damages and settled for an undisclosed amount in punitive damages. In this case, Talbott's physician treatment program coerced the client into alcoholism treatment through threats to his medical license, combined with a bogus diagnosis of alcohol dependence (which is typical for those who are assessed in alcohol treatment programs; cf. Sharkey, 1994). Talbott and a number of colleagues were found liable for fraud, malpractice, and a novel claim—false imprisonment (Ursery, 1999b). The fraud judgment required a finding that errors in the diagnosis were intentional.

Talbott's and his colleagues' diagnosis of the plaintiff did not meet the standard of care. Moreover, in line with the trend noted above, in malpractice claims against substance abuse programs, informed consent could be cited (although it apparently was not in the Talbott case) as an essential and required element of care, and failure to gain full consent used as evidence of malpractice. As with an ethics complaint, however, a malpractice action cannot be brought against an unlicensed psychotherapist or most CACs, who have few or no professional standards to violate.

Violation of Medical Principles in Addiction Treatment

Differential Diagnosis and Treatment

Given the widespread insistence in the U.S. that alcoholism and other addictions are diseases to be managed medically, one would expect that they would be dealt with like other medical conditions, according to established medical principles and procedures. For example, the scientific framework of medicine would require documentation of treatment efficacy and individualized treatment planning. Individualized planning would, in turn, indicate that therapeutic measures correspond to the severity of the condition. Thus, treatment of a person who is occasionally bingeing, particularly when the person is young, would be entirely different from treatment given to a chronic, middle-aged alcoholic. A parallel is often drawn by those seeking reforms in alcohol treatment to "step care" for cholesterolemia (see Institute of Medicine, 1990), in which mildly elevated cholesterol is dealt with through dietary recommendations, and more severe cases through increasingly potent medications. Analogously, in the case of alcohol problems, young people with incipient problems would be administered a "secondary prevention" program, emphasizing training to avoid binge situations and to drink moderately on social occasions (Marlatt et al., 1998).

Absence of Informed Consent in Addiction Treatment

Just as a genuine medical model of clinical treatment is based on differential diagnoses and graduated levels of intensity of care, the legal and ethical framework of medicine would require a patient's informed consent to treatment. Fully informed consent involves assenting, first, to any treatment at all, and, second, to a particular form of treatment. Yet, just as step care and secondary prevention programs are rarely considered in standard alcohol and drug programs, informed consent is likewise almost completely ignored.

These lacunae in the real world of addiction treatment in the U.S. occur due to the ideologically charged nature of drug and alcohol abuse/dependency. Here the legal and ethical tenets of the clinical professions, like their scientific foundations, are honored in the breach rather than the observance. Each year hundreds of thousands of people are routinely mandated into treatment by the courts or coerced by private employers (Brodsky & Peele, 1991; Weisner, 1990) (see Chapter 1). The vast majority of these are given no meaningful choice of treatment. Specifically, they are not informed about alternative treatments that have had better outcome records in clinical research (Miller et al., 1995). Issues of outpatient versus inpatient treatment are similarly decided based on what the program offers (and the patient's insurance coverage) rather than on proven efficacy (Miller & Hester, 1986).

This failure to implement a true medical model across the board has occurred in part because the prevailing model of addiction treatment in the U.S. is primarily rooted not in science but in religion, or in quasi-religious "spiritual" folklore. As such, its practitioners promote it—and it has largely been accepted—as received wisdom, not as an issue for empirical study. Although Alcoholics Anonymous and like-minded voluntary mutual-support fellowships disavow any coercive intent, many of those in clinical, administrative, and referring roles in public and private institutions are true believers in AA's 12-step model who see it as the only way to approach addictions problems, and who brook no opposition.

Moreover, although the disease model disclaims moralistic intent, substance abuse and addiction are often nonetheless seen in moral terms. This perception derives in part from actual risks of violence, accidents, and deteriorating health (which in a true medical model would be assessed case by case) and in part from an ingrained cultural prejudice against states of intoxication as *ipso facto* sinful and dangerous. Supposed addiction experts' views are highly colored by their personal experiences. A large majority would likely agree with G. Douglas Talbott, who declares: "The ultimate consequences for a drinking alcoholic are these three: he or she will end up in jail, in a hospital, or in a graveyard" (quoted in Wholey, 1984, p. 19—and a direct echo of the AA belief that alcoholics' only alternatives to AA are "jails, institutions, or death").

Based on such claims, treatment providers feel justified in applying any sort of pressure to coerce an "addict" into treatment. But in fact, many people overcome drinking and drug use problems on their own, without treatment (see Chapter 2).

The most intense types of coercion are interventions, in which the individual is surrounded by friends and family (and usually addictions professionals) who insist that he or she is out of control; such sessions normally end with the person being whisked off to a treatment center. To say that such interventions violate standard practices of informed consent is, once again, a serious understatement. Interventions employ practices that are quite similar to the kinds of group-think pressures that occur in cults and that amount to brainwashing (see Bufe, 1998; Gerstel, 1982; Lifton, 1969; Ragge, 1998). It is unthinkable that any form of therapy other than that for drug and alcohol abuse would utilize this as a treatment modality. Yet leading practitioners in the field (see Johnson, 1980) strongly endorse interventions. Indeed, in his book about the excesses of chemical dependency and other mental health treatment, Sharkey (1994) described how, in Texas, treatment centers actually employed private security guards to round up suspected substance abusers. Assuming that they were being arrested, these unsuspecting individuals were then deposited in for-profit hospitals. Eventually, prodded by state senator Frank Tejeda, Texas became the first state to crack down on some of the excesses involved in private psychiatric hospitalizations.

American Society of Addiction Medicine Principles of Ethics

Substance abuse and dependency as well as alcohol abuse and dependency are defined as psychiatric disorders in *DSM-IV.* State laws provide that if a mentally ill person is to be deprived of the right to make personal choices including that of giving informed consent to treatment, a court hearing must be held to determine that the person is incompetent (cf. *Kaimowitz v. Michigan Department of Mental Health,* 1973). If the person is to be deprived of physical freedom through involuntary hospitalization, hearings must be held at specified intervals to determine that the person is dangerous to self or others. As a rule, even an involuntarily committed person is presumed competent unless a court rules otherwise (Bursztajn et al., 1991).

Why are these legal safeguards routinely overridden in consigning people *en masse* to addiction treatment? Two elements of the addiction ideology provide an explicit or implicit rationale for this legal bypass. First, *loss of control* is a defining element in the 12-step definition of addiction or dependence, although it is not in *DSM-IV* (see Chapter 1). Like other aspects of addiction as popularly conceived (which have in turn imprinted themselves on medicine and law) and as promoted by treatment providers, loss of control over one's behavior is seen in all-or-nothing terms—as a dichotomy rather than a continuum. Moreover, this concept is applied quite loosely and inclusively, not only to addicted (or substance-dependent) persons, but also to many who would qualify for lesser diagnoses as mere substance abusers. Once any such person has been classified as having lost behavioral discretion, he or she will be claimed to be a danger to self or others.

Second, *denial* has become fundamental in U.S. addiction ortho-doxy—a concept that, from the outset, excludes the person so labeled from having a say in treatment choices. Denial is listed as the first element in the first section in the Principles of Medical Ethics adopted by the American Society of Addiction Medicine (ASAM). (It is important to note that addiction medicine is not a recognized medical specialty, but is rather a self-designation on the part of the group's members.) ASAM's Principles read:

> Because of the prominence of denial in patients suffering from chemical dependence, treatment may be mandated or offered as an alternative to sanctions of some kind. In other circumstances, a chemically dependent person whose judgment is impaired by intoxi-cation may be brought to treatment when unable to make a reasoned decision, or may be treated on an involuntary basis.

(American Society of Addiction Medicine, 1992)

Even ASAM, however, recognizes that use of the concept places them in a somewhat awkward position in regard to ordinary medical ethics. Thus, in the same place in its Principles statement, it continues:

> It is the duty of the addictionist to advocate on behalf of the patient's best interest and to prevent any abuse of this coercive element. The goal for patients is to restore, as quickly and safely as possible, their ability to make responsible decisions about their own recoveries.

However, in forensic psychiatry, even a person diagnosed with a psychosis can be found to retain decision-making capacity in some life functions (Appelbaum & Gutheil, 1991). By contrast, in the world of addiction services as actually practiced, being "in denial" about one's illness is assumed to render one incompetent to make decisions about that illness. This blanket, *a priori* determination is then employed as a substitute for a court hearing. Thus, the two criteria applied in mental health law to deprive a person of normal personal liberties and prerogatives—namely, dangerousness and incompetence—are routinely ignored in favor of the principles of loss of control and denial. In this way, standard treatments for substance abuse in the U.S. circumvent informed consent.

Among the interesting aspects of the ASAM ethics code is that it says nothing about whether a particular *type* of treatment may be mandated or refused. This is because, essentially, the ASAM reckons that there is only one possible type of treatment for substance abuse.

In other areas of the ASAM Principles, vacuous assertions are made that in fact are regularly violated. The Principles specify that the patient is to be treated with respect, "regardless of possible conflicts in values between patient and physician." Furthermore, the physician has a duty to uphold patient rights while working in an interdisciplinary team and "should not delegate to any nonmedical person any matter requiring the exercise of professional medical judgment." This element of the code is routinely disregarded through the reliance of treatment programs on alcoholism and addiction counselors who are themselves AA members preoccupied with their own recovery. As an example, G. Douglas Talbott and "many physicians on the Talbott team are recovering alcoholics" (Sibley, 1999).

Similarly notable, more for their violation than observance, are the code's injunctions to physicians to conduct public education "without any potential exploitation of patients through emotional appeals or misrepresentations" and, in public consultations, to "make clear whether their statements are based on scientific evidence, individual profession[al] or personal experience, or personal belief." Indeed, much of the code sounds as if it were derived from a list of common abuses in the field. In particular, the ASAM ethics code affirms the necessity of informed consent in standard medico/legal/ethical terms:

> Addictionists should treat individuals only with their consent, except in emergency and extraordinary circumstances in which the patient cannot give consent and in which the withholding of treatment would have permanent and significant consequences for life and health. In cases where the patient has been found to be incompetent by appropriate mental health professionals and/or by the judicial system, physicians may assist in their care.

> (American Society of Addiction Medicine, 1992)

It is difficult to reconcile this statement either with some of those made elsewhere in the Principles or with actual practice. In Chapter 6, we review the case of G. Douglas Talbott. Talbott, Past President and board member of ASAM (along with a number of professional colleagues) seemingly violated, without compunction, informed consent and other of what ASAM claims to be its ethical principles. There is additional irony in that Talbott's program is for "impaired" physicians and other health professionals, and that he is co-author of the definitive chapter in ASAM's *Principles of Addiction Medicine* concerning treatment of such professionals (Angres et al., 1998).

The best hope of reconciling practice in this area of medicine and therapy with the more broadly accepted (and legally enforced) standards of the medical profession may lie in the ASAM ethics claim that addictionists "carry the responsibility to be aware of the laws that govern both their professional practice and everyday lives and to respect and obey these laws." If those supposedly bound by ASAM's Principles took this guidance seriously in regard to the laws on informed consent, we would see an end to the special status of addiction treatment as a *de facto* exception to those laws.

ACKNOWLEDGMENTS: The authors are indebted to Harold J. Bursztajn, M.D., and Thomas G. Gutheil, M.D., for essential background information about informed consent in mental health treatment.

6

A Prototypical Case of Alcoholism Treatment and Coercion: G. Douglas Talbott

by Stanton Peele

G. Douglas Talbott is a physician and recovering alcoholic. He has been one of the most forceful voices—perhaps *the* most forceful—in American medicine in advocating the recognition of alcoholism as a disease à la the AA and 12-step approach. Moreover, he has been a pioneer in educating physicians about substance abuse problems, and in offering substance abuse care to them. In particular, he has emphasized the need to confront doctors with such problems and to compel them to enter treatment.

Talbott has used several mechanisms to accomplish this. He organized and has been a prominent member of the American Society of Addiction Medicine (ASAM, 1999), "the nation's medical specialty society dedicated to educating physicians and improving the treatment of individuals suffering from alcoholism or other addictions." Addiction medicine is not a recognized specialty, so one of ASAM's goals is to "establish addiction medicine as a specialty recognized by the American Board of Medical Specialties."

Talbott was President of ASAM from 1997 to 1999, when (in April of 1999) he took office as immediate Past President. But his involvement with the organization is more fundamental than his official positions alone would indicate. After graduating from Columbia Medical School in 1949 and completing his residency program in 1953, Talbott served three years in the U.S. Air Force during the Korean War. In 1956, he returned to his hometown of Dayton, Ohio, where he entered private practice in internal medicine and cardiology. In 1969, Talbott switched into the field of addiction medicine (presumably, in good part, because of drug and alcohol problems he has admitted). In 1971, he became medical director of the Baltimore Public Inebriate Program for skid row alcoholics, following which he created an alcohol and drug program at DeKalb General Hospital for DeKalb County (Georgia) and the city of Atlanta.

Talbott was also a formative figure in the AMA's Impaired Physicians Program. This led Talbott to create the DeKalb County Impaired Physicians Committee, which became the official program for the Medical Association of Georgia. This program then became a national model for treating impaired physicians and other health professionals. In 1976, he entered the private treatment business with a program he created at Ridgeview Institute, also in metropolitan Atlanta. Talbott was central in the founding of the American Society of Addiction Medicine in 1988.[1] Later, he was co-founder of the Talbott Recovery Campus in 1989. This campus serves as a National Impaired Health Professionals Treatment Program for physicians, nurses, dentists, pharmacists, and health therapists. In addition to his offices in ASAM, Douglas Talbott is medical director of the Talbott Recovery Campus. (Talbott's biography is available at the Talbott Recovery Campus web site: http://www.talbottcampus.com.)

A Troubled Program

From the start, Talbott and his treatment program's insistence on confrontational techniques raised questions, although rarely from within the addiction medicine field. In one four-year period, according to the *Atlanta Journal and Constitution*, five health care professionals committed suicide at Ridgeview (Durcanin, 1987). But this was only the tip of the iceberg; according to the paper (Durcanin & King, 1987): "At least 20 doctors, nurses and other health professionals who have gone through the Ridgeview Institute's nationally acclaimed treatment program over the past 12 years have killed themselves since leaving the hospital. . . ." In 1987, a jury awarded $1.3 million to the widow of one of the deceased physicians against Ridgeview and Dr. James W. Blevins, a staff psychiatrist, although a Superior Court judge later set aside the verdict (Ricks,

---

1. ASAM formerly existed as the New York City Medical Society on Alcoholism, the American Medical Society on Alcoholism, and the American Society on Alcoholism and Other Drug Dependencies.

1987). Other suits initiated on behalf of the suicides were settled out of court (Durcanin, 1987).

Another article in a four-part series in the *Journal and Constitution* (King & Durcanin, 1987a) noted that the Ridgeview hospital had removed Talbott as director of the addiction treatment program he founded. Some questioned the tough philosophy Talbott practiced. For his part, Talbott defended his confrontational approach: "Every physician I've got here thinks he's his own doctor," said Talbott. "I tell them if that's the case they've got a fool for a patient." The article continues, "'I'm not much for the bullying that goes along with some of these programs,' said Dr. LeClair Bissell. . . ." Bissell, a psychiatrist who has written about and administered programs for impaired physicians and nurses, was one of the few who wasn't afraid to speak her mind about Talbott and his approach: "When you've got them by the license, that's pretty strong leverage. You shouldn't have to pound on them so much. You could be asking for trouble."

Another article in the series (King & Durcanin, 1987b) reported that doctors entered the treatment program because of threats that they would lose their licenses, "even when they would prefer treatment that is cheaper and closer to home. . . . Ridgeview also enjoys unparalleled connections with many local and state medical societies that work with troubled doctors to save their licenses. Their membership often includes physicians who themselves have successfully completed Ridgeview's program. Licensing boards often seek recommendations from such groups in devising an approved treatment plan for a troubled physician. And that is how many such doctors wind up at Ridgeview." The cost of a 28-day program for nonprofessionals at Ridgeview in 1987 was $10,000 (compared with $6,000 for the Betty Ford Center and $4,300 for Hazelden), while the cost was "higher for those going through impaired-health professionals programs," which lasted months rather than 28 days (Durcanin & King, 1987).

Physicians who questioned the Talbott-Ridgeview method faced serious trouble. "One South Georgia physician who decided to seek treatment elsewhere wound up in a protracted battle for his license. 'I refused to humble to Ridgeview,' said the physician. 'Back then no one had ever fought Ridgeview, but I did and it cost me four years before my license was reinstated'" (King & Durcanin, 1987b). Talbott, of course, felt there was no problem: "[W]e know more about impaired professionals than anyone else." But some experts in the field say the threat of losing licenses amounts to intimidation. "There's a lot of debate in the field over whether treatment imposed by threats is worthwhile," according to Bissell. "To a large degree a person has to seek the treatment on his own accord before it will work for him."

Another Talbott-Ridgeview method for dealing with doctors who expressed a desire to map an independent path was to expel them. "For instance, a Virginia therapist was asked to leave on the 25th day of the 28-day program after she told her physician she wanted to complete the second phase of a rehabilitation program closer to home. On the 27th day of the program, a retired Maryland physician was given 90 minutes to leave the hospital. 'If anyone was ever going to kill himself over something, it would be the shock of someone coming up to you and saying you're out now,' he said. 'If they had picked the wrong person, they could have really set someone off'" (King & Durcanin, 1987b).

Accusations against Talbott and programs in Georgia with which he was associated were not limited to patients. In an extremely serious charge, Dr. Paul G. Cohen asserted that Talbott and doctors at Northside Hospital began alleging in 1982 that he had an alcohol or drug problem. Their reason for doing so, according to a suit he brought, was that he "repeatedly found fault with doctors or the hospital over deficiencies in patient care. . . . Dr. Cohen claims in the suit, which specifies no monetary damages, that he underwent at least five psychiatric evaluations and more than 30 drug tests, and none showed any addiction to alcohol or drugs" (McIntosh, 1989).

The Talbott Philosophy and Its Sources

Talbott regards doctors as overly impressed with themselves and their ability to heal themselves, a view he took special satisfaction in rooting out of his patients. "Talbott said the sessions, which are often highly emotional, are designed to force patients to admit their addiction and to talk about their problems instead of bottling them up inside. They go a long way, he said, toward destroying the 'M.D.eity' of impaired physicians—the feeling that they are unique, invulnerable to addiction, and capable of curing themselves. . . . Impaired doctors must first acknowledge their addiction and overcome their 'terminal uniqueness' before they can deal with a drug or alcohol problem, he said. 'Terminal uniqueness' is the phrase Talbott's group uses to describe doctors' tendency to think they can heal themselves" (King & Durcanin, 1987a).

This attitude, according to some critics, stems from the personal histories of the treatment staff, including Talbott. One such critic was

Assistant Surgeon General John C. Duffy, who was a pioneer in addressing impaired physicians. "Duffy, who has followed the Ridgeview approach for years, said the hospital suffers from a 'boot-camp mentality' when it comes to treating alcoholic and drug-addicted physicians. . . . He blames the program's attitude, in part, on the fact that former addicts are at the helm of the treatment program. . . . 'They assume every physician suffering from substance abuse is the same lying, stealing, cheating, manipulating individual they were when they had the illness. Certainly some physicians are manipulative, but it's naive to label all physicians with these problems'" (Durcanin & King, 1987).

"Talbott himself is no stranger to the problems of impaired physicians. His own addiction to alcohol and drugs led to the disintegration of a successful career as a cardiologist in Dayton, Ohio, and the near destruction of his marriage and family. After overcoming his addiction, he founded the program that to this day relies heavily on elements of the Alcoholics Anonymous philosophy. Talbott is no stranger to the dangers of suicide, either. In 1981, a Little Rock, Arkansas psychiatrist, Dr. Martha Morrison, attempted to kill herself shortly after entering the Ridgeview program. The attempt failed when the belt she was using snapped while she was trying to hang herself from a tree on the hospital grounds. Dr. Morrison went on to become the director of Ridgeview's programs for addicted adolescents. She also married Douglas Talbott Jr." (King & Durcanin, 1987a).

Obviously, key members of Talbott's staff are dedicated beyond question to his approach. And Talbott himself brooks no opposition to the AA/12-step model. In an interview on impaired physicians, in response to the question, "Is Alcoholics Anonymous essential for physicians, nurses, and other health professionals?" Talbott responded, "Of course it is" (Physicians for Prevention, 1999).

For well over a decade there have been many danger signs that Talbott and his colleagues are true believers verging on zealots who have no real respect for their patients' points of view or alternative approaches to drinking problems. They have shown themselves more than willing to rely on coercion and threats to get and keep patients in their program. Yet surprisingly little opposition has been raised within the field to Talbott, his program, or his approach. Well after the series of suicides and newspaper analyses of Talbott's single-minded treatment style, he was elected president of ASAM in 1997. There were no signs that he was ever called to task professionally for what seems to be his complete disregard for ethical and legal principles such as informed consent. This concept, which is imbedded in the ASAM's (1999) Principles of Medical Ethics, requires that a physician allow prospective patients to choose their treatment freely, other than in exceptional life-threatening emergencies (see Chapter 5 and Appendix A).

In part, Talbott was protected by the fact that it was exceedingly difficult for a physician to challenge him or his program. Given that physicians and other health professionals were referred to the program under threat of revocation of their licenses, it was rare that a doctor would challenge the treatment. Even after physicians left the program, there was little to be gained from challenging its value or its methods.

The Masters Case

Dr. Leonard Masters of Jacksonville, Florida, and his wife sued "Talbott Recovery [which Talbott established in 1989 after leaving Ridgeview], its founder, Dr. G. Douglas Talbott, Anchor Hospital and 13 others, including doctors and counselors who treated Masters during his hospitalization and treatment center stay" (Ursery, 1999a). The elements of Masters' suit resemble complaints lodged against Talbott's program at Ridgeview, to which Talbott and colleagues claimed they had responded with adjustments in their program. Whether or not the Ridgeview suicides and Talbott's take-no-prisoners approach were related, the Masters' suit certainly challenged whether Talbott practiced in accordance with ASAM's Principles of Medical Ethics.

Masters admitted to being a fairly heavy drinker, saying that "he drank a fifth of scotch . . . plus four or five glasses of wine a week" (Ursery, 1999a). But no one ever reported him for having a drinking problem, according to his attorneys, "not his friends, not his wife, not his seven children, not his fellow doctors, not his employees, not his employers. No one." Talbott and the other defendants did not contradict this testimony. Rather, both sides agreed, Masters wound up in treatment after a physician who had attended the Talbott program, and who headed the Florida Physicians Recovery Network, referred Masters for an evaluation. Masters was told "he'd been accused of prescribing too many narcotics to his chronic pain patients." The physician "told Masters that he could either surrender his medical license until he could disprove the allegations or go to Anchor in Atlanta for a 96-hour evaluation."

However, once at the Anchor Hospital, Masters was quickly assessed as being alcohol dependent and was immersed in four months of treatment in the Talbott Recovery System. Masters described how he told inmates at Anchor Hospital he was only there for an evaluation: "Two patients laughed when Masters mentioned he'd be going home soon," according to his attorney (Sibley, 1999). Furthermore, "family members, employees and longtime friends, including his first wife, testified they were stunned at the diagnosis" (Sibley, 1999). Masters' attorney said he "was afraid to leave the program because 'if any doctor dared to dispute the team's diagnosis, if they wanted to leave and go home, or even consent to get treatment in their home state,' Talbott Recovery personnel 'would threaten to report that doctor to his or her state board of medicine . . . as being an impaired physician, leaving necessary treatment against medical advice'" (Ursery, 1999a).

In other words, Masters experienced exactly the same coercive techniques that Talbott's Ridgeview program had been accused of years earlier. Other physician patients in Talbott's program testified on behalf of Masters. The transcripts of *Masters v. Talbott* (1994) were sealed. This could have been due to the terms of the settlement, but it probably also was in part to protect witnesses who testified that their medical licenses were threatened or suspended by Talbott and his organization.

On his release, Masters was forced to sign a five-year continuing care contract, which included attendance at AA. Masters actually attended these meetings and "admitted" he was an alcoholic. This and other evidence was used by the defense to show that, initially, Masters bought into his own diagnosis. A key witness for Masters was Dr. Anne Geller, former director of the Smithers Institute in New York City and president of ASAM prior to Talbott! Geller testified that the Talbott program's diagnosis of alcohol dependence against Masters deviated from the professional standard of care. While Masters was a heavy drinker, he showed no signs of withdrawal, loss of control, or other life detriments from his drinking required for a diagnosis of alcohol dependence (Ursery, 1999a).

In May 1999, the jury awarded Masters $1.3 million in actual, or compensatory, damages. (He had asked for $930,000 before trial.) Before the jury could reach a figure for punitive damages, however, the defendants settled on this aspect of the judgment. The punitive figure might easily have exceeded the compensatory damages. The jurors found Drs. G. Douglas Talbott and his daughter-in-law, Martha A. Morrison, liable for fraud in the form of breach of fiduciary duty.

A finding of fraud obligated the jurors to decide that the defendants had acted intentionally. The jury also found "that at least one of three doctors . . . —Talbott, Dr. James W. Blevins [a recovering alcoholic whom a jury had earlier found liable in a Talbott patient's suicide] and Dr. John P. Keppler—misdiagnosed Masters as an alcoholic," which amounted to malpractice. Talbott and Keppler were also liable for a novel claim for false imprisonment. No specific charges were related to the defendants' failure to provide informed consent, although potentially this could have contributed to the malpractice finding (see Chapter 5). Since the jury found that Talbott and Morrison were agents of Anchor Hospital and Talbott Recovery Systems, these two institutional defendants were liable for damages as well (Ursery, 1999b).

What the Masters Case and Judgment Tell Us

Talbott and His Followers Are True Believers

Notwithstanding the jury's finding of fraud in *Masters v. Talbott*, and that Talbott and his colleagues, as well as associated programs and institutions, profited greatly from these practices, their actions are best understood as expressions of a genuine belief system. In a sense, this makes Talbott and his associates much more frightening. They could strike out at physicians, like Dr. Cohen, who question any aspect of the care they provide. More directly, Talbott, Morrison, Blevins, et al. felt that patients had to follow the 12-step precepts of confession and contrition in order to get better, because they themselves had succeeded by using this method. If the targeted person doesn't own up, professionals like these believe, they are justified in applying—indeed obligated to apply—a range of coercive techniques, from peer group pressure to the threat of licensure action. In this way, Talbott and his co-defendants were not acting as health care professionals; they were too emotionally involved to exercise sound and objective clinical judgment.

Patients Themselves Often Take On the Addict Identity

Masters admitted attending AA and standing up in front of others to say he was an alcoholic. Indeed, at the Anchor Hospital, Masters reported that, in alcoholism treatment groups, he broke down. "I was no longer me," he testified (Ursery, 1999b). This type of response is to be expected when individuals are isolated, separated from their families, and subjected to repeated group and therapist pressure to identify themselves as alcoholics. (Masters eventually resumed drinking, but at a much reduced level.)

Talbott's Practices Are Widely Accepted in the Field

Talbott and his program are certainly not alone in their insistence that patients admit that they are alcoholics or addicts against their own better judgment and that they enter a 12-step program; this is standard practice in the field. Nor is Talbott likely to be alone in his excesses. Sharkey (1994) described rampant hard-selling techniques —up to and including physical force—to recruit patients. Among others, he related the case of resident anesthesiologist Ronald L. Hedderich, who was reported for drug abuse based on his irascible personality in the operating room. (Missing morphine played a part in the accusation, but the missing drug was soon located.) Hedderich was "repeatedly confronted" with the demand that he either admit his drug addiction or lose his residency. He was then driven directly to an inpatient treatment facility for an assessment. Although all drug tests were negative, Hedderich could not escape the hospital and a vague diagnosis of "opioid abuse—unspec." Hedderich left the hospital later against advice and sued; the defendants denied his allegations, and the case was settled out of court. Like laws allowing police to confiscate property of suspected drug dealers, the treatment system requires innocent people to prove that they are not guilty. Although reformers look to treatment as a humane way to ameliorate the effects of unjust drug laws, it is among the most individuality- and freedom-denying mechanisms in our society.

The Deck Is Stacked Against Licensed Professionals Charged with Substance Abuse

Masters' damages occurred because he lost his job while he was in treatment in 1992; but he retired in 1994. Most doctors accused of substance abuse problems are obviously earlier in their careers and have more to lose. For these and other health care professionals, the costs of challenging a treatment program and the consequences likely to be imposed by their medical board or licensing body are typically prohibitive. Thus most such individuals simply bite the bullet and play the role of recovering alcoholic, as demanded of them. Likewise, airline and ship pilots whose careers and livelihoods can be destroyed by the action of a licensing body have little leeway to challenge the decisions of treatment providers, no matter how irrational these are (see Appendix A). Nonetheless, this book is based on the idea that reason, law, and science can and do make a difference, and that it is worth standing up for oneself and making a case for reasonable therapeutic and professional treatment.

Addiction Medicine Providers Do Not Care About Issues of Informed Consent, Ethics, and Individual Choice

ASAM's volume, *Principles of Addiction Medicine* (Graham & Schultz, 1998), while including a chapter on recovery for health professionals by Talbott and others (Angres et al., 1998), devotes no space to informed consent or other ethical principles that are commonly violated by addiction professionals. And, while it remains to be seen how ASAM and related professionals respond to this latest revelation about addiction treatment—Enoch Gordis, director of the National Institute on Alcohol Abuse and Alcoholism, and Alan Leshner, Director of the National Institute on Drug Abuse, wrote introductions to the ASAM volume—such leading figures have never yet come forward to criticize member misconduct or ethical deficiencies in their field. We should note, however, such courageous exceptions as Drs. Anne Geller and the irrepressible LeClair Bissell.

ASAM's (1992) Principles of Medical Ethics Are Meaningless

A thoroughgoing review of physician conduct with respect to ASAM's (1992) ethical principles is outlined in Appendix A. These principles state: "Addictionists should treat individuals only with their consent, except in emergency and extraordinary circumstances in which the patient cannot give consent and in which the withholding of treatment would have permanent and significant consequences for life and health." But how has ASAM maintained these principles in regard to the actions of its own president, even as he openly denies their validity in his treatment philosophy and his program's actions? Similarly, other violations of ASAM's stated principles—such as that the patient is to be treated with respect, "regardless of possible conflicts in values between patient and physician"—are the rule in addiction treatment. What's more, the principles note that the physician has a duty to uphold patient rights while working in an interdisciplinary team and "should not delegate to any nonmedical person any matter requiring the exercise of professional medical judgment," but ASAM physicians typically hand off patients to recovering alcoholism counselors (that is, to AA or NA members with little if any medical training).

The answer to these abuses may be that, as demonstrated in *Masters v. Talbott*, juries can respond to the blatant violations of individual rights, medical principles, and therapeutic responsibility that pervade American addiction practice. Multimillion-dollar judgments may be the only argument that true-believing, coercive "addictionists" will understand.

ASAM has not yet (as of November, 1999) communicated to its members any concerns about or changes in the practice of addiction medicine based on the Talbott case judgment. It may be that, just as occurred after the Ridgeview Institute suicides were revealed, Talbott and the entire addictions field will proceed as usual.

The following chapter reduces the contents of this book to a few pages. The purpose of this reduction is to allow readers to communicate the book's content quickly to anyone who could benefit from it. This includes corrections officials, judges, employers, human resource officers, substance abuse program managers for the armed forces and other government agencies, and anyone who has a decision-making role in creating treatment options or in compelling individuals to attend treatment. In addition, readers can use this chapter to alert attorneys or other sympathetic professionals to the state of the law and to clinical issues involved in mandatory AA/12-step and/or abstinence treatment. Finally, this chapter can provide necessary background in public discussions that tend to be dominated by assumptions that AA and the 12 steps are the only path to recovery.

Summary of Legal and Clinical Objections to Compulsory AA, 12-Step, and Abstinence Treatment

Dear Decision Maker:

This chapter is a summation of the book, *Resisting 12-Step Coercion,* by Stanton Peele, Charles Bufe, and Archie Brodsky, which deals with the legal and clinical pitfalls of mandating treatment for substance abuse, and particularly AA, NA, or 12-step treatment. As part of this summary, this chapter reviews the evidence on the efficacy and appropriateness of forcing people to abstain from alcohol. Finally, this chapter suggests alternative methods of dealing with people who abuse drugs or alcohol. Please take note of this material when considering the appropriateness of your substance abuse services/ regulations.

There are two aspects to the mandate to attend AA or 12-step-based treatment (and to abstain from alcohol) by a state-operated agency (such as the courts). These are legal and therapeutic:

Legal Issues

Coercion into AA and 12-Step Programs

Four higher courts have evaluated cases in which corrections departments, correctional institutions, and conditions of probation have required attendance at Alcoholics Anonymous, Narcotics

Anonymous, or therapy based on AA's 12 steps. In these cases, the failure to comply carried serious penalties (i.e., return to prison, loss of parole opportunities or major benefits such as family visits). All of these cases have been decided since 1996. *Uniformly, the courts have decided that such mandated attendance violates the First Amendment of the U.S. Constitution.* The Bill of Rights begins with the statement that, "Congress shall make no law respecting the establishment of religion or prohibiting the free exercise thereof. . . ." The first part of this statement is referred to as the "Establishment Clause" and has been interpreted by the U.S. Supreme Court to mean that no government body can require or encourage religious observance of any type. (This is also known as the separation of church and state.) It is this clause which two Federal circuit courts (the appeals courts just below the U.S. Supreme Court) and two state high courts (Tennessee and New York) have found were violated when prisons or courts required that inmates or defendants undergo 12-step therapy or participate in 12-step support groups.

Kerr v. Farrey (1996)

The United States Court of Appeals For the Seventh Circuit, reversing a district court decision, unanimously held "that the state . . . impermissibly coerced inmates to participate in a religious program, thus violating the Establishment Clause." In this case, an inmate at Oakhill Correctional Institution in Wisconsin was threatened with being sent to a higher security prison and with rejection of his parole application for refusing to attend Narcotics Anonymous meetings.

Warner v. Orange County Department of Probation (1999)

The United States Court of Appeals for the Second Circuit affirmed, 2-1, a Southern District of New York ruling that requiring an inmate plaintiff's participation in Alcoholics Anonymous as a condition of probation violated the Establishment Clause of the First Amendment to the U.S. Constitution. The plaintiff received nominal monetary damages. The dissenting Second Circuit Court judge indicated that the Free Exercise Clause of the First Amendment was a better basis for protecting Warner's (the plaintiff's) rights, and warned of the great possibilities for finding liability created by a decision that mandatory AA sentences without alternatives violate the Constitution. The circuit court took the unusual step of vacating its own decision and of remanding the case to the district court to decide whether the plaintiff had waived his right to object to the religious nature of AA. The District Court decided that Warner had not waived his First Amendment right, and the Second Circuit Court again upheld the decision.

Griffin v. Coughlin (1996)

New York's highest court, the Court of Appeals, prohibited (in a 5-2 decision) the state corrections department from making a prisoner's participation in the family reunion program conditional on his attendance in the prison's 12-step-based alcohol and substance abuse treatment program. The court ruled that such participation violated the Establishment Clause. This ban would apply to any compulsion to participate in "a curriculum which adopts in major part the religious-oriented practices and precepts of Alcoholics Anonymous." The decision emphasized the "proven effectiveness of the A.A. approach to alcoholism or drug addiction rehabilitation" and the acceptability of "a noncoercive use of A.A.'s 12-step regimen as part of an alternative prisoner drug and alcohol abuse treatment effort . . . , providing it offered a secular alternative to the A.A. component." The American Jewish Congress filed a friend-of-the-court brief in support of the inmate's claims.

Evans v. Tennessee Board of Paroles (1997)

The Supreme Court of Tennessee, responding to petitions from two inmates regarding their failed parole hearings, found unanimously that the trial court erred in dismissing one of the inmates' (Anthony Evans') claim for injunctive relief from the Board's requirement that he participate in Alcoholics Anonymous. The court remanded the case to the trial court to determine whether AA was religious in nature, while citing case evidence that this was indeed true.

Conclusions

Court decisions, strictly speaking, are limited in their applicability to the jurisdictions in which they are made. On the other hand, courts often turn to sister jurisdictions for guidance; and federal courts, in particular, can accept precedents from other district or circuit courts in the absence of applicable decisions in their own jurisdictions.

Based on existing precedent, courts are obligated to require alternatives to AA or 12-step programs, and specifically non-religious alternatives such as SMART Recovery and Rational Recovery, where state agencies require or encourage (through imposition of benefits or penalties) substance abuse treatment. Any court should recognize this obligation, and a person should be able to present a reasonable alternative option that he or she genuinely wishes to pursue. When people are required to create and follow programs of their own choosing, of course, society and its agencies can properly require adherence to the designated program and responsible behavior as conditions of continued freedom.

Informed Consent

Overview

During the past several decades, informed consent has become an established principle of health law as well as clinical ethics (Appelbaum, 1997). The courts have repeatedly reaffirmed that a person (even one who is hospitalized for mental illness, if competent) has the right to refuse any and all medical treatment. The requirement that a person give informed consent to medical treatment is based on a widespread social consensus that people have the right to control access to their own bodies and make decisions about their own health and well-being—decisions with which others might disagree—and live or die with the consequences.

Legal Requirements

Although statute and case law concerning the scope and application of informed consent vary from one jurisdiction to another, the basic principles are consistent. The right to give or withhold informed consent is one possessed by competent adults. Besides competence, two main requirements must be met for informed consent to take place: *information* and *voluntariness*. In order to be able to make an informed decision, a person must be informed about the nature of the treatment offered, its risks and benefits (i.e., possible outcomes, including side effects, and their probability of occurrence), and possible alternative treatments. The risks and benefits of no treatment at all must also be considered. The requirement of voluntariness means that consent must be given freely and may not be coerced.

Physical coercion clearly violates this stipulation, as do psychological or emotional coercion—though their presence or absence is at least to some degree a matter of interpretation.

Exceptions to the informed-consent requirement mainly involve emergencies in which the need to act quickly overrides the need for consent. The right to informed consent may also be overridden or compromised when others are directly endangered by a person's decisions. But this does not justify the denial of the opportunity for full consent by virtually all patients who enter alcoholism treatment, and particularly *after* they have overcome a specific drinking crisis. The treatment industry typically relies on the concepts of *denial* and *loss of control* to override the right of the patient to decide what is best for him or her and to select a treatment option—or no treatment—based on his or her values. This issue has not been resolved in the courts. But even the American Society of Addiction Medicine (ASAM) (1992) has recognized only a very narrow range of circumstances in which the treatment provider may proceed without obtaining informed consent: "Addictionists should treat individuals only with their consent, except in emergency and extraordinary circumstances in which the patient cannot give consent and in which the withholding of treatment would have permanent and significant consequences for life and health."

At the same time, it is also true that most alcohol and drug treatment professionals do not recognize any kind of treatment other than 12-step treatment, or that any other treatment can be effective. In a survey of all alcohol treatment providers listed in the San Diego Yellow Pages in October, 1998, Tom Horvath and Jeff Jones found that 45 percent of the centers stated that 12-step treatment was the only available approach, while 47 percent acknowledged that alternatives existed but claimed these were not effective (cf. Horvath, 1999). Only in addiction treatment is such self-serving ignorance common.

Therapeutic Issues

Efficacy

In deciding that mandatory AA attendance is illegal, courts often note the "proven effectiveness" of AA and standard 12-step programs. However, research does not support this supposition. A group of researchers working with William Miller, of the University of New Mexico, reviewed all controlled clinical research on alcoholism treatment. Using a summing technique called "meta-analysis," they rated therapies as follows (the higher the score, the higher the indicated effectiveness):

Table 1

Most and Least Effective Alcoholism Treatments

Highest Rated

Brief interventions	+239
Social skills training	+128
Motivation enhancement	+ 87
Community reinforcement	+ 80
Behavioral contracting	+ 73

Lowest Rated

Metronidazole	− 102
Relaxation training	− 109
Confrontational counseling	− 125
Psychotherapy	− 127
General alcohol counseling	− 214
Alcoholism education programs	− 239

Methods with Too Few Tests to be Reliably Rated

Sensory deprivation	+ 40
Developmental counseling	+ 28
Acupuncture	+ 20
Calcium Carbamide	− 32
Antipsychotic medication	− 36
Alcoholics Anonymous	− 52

Source: Hester & Miller (1995)

The ratings combine assessments both of the quality of the studies in support of a therapy's effectiveness and the degree of superiority (or inferiority) found for the target treatment compared in the studies to other treatments. Note that, almost uniformly, it is the ineffective therapies (AA, alcohol education and counseling) that are employed in court-mandated programs.

The Requirement of Abstinence

Therapy in the U.S. is oriented almost exclusively towards abstinence. Thus, as a condition for probation, parole, etc., an individual is often ordered to abstain from alcohol. This requirement is supported unwaveringly by the mainstays of the medical treatment establishment, including the American Society of Addiction Medicine (1974), whose very first policy statement was on the absolute necessity of abstinence for recovery, and by Enoch Gordis, director of the National Institute on Alcohol Abuse and Alcoholism (NIAAA). This requirement can be objected to on several grounds, the two most important being:

1) **Without a clinical diagnosis of alcohol dependence, the requirement of abstinence makes no sense even according to 12-step treatment providers.** That is, when such groups and individuals note that someone has obviously returned to moderate drinking, they maintain that the person was only a problem drinker and not alcohol dependent, and for such an individual a reduction in drinking is unexceptional. For example, when *U.S. News and World Report* ran a cover story indicating that controlled drinking was an option for most problem drinkers (Shute, 1997), G. Douglas Talbott (1997), then president of ASAM, wrote a letter chastising the periodical for claiming "that treatment for alcoholics is based on 'folklore,' rather than science." Nonetheless, Talbott acknowledged, "moderation management is acceptable for abusive problem drinking." Therefore, a coerced individual should insist on receiving a formal, written diagnosis, whether of alcohol dependence or alcohol abuse/problem drinking. This document allows the individual to have another expert independently evaluate the diagnosis.

2) **In fact, no study finds that abstinence is required or particularly effective in dealing with any type of alcohol problem.** Recently, the entire abstinence requirement has been challenged by research from an unexpected source—the NIAAA. This organization organized

Project MATCH (1997), whose goal was to discover whether alcoholic persons did better when referred to treatments matching certain of their key characteristics—personality, severity of problem, etc. In fact, matching results were not particularly significant, but the NIAAA hierarchy and Project MATCH directors noted the great improvement by subjects in all the treatments included in the study. The subjects—virtually all of whom were alcohol-dependent—reduced their drinking at 18 months after treatment from, on average, 25 to 6 days per month, and from 15 to 3 drinks per drinking episode. In other words, abstinence was of secondary importance in improved outcomes in the most expensive clinical alcoholism study ever conducted, involving therapy designed and administered by the most important treatment researchers in the U.S.

Treatment Choice

Paralleling the legal and ethical issue of informed consent, there are therapeutic grounds for encouraging patient choice of treatment. A great deal of evidence supports allowing alcoholics to select treatment types and goals based on their values and beliefs. This research indicates that commitment to therapy and successful outcomes are encouraged by providing the patient with options—for example, to pursue controlled drinking or abstinence (Booth et al., 1992; Elal-Lawrence et al., 1986; Orford & Keddie, 1986; Sanchez-Craig & Lei, 1986; Sobell et al., 1992).

The Necessity of Treatment

The requirement of attending treatment, whether in a legal, correctional, or private context, is based on the idea that no one can recover from any sort of an alcohol problem without treatment. Once again, results from the NIAAA's own research proves this notion wrong. The National Longitudinal Alcohol Epidemiologic Survey (NLAES), which surveyed over 40,000 Americans about their drinking habits, focused on approximately 4,500 subjects who had been alcohol dependent at some time in their lives. In the first place, only 1,233 were treated, compared with 3,309 who were not. But the untreated subjects were actually more likely to have recovered from alcohol abuse or dependence than those treated!

Table 2

National Longitudinal Alcohol Epidemiologic Survey (NLAES) Data on Alcohol Dependent Subjects

Drinking over prior year	Treated	Untreated	Total
drinking with abuse/dependence	33%	26%	28%
abstinent	39%	16%	22%
drinking w/o abuse/dependence	28%	58%	50%

Source: Dawson (1996)

Note that this superiority in outcome is because many more untreated than treated alcoholics are able to reduce or control their drinking. These results agree with the NIAAA-funded Project MATCH results, which NIAAA director Enoch Gordis likewise disregards. Responding to the article noted in *U.S. News and World Report,* which indicated that problem drinkers (but not alcoholics—that is, alcohol-dependent persons) can moderate their drinking, Gordis (1997) declared, "Regarding the need for abstinence as a treatment goal, *current evidence* supports abstinence as the appropriate goal for persons with the medical disorder 'alcohol dependence' (alcoholism)." But this evidence does not include two enormous research projects, Project MATCH and NLAES, funded and/or conducted by Gordis's own agency. Once again, the head of the leading alcoholism research and treatment agency in the world declared his allegiance to conventional bureaucratic "truths" rather than scientific evidence.

Alternative Programs

Of course, one difficulty in providing or allowing alternatives to AA and 12-step programs is their relative dearth in America (see Horvath, 1999). But because there is a real need for them, "alternative" self-help groups such as SMART Recovery and Rational Recovery, as well as non-12-step treatment programs, will continue to grow in popularity (see Appendix B). We hope that the legal and clinical findings summarized in this chapter and book will encourage this trend. However, for the time being, it is not safe to assume that alternatives to 12-step programs will be available in your area. Likewise, even prevention or secondary-prevention alcohol abuse programs are currently almost exclusively 12-step and disease-oriented. (Secondary prevention means educating people to drink moderately after they have already displayed signs of abusing alcohol.)

A provider, payor, or patient may be asked to provide an alternative program. One such secondary prevention program has been developed by Alan Marlatt and his colleagues at the University of Washington; it's based on providing sensible information about alcohol's effects and how these effects are influenced by the individual's expectations, the environment, and cues surrounding the drinker's consumption of alcohol. (Such an approach is called "cognitive-behavioral" or "social-learning.") The drinker is then helped to develop accurate and realistic standards for drinking levels, and to develop the skills with which to adhere to these standards (Dimeff et al., 1998). Self-management skills are steeped in an important concept termed "self-efficacy," the belief that one can control one's existence and bring about beneficial outcomes for oneself. Marlatt and his colleagues (1998) have reported significant positive results from such programs with college problem drinkers. Another such program is outlined by a naval clinical psychologist in a letter to one of us (S.P.):

> My most frequent clients on the ship are young men between the ages of 18–25. We have female crew members on the ship, but they certainly get in less trouble. There is some documentation that in the military in general we have a greater portion of people with childhood problems. It certainly is extremely common for us to hear people say that they joined the military to get away from a bad home life or a dismal future. This takes them geographically away from the troubled family or bad neighborhood, and places them in a highly structured environment with clear rules.
>
> Many people adapt and are better off with the structure and rules. Others have great difficulty trusting anyone in authority, complying with rules, and living up to adult responsibilities. These are reasons why I think a Life Process program (Peele et al., 1991) that encourages self-awareness, acceptance of personal responsibility, clarification and development of values, and recognition of the importance of our role within the larger culture is fruitful. I taught a "Risk Reduction" program—a brief psychoeducational group—that was very well received and was non-specific for the type of trouble people had gotten into. It was also not focused on telling people to change, but everyone signed up wanting to change.

A further five-week program (with the Navy or similar setting in mind) for brief education, prevention, or secondary prevention is outlined here. Each weekly unit is designed for a two-hour session with two hours of preparation. (Reading materials are available at Peele & Sas, 1999.) While the program is ostensibly about alcohol, it actually prompts a more inclusive analysis of lives, habits, goals, and self-management principles. The sessions comprise the following:

1) *Environmental analysis:* Analysis of special nature of the setting in which drinkers are placed—in terms of a ship, bursts of intermittent activity broken by free time; dangers of environment, such as pitching and dark decks; loneliness and absence of family; the range of excessive behaviors in which people engage and negative emotions people experience; and so on.

2) *Positive drinking and other habits:* Review of positive drinking habits such as moderate consumption involved with other activities, such as meals and social conversation; review of the dangers of bursts of excessive consumption during intermittent free periods and of heavy total consumption resulting from drinking over many free breaks; review of drinking for relaxation and leisure versus drinking for escape that muddles feelings, hurts concentration and reflexes; and so on.

3) *Realistic positive activities:* running and exercise, reading and computers, educational opportunities, social time and support groups, and so on.

4) *Planning for the future:* Developing life goals and the means needed to achieve these. For example, in the Navy, understanding the sailor's role in larger ship operations and in the overall command; military career opportunities and planning; post-career options; and so on.

5) *Addictive behaviors:* What are addictive behaviors and how do we recognize them, whether to alcohol, drugs, or anything else; what are the causes of addiction; how can people prevent the development of such problems rather than addressing them only after they become fully addicted or alcohol dependent?

Appendix A

A Complaint Regarding Alcoholism Therapist Misconduct

The following is a slightly edited version of an actual complaint filed with the American Society of Addiction Medicine in August 1999 by Stanton Peele. The names "Smythe," "Jones," "Kramer," and "Walton" are pseudonyms; all others are actual names.

James F. Callahan, DPA, Executive Vice-President/CEO
American Society of Addiction Medicine
c/o Cammy Davidge
American Society of Addiction Medicine
4601 N. Park Avenue; Upper Arcade Suite #101
Chevy Chase, MD 20815

Dear Dr. Callahan:

You may recall that I wrote to you previously, as directed by ASAM President, Dr. Marc Galanter, to inquire about the ASAM's position regarding the judgment of liability for false imprisonment, fraud, and malpractice against Dr. G. Douglas Talbott [Chapter 6]. Is ASAM discussing the implications of this decision against its past president and founder? I am in touch with a physician member of ASAM, who informs me that he has seen nothing about the case in any of your publications.

At the time I contacted you, I also inquired to whom an ethics complaint concerning an ASAM member must be submitted. You did not answer that question, and so I am advising Captain William Smythe to mail directly to you a complaint he wishes to submit against ____, M.D., FASAM, who is listed as an ASAM fellow at the ASAM web site. I have written this report at the behest of Captain Smythe in support of his complaint.

I have reviewed the case of Captain Smythe. Capt. Smythe completed a residential treatment program at the _____ Treatment Center. He was compelled to attend this program by his employer, ABC Corp. (ABC hereafter), under threat of losing his job and his ship's pilot's license. The basis for this treatment was a diagnosis of alcohol dependence by Dr. ____, to whom Capt. Smythe was referred by ABC and its EAP, headed by Ms. Ann Jones. Dr. ____ further indicated to Capt. Smythe that he was required to create a follow-up therapeutic/rehabilitation plan with him.

I have reviewed the records of this case, including an evaluation of Capt. Smythe by Dr. ____ (June 22, 1998); Capt. Smythe's written narrative of these events, including a statement by his wife; Capt. Smythe's rejection of a therapeutic agreement with Dr. ____ (dated September 23, 1998); Capt. Smythe's offer of his own therapeutic agreement with Dr. Kramer (dated October 27, 1998) and accompanying rehabilitation agreement, which was subsequently rejected by ABC through its attorney (October 30, 1998); Dr. Kramer's interview and diagnosis notes on this case; Capt. Smythe's subsequent proffer of an additional therapeutic/rehabilitation agreement with Dr. Walton (no date noted); and the subsequent acceptance (with some additional conditions) of this last agreement by ABC through its attorney (November 10, 1998).

Narrative (as provided by Capt. Smythe)

In May of 1998, Capt. Smythe was reported for having alcohol on his breath when he reported for duty as a ship's pilot, although the complainant has never been identified. Capt. Smythe's partner, who traveled with him for some hours on the way to work, and other people at his workplace have stated that they did not smell alcohol on Capt. Smythe's breath or notice any strange behavior on his part that night (as described in Dr. ____'s report). Capt. Smythe had not consumed alcohol since dinner, five hours before reporting to work and nine hours before actually piloting the boat. He has never seen this initial complaint. I have not seen this complaint.

(Capt. Smythe ceased drinking and has not consumed any alcohol since this incident, which I confirmed independently in a phone call with his wife. The primary reasons for this abstinence were Capt. Smythe's and his wife's concern over the child they were adopting, as well as his concern over his pilot's license.)

Two days following this incident, the ABC directors asked to meet with Capt. Smythe. They indicated that he must see the company EAP counselor for an assessment and that if he refused to go he would be fired. Two weeks later, Capt. Smythe met with the EAP counselor, whom he saw two times. This counselor repeatedly stated that their interview was confidential. Following their two sessions, the counselor stated she felt everything was fine and that Capt. Smythe would be permitted to return to work. However, since Capt. Smythe had been on medical leave during this process, she told him it was first necessary for him to meet with Dr. ____ in order to return to work.

During an initial phone call, Dr. ____'s office informed Capt. Smythe that the fee for Dr. ____'s services and tests would be $1500. Capt. Smythe indicated that this bill should be sent to ABC. Capt. Smythe then met with Dr. ____ for about 30 minutes. During this meeting, according to Dr. ____'s report, he explained to Capt. Smythe that "we do not have a true doctor-patient relationship; I will compose a report based upon the information acquired during the assessment; and the report will go to the party who has contracted with me to perform this service." Dr. ____ indicated that Capt. Smythe signed this informed consent notice. Capt. Smythe, however, does not recall signing such a form. He claims, instead, that Dr. ____ assured him their meeting and its results were completely confidential. Capt. Smythe has repeatedly requested this signed form from Dr. ____ and from the EAP, but he has not received a copy.

Dr. ____ subsequently interviewed Capt. Smythe's wife briefly by phone. In a letter signed by Mrs. Smythe (which I confirmed in a phone conversation), she says that she does not believe Capt. Smythe has ever lost control of his drinking or suffered negative consequences from this drinking as claimed in Dr. ____'s report, and that Dr. ____ misattributed these statements to her.

About 20 days after the interview with Dr. ____, Capt. Smythe called the EAP to find out his status, but got no return call. About this time, when he thought he was about to resume work, Capt. Smythe contacted an ABC director, who informed him that he would not be permitted to return to work. This was the first time Capt. Smythe had any indication this was to be the case.

Capt. Smythe then attempted several times to contact the EAP. When he finally reached the EAP, Ms. Jones informed Capt. Smythe that she had Dr. ____'s report declaring that Capt. Smythe was alcohol dependent, and that he would have to enter a treatment center for four weeks. Capt. Smythe objected, and a meeting was scheduled with the directors of ABC. In the meantime, Capt. Smythe contacted Dr. ____. Dr. ____ indicated that there was "some evidence of dependency and you have to go through an intense four-week program with a follow up of twice-weekly visits to him and weekly AA meetings." Dr. ____ further stated that the treatment and aftercare process was required given Capt. Smythe's safety-sensitive job. Capt. Smythe started to ask questions, but Dr. ____ brushed them off and hung up.

When Capt. Smythe met with his directors, they indicated that his pay was cut off as of the last day he worked in May, and that the money he had been paid in benefits was to be treated as a loan and would have to be paid back to ABC. During this meeting, one of the directors blurted out, "Well, Dr. ____ told us that you are only in the very early stages of dependency and you have a better than 90 percent chance of a full recovery!" Capt. Smythe looked at him and asked, "How did you know that?" The director said, "The doctor and Ms. Jones had a meeting with us and told us that you were alcohol dependent and stand a good chance of a full recovery." The directors then threatened Capt. Smythe, telling him his pilot's license could be suspended, perhaps permanently. In fact, he learned during the meeting that his licensing organization had been told of ____'s diagnosis.

Capt. Smythe was naturally concerned about losing his license. In addition, he and his wife were in the process of adopting a child. As a result, he agreed to enter a treatment program. He considered several. When he mentioned one to Ms. Jones, she said that that center was not 12-step-oriented and that Dr. ____ insisted that he enter a 12-step center, and that he was to comply with Dr. ____'s orders. Ultimately, Capt. Smythe entered the ____ Treatment Center.

At ____, Capt. Smythe encountered numerous patients who had been in treatment previously—one young woman said it was her eleventh time in treatment. Capt. Smythe completed the program (of the 33 people who entered along with him, 12 either left or were thrown out for drinking or using drugs, thus belying ____'s claims to patients that it had a 95 percent success rate). Ten days after he returned home, he was informed that he had to contact Dr. ____ again in order to be certified for work. In the meantime, Capt. Smythe did research on his own and discovered that there was strong disagreement about approaches to alcoholism treatment in the addictions literature. Among other programs and practitioners, he contacted Rational Recovery—a non-12-step, non-spiritual recovery group—and myself.

When Capt. Smythe met with Dr. ____ following treatment, he was informed that he had to enter into a two-year contract with Dr. ____ and with ABC. Dr. ____ elaborated, "It's a therapeutic contract between me and you and you're going to do certain things for me. If you are in violation of our contract then the employer will be notified and you'll have to answer to them. This is what you are going to do for me. First you will attend at least three AA meetings a week. You will be involved with a weekly step group and a weekly home group. You will get yourself a sponsor. You will provide us with urine and blood samples on a regular and random basis at my lab. You will see me every two weeks until I feel you're doing all right, then we'll increase the time in between visits. You are responsible for all the associated costs." Dr. ____ indicated to Capt. Smythe that the Captain was fortunate, because his contract was for only two years, while some contracts were for five years.

However, Capt. Smythe was now in a position where, if he did not sign the contract with Dr. ____, he could not return to work. If he did sign the contract, if he missed so much as a single AA meeting, he would be in violation of the contract. At the same meeting where Dr. ____ reviewed the contract with him, Capt. Smythe complained that officers of ABC and other employees knew details about his diagnosis and had apparently seen Dr. ____'s report. Dr. ____ at first denied that he had turned over such information to ABC, saying it would be an ethical violation to do so. Capt. Smythe then asked for Dr. ____'s medical report. At this point, Dr. ____ indicated he couldn't give Capt. Smythe this report because whoever purchased his services "owned" the report. This was the first that Capt. Smythe was aware that this was the case. After the meeting, Capt. Smythe immediately called and left a message for Ms. Jones saying he wanted a copy of the report as soon as possible.

Meanwhile, Capt. Smythe received a call from one of ABC's directors. In a highly aggressive manner, the director told him, "Ms. Jones just called and said you wanted the medical report. You can't have it! It's not yours. We own it and you can't have it!" Capt. Smythe consulted with an attorney about the contract and searched for alternative providers of his contracted posttreatment plan. He and his lawyer developed an alternative plan with fewer meetings, and involving a Rational Recovery group rather than AA. In addition, Capt. Smythe contacted a family physician, Dr. Lawrence Kramer, who had been medical director of a detoxification/substance abuse clinic for seven years and had seen hundreds of patients with substance abuse problems over 15 years in private practice. This physician was not a 12-step practitioner—indeed, he opposed this approach. Capt. Smythe met with this provider twice and found his approach amenable. Dr. Kramer diagnosed Capt. Smythe (according to Dr. Kramer's notes) as a "habitual but not compulsive" drinker, and later indicated in a letter that he did not find Capt. Smythe to be alcohol dependent.

ABC had meanwhile written Ms. Jones and copied Capt. Smythe a release for Dr. _____'s report. At the same time, ABC was threatening Capt. Smythe with consequences if he did not sign the contract proposed by Dr. _____. Capt. Smythe responded with the alternative contract and aftercare provider. Capt. Smythe continued to try to get Dr. _____'s report from Ms. Jones. Capt. Smythe finally received a fax of Dr. _____'s report after the initial deadline he had been given to sign the contract with Dr. _____ and ABC. Capt. Smythe sent this report to Dr. Stanton Peele, whom he had contacted in the interim.

ABC refused to accept Dr. Kramer, saying he was unqualified, and insisted that Capt. Smythe sign an aftercare agreement with Dr. _____. However, after the initial deadline had passed, ABC now provided a list of 15 additional providers. One of these providers worked in a rundown part of town and was not a 12-step practitioner, but also specialized in drug-addicted AIDS patients. Capt. Smythe agreed to aftercare with this physician, Dr. Walton. Dr. Walton, as had Dr. Kramer, did not find Capt. Smythe to be alcohol dependent. Nonetheless, he signed an aftercare agreement with Capt. Smythe that was accepted by ABC.

My Assessment of the Report (see Attachment)

A single alcohol-related incident was reported in connection with Capt. Smythe's employment as a ship's pilot. Capt. Smythe reported to work at 11:00 p.m., when an agent smelled alcohol on his breath. Dr. _____'s evaluation indicates that Capt. Smythe said that he had two beers at dinner approximately five hours before reporting, and nine hours before he piloted the ship. (In a phone call, Mrs. Smythe told me that Capt. Smythe had three beers with dinner, was not intoxicated when he left for work, and that he was not to pilot a ship until 3:00 a.m. the next morning. Capt. Smythe told me, and his wife corroborated, that the Captain did not drink on working days.) He had had a total of six beers that day. As far as the record indicates, no breathalyzer or blood test was administered, so that no BAL (blood alcohol level) was determined. A fellow pilot who accompanied Capt. Smythe reported that he noted no impairments in Capt. Smythe's behavior or performance (this is included in Dr. _____'s report).

From both a legal and a clinical standpoint, I would judge that this incident did not provide sufficient cause for either legal or mandatory clinical action. In fact, it prompted the subsequent examination by Dr. ____, in which a diagnosis of alcohol dependence was made. But a diagnosis of alcohol dependence is not, in my judgment, established by Dr. _____'s report.

Violations of ASAM Principles of Medical Ethics

I proceed in this section by matching the performance of Dr. ____ against the Principles of Medical Ethics listed at the ASAM web site (ASAM, 1992). (Only those sections of the ASAM principles relevant to Captain Smythe's ethics complaint are reproduced here, and particularly relevant passages appear in bold italics.)

Preamble:

The American Society of Addiction Medicine supports a body of ethical statements developed primarily for the benefit of the patient.

It can certainly be said that Dr. ____ was not primarily oriented towards the betterment of the patient, or towards Capt. Smythe at all. Dr. ____ did not communicate his diagnosis directly to Capt. Smythe, did not respect Capt. Smythe's preferences for treatment or requests for information, and seemed most directly concerned with the EAP's and employer's needs, as well as his own financial benefits (see *Conflict of Interest* below). Capt. Smythe appears in this matter to have been a recipient of secondary consideration throughout.

Section I:

1. Because of the prominence of denial in patients suffering from chemical dependence, treatment may be mandated or offered as an alternative to sanctions of some kind. In other circumstances, a chemically dependent person whose judgment is impaired by intoxication may be brought to treatment when unable to make a reasoned decision, or may be treated on an involuntary basis. *It is the duty of the addictionist to advocate on behalf of the patient's best interest and to prevent any abuse of this coercive element. The goal for patients is to*

restore, as quickly and safely as possible, their ability to make responsible decisions about their own recoveries.

Capt. Smythe's treatment was mandated. Alcohol dependence was diagnosed, although I seriously question this diagnosis (see Attachment). In any case, Dr. _____'s self-centered, dictatorial, nonresponsive, and paternalistic approach continued well past treatment. Captain Smythe was not in a medical emergency when he was referred to treatment, having ceased drinking a month earlier. Yet he was not allowed to select a treatment program he felt was best for him. Moreover, any potential emergency was certainly well past after he had completed treatment. Nonetheless, Dr. _____ refused to allow Capt. Smythe any say in his treatment and aftercare arrangement (e.g., particularly in regards to his preference for alternatives to AA and 12-step treatment), and to allow Capt. Smythe free choice of a provider with whom to create an aftercare contract.

2. All patients with problems of chemical dependence, regardless of how dysfunctional they may appear, retain the right to be treated with respect. *The physician practicing addiction medicine will maintain a decorum that recognizes each patient's dignity regardless of possible conflicts in values between patient and physician.*

Dr. _____ displayed no concern for Capt. Smythe's values, in regard either to his desire for full disclosure or his treatment preferences. Dr. _____ appears fully committed to the 12-step model of alcoholism treatment. Capt. Smythe found this offensive to his values. Dr. _____ seemed incapable, as a professional, of acknowledging and respecting this difference between his and his patient's values.

Section II, Preamble:

A physician shall deal honestly with patients and colleagues and shall attempt to notify appropriate authorities promptly regarding those physicians whose conduct is illegal, unethical or incompetent or who engage in fraud or deception.

Capt. Smythe contends that Dr. _____ lied to him—primarily (but not exclusively) about what Dr. _____ communicated to Capt. Smythe's employers. That is, Dr. _____ had no compunction about conveying his diagnoses directly to the EAP and ultimately to Capt. Smythe's employer. Dr. _____ says he had Capt. Smythe sign an informed consent agreement, one that Capt. Smythe has not subsequently been able to obtain. Instead, Capt. Smythe maintains, Dr. _____ initially told him their consultation was confidential and then attempted to obfuscate who would receive—and had received—Dr. _____'s report.

3. Addiction treatment services, like all medical services, are dispensed in the context of a contractual arrangement between physician and patient and which is binding on both. *Addictionists should avoid misrepresenting to patients or families either the nature, length or cost of treatment recommended. This is particularly important when the physician may profit from the recommendation or when the physician holds power over a patient's legal or professional status* **or when the physician's income is based on census within an institution as opposed to services rendered to patients.**

Dr. _____ did reveal the costs of the various services he was to perform for Capt. Smythe. However, Capt. Smythe was anything but free to accept or reject this proposed arrangement and to seek alternative services and/or providers. Capt. Smythe's initial selection of a non-12-step treatment program was rejected by the EAP on an understanding that Dr. _____ would not accept such a program. Capt. Smythe's employer negotiated consistently to compel Capt. Smythe to adopt the aftercare contract proffered by Dr. _____. It is hard to avoid the conclusion that ABC and Dr. _____ were in contact—not to say in collusion—in their efforts to force Capt. Smythe to accept Dr. _____'s contract.

Section III:

2. *Addictionists are often in the position of acting as role models for recovering patients. As such, they carry the responsibility to be aware of the laws that govern both their professional practice and everyday lives and to respect and obey these laws.* **While most unlawful behaviors would have a direct or indirect bearing on suitability to practice, there may be situations such as an act of civil disobedience in protest against social injustice in which unlawful activity might not automatically be equivalent to professionally unethical conduct.**

Dr. _____'s conduct regularly clashes with these Principles of Medical Ethics. He repeatedly violated, among other medical and ethical precepts, confidentiality and informed consent. Confidentiality is a separate part of the ASAM's Principles of Medical Ethics (see below).

Section IV, Preamble:

A physician shall respect the rights of patients, of colleagues and of other health professionals and shall safeguard patient confidences within the constrains [sic] of the laws.

1. Physicians practicing addiction medicine often treat patients who feel stigmatized and are reluctant to disclose medically necessary information because of suspicion, fear and distrust. *In this special physician patient relationship, it is essential that the rights of the patient be recognized, respected and protected by the treating physicians.*

2. *When addicted patients are coerced into treatment by external agencies and are under threat of legal, social or professional sanctions, demands for information from these agencies may at times conflict with a patient's desire for confidentiality. The physician has the obligation to consider the short and long term consequences of disclosure and to advise the patient who must give consent.* The patient's right to limit the content, purpose and duration of consent should be respected within the limits of the law.

Dr. ____'s June 22, 1998 report is labeled an "Independent Medical Evaluation." However, the report was authored at the behest of the ABC and/or its representative, Ann Jones, expressly for the purpose of deciding whether Capt. Smythe should be compelled to undergo treatment and for the purposes of work assignment. In and of itself (other than mislabeling the assessment "independent"), this is of course a legitimate company function. However, the recipient of such an evaluation must be informed in some clear and unmistakable way that this is the case. Capt. Smythe maintains that this never happened, and that he was repeatedly assured that his consultation with Dr. ____ was confidential, and that Dr. ____ only told Capt. Smythe otherwise later, when confronted with his actions. Capt. Smythe maintains that Dr. ____'s assurance in his report that "I explained the nature of this evaluation" was thus a misrepresentation, and that in any case he was never cognizant of the purpose of the evaluation and a report based on it. This situation is compounded in that the report or its contents were apparently conveyed to Capt. Smythe's licensing body.

The principle that a patient must be informed if an interview with a professional is intended—or can potentially be used—for legal or employment actions is acknowledged ordinarily by a so-called Lamb warning. A standard Lamb warning reads as follows:

> I am retained by _____. I am not your doctor/therapist, and this is not treatment/therapy. What you say to me is not confidential and I may report it to [the retaining party] and what you tell me may be used in court. Thus, what you say can benefit or harm your case, or have no effect on it. You are free not to answer any questions but I may make note of that fact in my report.

Section IV:

3. *Addictionists should treat individuals only with their consent, except in emergency and extraordinary circumstances in which the patient cannot give consent and in which the withholding of treatment would have permanent and significant consequences for life and health.* **In cases where the patient has been found to be incompetent by appropriate mental health professionals and/or by the judicial system, physicians may assist in their care.**

Dr. ____'s assurance in his report that "informed consent" standards were being followed is inaccurate in as much as this term is usually understood very differently (see Chapter 5). Clearly, Capt. Smythe was not given a free choice about whether to enter treatment, based on Dr. _____'s diagnosis of alcohol dependence. The attachment to this letter makes clear that this diagnosis is flawed. If treatment was recommended, clearly an outpatient alternative should have been considered. Informed consent not only requires gaining the patient's consent for his or her treatment, it also requires full disclosure of the patient's diagnosis, the nature of the proposed treatment, and possible alternative treatments. Informed consent then requires that the patient's judgment and decisions be respected with regard to treatment. Dr. ____ provided none of this information; nor did he respect Capt. Smythe's choices. He did not explain the nature of 12-step treatment and its alternatives to Capt. Smythe. Indeed, it is clear that Dr. ____ would accept only a 12-step treatment program. After Capt. Smythe learned of such alternatives, in fact, Dr. ____ resisted all initiatives by Capt. Smythe to seek alternatives to 12-step aftercare.

Section VII:

4. *The physician will be extremely careful of any dual role relationships with patients.* Assuming the doctor-patient role with employees, business associates and vendors, students, family members and others may compromise professional judgment. Conflict of interest or an advantage of power over the patient outside of the treatment relationship can lead to exploitation or interfere with the fiduciary nature of the professional relationship. While such treatment is not frankly unethical, there are potential dangers and conflicts in such roles and the physician should enter into them only with great caution.

Dr. _____ evinced several conflicts in his dealings with Capt. Smythe (see Strasburger et al., 1997). Initially, Dr. _____ had a stake in assessing, in a supposedly "independent" evaluation for an employer and EAP, that Capt. Smythe was alcohol dependent, since Capt. Smythe was required to sign an aftercare arrangement with Dr. _____. Dr. _____'s refusal (operating through the employer's negotiations with Capt. Smythe in the creation of an aftercare contract) to allow alternative treatments or providers was clearly financially and professionally self-serving for Dr. _____. Furthermore, requiring that Capt. Smythe sign a rehabilitation agreement with him while in fact he was employed by ABC Corp. to make decisions regarding Capt. Smythe's employment and professional status is an additional conflict.

Misdiagnosis of Alcohol Dependence

The ASAM is aware, I know from my prior correspondence with you, that its past president, Dr. G. Douglas Talbott, was found liable in his treatment of a patient for fraud, false imprisonment, and malpractice. An essential element of this judgment was the decision by the jury that the patient, Dr. Leonard Masters, was misdiagnosed as alcohol dependent, on the basis of which the defendants coerced him into treatment at the Talbott-Marsh Recovery Campus (now the Talbott Recovery Campus). As you may know, Dr. Anne Geller, president of ASAM prior to Dr. Talbott, testified for the plaintiffs in support of the argument that Dr. Masters was misdiagnosed. Among the points Dr. Geller made were that the defendants neglected to interview Masters' family, friends, and colleagues (Ursery, 1999b); and that Dr. Masters' record gave no evidence of loss of control, of an increase in drinking (tolerance), or of withdrawal (Ursery, 1999a).

It is my contention (see Attachment) that Capt. Smythe's was an even more blatant case of misdiagnosis, displaying the same limitations and oversights as Dr. Geller pointed out in the Masters diagnosis—and more.

Although the record does not rule out the possibility of excessive drinking or a diagnosis of alcohol abuse on Capt. Smythe's part, clearly the diagnosis of alcohol dependence on which Dr. _____'s actions and Capt. Smythe's treatment were predicated is not justified by the record or by Dr. _____'s report. More importantly, the record establishes a host of violations of proper clinical procedures and professional ethics in this case.

Yours sincerely,

Stanton Peele, Ph.D., Esq.

Attachment: Dr. _____'s Assessment of Captain Smythe

Dr. _____ authored what is titled an "Independent" Medical Evaluation. I elsewhere address what is meant in this instance by "independent." The assessment also includes what it claims is an "informed consent" clause. I address this claim elsewhere as well. The assessment cites the one above-mentioned incident. Its past medical history comprises seven lines, and refers to a motor vehicle accident in which alcohol was not involved, and a mild case of hepatitis, in which, Dr. _____ reports (according to Capt. Smythe's family physician), "Alcohol may have been an exacerbating factor." No independent record of this physician's assessment is provided. Capt. Smythe maintains that Dr. _____ never spoke to this family physician, and so I remain puzzled about the source of this information. The report notes that Capt. Smythe had his last drink a month prior (confirmed by his wife and a negative alcohol screen), which would be clinically relevant to a diagnosis of alcohol dependence.

Collateral reports. The pilot who accompanied Capt. Smythe the evening of the reported incident indicated he did not believe Capt. Smythe had an alcohol problem. The only other collateral contacted was the subject's wife of 17 years, Susan, who Dr. _____ reports "has been concerned about his drinking for several years." Dr. _____

reports that she expresses "the belief that Capt. Smythe has a drinking problem" and that "he appears on occasion to lose control of his drinking and suffer negative consequences from his drinking." However, I have a copy of an independent statement from Susan Smythe that maintains these statements were purportedly taken from a phone call and were, she says, "either taken out of context or were distorted." According to the document I have, Mrs. Smythe reported that her husband has never lost control of his drinking and that "I do not recall Capt. Smythe suffering any negative consequences" (from his drinking).

(I spoke by phone with Mrs. Smythe, when Capt. Smythe was not present. She agreed that she felt Capt. Smythe was drinking too much, but that he displayed no negative consequences from his drinking and always remained in control of it. Mrs. Smythe confirmed that Capt. Smythe quit drinking after the incident and has not drunk again, that he never drank on days when he worked, and that he had three beers with dinner the night before piloting the boat as scheduled during the reported incident. She was always confident Capt. Smythe could quit drinking, because "he has extremely strong will power," citing his successful loss of 60 pounds two to three years earlier. She confirmed for me the contents of her letter in regard to her interview with Dr. _____. She said this about what he subsequently wrote in his report: "Dr. _____ wanted to hear that my husband loses control when he drinks, but he doesn't." In regard to Dr. _____'s report, she told me: "It was like he was taking me out of context, and trying to twist what I said around.")

Negative consequences. Negative consequences are often summed in assessments of alcohol dependence, and so the total number of negative consequences and their nature/severity are clinically relevant. Dr. _____ lists a total of four such consequences: "[A]bout 15 years ago . . . He was charged with failing to provide a breath sample [no details provided]. He has had medical consequences in that his hepatitis was likely [above Dr. _____ states that the reporting physician said "may have been"] made worse by his continued drinking. His wife Susan has been concerned about his drinking for several years. He has had vocational consequences [the single incident above], resulting in this assessment." This list of consequences, even without the alternative/additional information provided here, does not justify a diagnosis of alcohol dependence.

Quantity drunk/test results. Dr. _____ reports that Capt. Smythe typically drinks nine beers per day, and occasionally more at parties. He notes that this drinking is characteristic of non-working days. Captain Smythe reports, and his wife confirms, that he does not drink at all on working days, which is both clinically and professionally relevant. Dr. _____ reports an AUDIT (screening) test score of 14, where cutoff of 8+ "makes a diagnosis of alcohol use disorder likely." Since this is a screening rather than a diagnostic test, it cannot assess alcohol dependence, as Dr. _____ notes.

Family history. Capt. Smythe presents no family history of parental alcohol abuse, but Mrs. Smythe does have a family background of alcoholism, which might make her highly sensitive to signs of alcohol abuse.

Overall health. Capt. Smythe is healthy, does not smoke or drink coffee, is not depressed, sleeps well, recently lost about 60 pounds, and displays no symptoms of chronic or acute illness (except as described in next section). Dr. _____ assesses his cognitive acuity and memory to be good, finds no signs of mood or thought disorder, and states that he displays no (other) obsessive or addictive behaviors.

Medical tests. Dr. _____ reports liver dysfunction indicating "excessive alcohol intake." Dr. _____ reports that Capt. Smythe had not drunk alcohol since May 18, 1998 (this was on June 22, so that Capt. Smythe had been abstinent over a month); it was two months after this point (in August) that Capt. Smythe entered inpatient treatment. Dr. _____ administered an alcohol drug screen, which was negative. Signs of an ulcer were noted.

Diagnosis of Capt. Smythe

Dr. _____, under "Diagnostic Impression," lists an axis 1 diagnosis of "alcohol dependence," based on "negative consequences + loss of control + compulsive use." Given Capt. Smythe's job as pilot, this diagnosis requires, according to Dr. _____, "thorough treatment and monitored follow-up." If not for this sensitive work, Capt. Smythe would still require "follow-up by an addictions counselor. . . and regular attendance at Alcoholics Anonymous . . ."

Alternate View of Diagnosis

Dr. _____'s assessment of alcohol dependence seems inadequate in a number of regards. No diagnostic test was administered, and no computation of alcohol dependence symptoms in reference to a set of diagnostic criteria (such as *DSM-IV*) is reported. Sources for many of his claims are inconsistent, unsubstantiated, or disputed. At this point, it may be valuable to review the *DSM-IV* description and criteria for substance dependence (alcohol is included here with other substances):

> The essential feature of Substance Dependence is a cluster of cognitive, behavioral, and physiological symptoms indicating that the individual continues use of the substance despite significant substance-related problems. There is a pattern of repeated self-administration that usually results in tolerance, withdrawal, and compulsive drug-taking behavior.
> (American Psychiatric Association, 1994, p. 176)

DSM-IV further elaborates:

> Individuals with Substance-Related Disorders frequently experience a deterioration of their general health. Malnutrition and other general medical conditions may result from improper diet and inadequate personal hygiene. Intoxication or Withdrawal may be complicated by trauma related to impaired motor coordination or faulty judgment.
>
> (pp. 189-190)

Capt. Smythe seems to be a far cry from this description.

DSM-IV lists a specific set of criteria:

> ***Criteria for substance dependence.*** A maladaptive pattern of substance use, leading to clinically significant impairment or distress, as manifested by three (or more) of the following, occurring at any time in the same 12-month period:
>
> 1. tolerance, as defined by either of the following:
>   a. a need for markedly increased amounts of the substance to achieve intoxication or desired effect
>   b. markedly diminished effect with continued use of the same amount of the substance

2. withdrawal, as manifested by either of the following:
   a. the characteristic withdrawal syndrome for the substance
   b. the same (or a closely related) substance is taken to relieve or avoid withdrawal symptoms

3. the substance is often taken in larger amounts or over a longer period than was intended

4. there is a persistent desire or unsuccessful efforts to cut down or control substance use

5. a great deal of time is spent in activities necessary to obtain the substance (e.g., visiting multiple doctors or driving long distances), use the substance (e.g., chain-smoking), or recover from its effects

6. important social, occupational, or recreational activities are given up or reduced because of substance use

7. the substance use is continued despite knowledge of having a persistent or recurrent physical or psychological problem that is likely to have been caused or exacerbated by the substance (e.g., current cocaine use despite recognition of cocaine-induced depression, or continued drinking despite recognition that an ulcer was made worse by alcohol consumption).

(APA, 1994, p. 181)

Note, first, that these symptoms must occur over the same 12-month period, and thus the unspecified refusal of the breath test 15 years ago would not be relevant to this diagnosis. Note also the descriptor, "clinically significant impairment or distress." Dr. _____ makes no representation that criteria (1)–(3) are met, i.e., tolerance, withdrawal, or increasing use. As to (4), no such unsuccessful efforts to quit or cut back are reported. Indeed, Dr. _____ notes at the time of his assessment that, prior to treatment and following the job incident, Capt. Smythe has ceased drinking, and Capt. Smythe reports having ceased drinking earlier in the year when he developed hepatitis. No reports of criterion (5) are included in Dr. _____'s assessment. In addition, as to criterion (6), no mention of sacrifice of work or any other activities in order to drink (other than the involuntary cessation of work caused by Dr. _____'s assessment itself) is made.

Note that, for a diagnosis of alcohol dependence, three of these *types* of criteria need to be met in the prior 12 months. In fact, three events are reported in Captain Smythe's case, but all fall within category (7), which is not sufficient to qualify a person for a diagnosis of alcohol dependence. And even these three events all have questionable elements, some dispositively so.[1] Arguably, drinking contributing to hepatitis would meet criterion (7), but Capt. Smythe claims instead to have ceased drinking when he learned of his hepatitis, and no report from his physician contradicts this. Once again, when a single job incident occurred, Capt. Smythe by Dr. _____'s own tests was shown to have abstained, which again refutes this criterion. All that remains is the claim that Capt. Smythe drinks despite his wife's objections, although his wife has subsequently denied central elements of Dr. _____'s report on his interview with her. Furthermore, Dr. _____ reports negative tests for depression and no other sign of psychological dysfunction, thereby contradicting the possibility of drinking despite "a persistent psychological problem."

Dr. _____ emphasizes "loss of control" and "compulsive use" in his report. These elements are approximated by items (3), (6), and (7) of the *DSM-IV* alcohol dependence criterion. The only basis for establishing loss of control in the case record is the claim made over the phone by Mrs. Smythe, the accuracy of which Capt. Smythe contests with a signed statement from his wife. (I have confirmed that she disagrees with the loss-of-control contention.) Loss of control indicates that, once an individual has begun drinking, he or she cannot halt until unconscious, intoxicated, or some similar state has been reached. In other words, he or she *cannot* drink moderately. But no case evidence is presented that Capt. Smythe *ever* had a single loss-of-control experience. This type of behavior is difficult to cover up, and would typically be widely noticed. Other case data included in Dr. _____'s report dispute the loss-of-control assessment, as well as that of compulsive use—not the least being Dr. _____'s report that Mrs. Smythe "believes he will be able to stop drinking," when, in fact, the case record indicates that Capt. Smythe had already done so and that he continued to do so for several more months prior to treatment. Previous contradictory indicators of compulsive use have been noted above in regards to criteria (3)–(7).

The failure to establish a solid alcohol-dependence diagnosis is significant. An inpatient program for alcoholism requires a very firm

---

1. Dispositively is a legal term, meaning that the evidence conclusively indicates something (that is, disposes of the issue).

diagnosis of this type, since the differential benefits for inpatient treatment for lesser degrees of alcohol problems are not established; in fact, what differences have been measured favor less intensive, or outpatient, treatment for such less severe alcohol abuse (Miller & Hester, 1986). It is my professional opinion that the original referral to an inpatient hospital program was not justified on the assessment reported here. An outpatient program would surely have been sufficient if any treatment were required. Likewise, the need for AA attendance—which presupposes a firm diagnosis of alcohol dependence or alcoholism—is simply not appropriately established by this assessment.

Postscript

ASAM referred this complaint to its attorney, Edward A. Scallet, of the firm LeBoeuf, Lamb, Greene & MacRae, who responded to Captain Smythe as follows:

"The ASAM Bylaws do not include a formal process for reviewing complaints against members. . . ." and that ASAM takes action only when "a member has been sanctioned by a licensing board" or has been convicted of a crime. The letter further indicates that "your complaint seems to be at least as focused on your employer and how your employer treats confidential information it receives in connection with its EAP[!]"

Thus, ASAM, which lists on its web site as a primary goal to "establish addiction medicine as a specialty recognized by the American Board of Medical Specialties," has no mechanisms in place to evaluate violations of its professional code of conduct short of commission of a felony (thus, allowing past president G. Douglas Talbott to escape readily from professional consequences for being found civilly liable for fraud and malpractice) and seems not to be concerned at all that a member might have committed malpractice by violating ASAM's own—and general medical—standards of care and ethical principles with respect to informed consent, confidentiality, and conflict of interest.

The complainant continues to pursue this matter with Dr. _____'s licensing body and potentially through legal action.

Appendix B

Secular Self-Help Groups

There are five important alternative (to AA) self-help groups in the United States. Unfortunately, none of them have been subjected to controlled studies, so there is no proof yet of their efficacy. We surmise that *all* of them are more effective than AA (if for no other reasons than that attendance at them is overwhelmingly voluntary and because they do not inculcate the harmful 12-step "powerless," "disease," and "loss of control" concepts); but, at present, there is no scientific evidence to support this belief.

For those coerced into AA, NA, MA, or CA participation, however, there is some good news: at various places in the United States attendance at the groups listed here is considered an acceptable alternative to 12-step group participation. Unfortunately, this situation varies widely from locale to locale, and alternative group meetings are not available in many places. Still, it's easy to find out if there are meetings in your area, and it's sometimes possible to persuade probation or parole officers that attending one of the alternatives is an acceptable substitute for 12-step group participation. Contact the following groups directly for information on meeting locations.

A brief description of the alternative groups, in alphabetical order, follows:

Moderation Management: MM, founded in 1994, suggests guidelines and limits for moderate drinking, and provides professionally advised meetings for those attempting to moderate. MM provides a supportive mutual-help environment that encourages people who are concerned about their drinking to cut back or quit drinking before their drinking problems become severe. For more information, or for groups in your area, call (425) 844-8228, or write to Moderation Management, P.O. Box 27558, Golden Valley, MN 55427. Web site: http://www.moderation.org

Rational Recovery: RR, founded in 1986, is based on Addictive Voice Recognition Technique (AVRT), and is a total abstinence program. RR advises that participation in recovery groups is not necessary for those who learn AVRT. For more information, or for groups in your area, call (530) 621-2667, or write to Rational Recovery, P.O. Box 800, Lotus, CA 95651. Web site: http://www.rational.org/recovery/

Secular Organizations for Sobriety: SOS, founded in 1985, believes that alcoholism is a disease, and thus takes a strict abstinence approach. Its program consists largely of the "Sobriety Priority," which is a daily acknowledgment that staying sober is one's highest priority. For more information, or for groups in your area, call (310) 821-8430, or write to SOS, 5521 Grosvenor Blvd., Marina del Rey, CA 90066. Web site: http://www.unhooked.com

SMART Recovery (Self-Management And Recovery Training): SMART was incorporated as a non-profit in 1992, and states that its teachings "are based on scientific knowledge, and evolve as scientific knowledge evolves." SMART is a time-limited, free, professionally advised abstinence program that views addictive behavior as learned behavior that can be unlearned by correcting inaccurate and self-defeating thinking. For more information or for groups in your area call (216) 292-0220, or write to SMART Recovery, 24000 Mercantile Road #11, Beachwood, OH, 44122.
Web site: http://www.smartrecovery.org

Women for Sobriety: WFS is the oldest—founded in 1975—of the modern (non-12-step) programs, and is dedicated to helping women overcome alcoholism and other addictions. WFS accepts the disease model and is an abstinence program. Its "New Life" program is specifically designed for women. For more information or for groups in your area call (215) 536-8026, or write to Women for Sobriety, P.O. Box 618, Quakertown, PA 18951.
Web site: http://www.womenforsobriety.org

Recovery Alternatives: An on-line clearinghouse for alternatives to AA, including these primary alternative groups as well as other groups and web sites. Web site: http://www.radial.com/night/

For a more thorough discussion of the alternatives to AA, see *Alcoholics Anonymous: Cult or Cure?*, (2nd Ed.) (Bufe, 1998), which contains detailed descriptions (in most cases self-descriptions) of the self-help groups listed here.

References

Addiction Research Foundation. (1998). How many people are alcoholic? [On-line]. Available: http://www.arf.org/isd/stats/alcohol.html

Alcoholics Anonymous. (1980). *Dr. Bob and the good oldtimers.* New York: Alcoholics Anonymous World Services.

Alcoholics Anonymous. (1984). *Pass it on.* New York: Alcoholics Anonymous World Services.

Alcoholics Anonymous. (1997). *Alcoholics Anonymous 1996 membership survey* [brochure]. New York: Alcoholics Anonymous World Services.

Alcoholics Anonymous. (1999). *Membership* [On-line]. Available: http://www.alcoholics-anonymous.org/em24doc4.html

Alcoholics Anonymous. (n.d., presumably 1990). *Comments on A.A.'s triennial surveys.* New York: Alcoholics Anonymous World Services.

American Psychiatric Association. (1994). *Diagnostic and statistical manual of mental disorders* (4th Ed.). Washington, DC: American Psychiatric Association.

American Society of Addiction Medicine. (1974, September). *Public policy: Abstinence* [On-line]. Available: http://www.asam.org

American Society of Addiction Medicine. (1992, October). *Public policy: Principles of medical ethics* [On-line]. Available: http://www.asam.org

Angres, D., Gallegos, K.V., & Talbott, G.D. (1998). Impairment and recovery in physicians and other health professionals. In A.W. Graham & T.K. Schultz (Eds.), *Principles of addiction medicine* (2nd ed., pp. 1263-1279). Chevy Chase, MD: American Society of Addiction Medicine.

Appelbaum, P.S. (1997). Informed consent to psychotherapy: Recent developments. *Psychiatric Services, 48,* 445-446.

Appelbaum, P.S., & Grisso, T. (1988). Assessing patients' capacities to consent to treatment. *New England Journal of Medicine, 319,* 1635-1638.

Appelbaum, P.S., & Gutheil, T.G. (1991). *Clinical handbook of psychiatry and the law* (2nd Ed.). Baltimore: Williams & Wilkins.

Argeriou, M., McCarty, D., & Blacker, E. (1985). Criminality among individuals arraigned for drinking and driving in Massachusetts. *Journal of Studies on Alcohol, 46,* 525–530.

Armor, D.J., Polich, J.M., & Stambul, H.B. (1976). *Alcoholism and treatment.* Santa Monica, CA: Rand Corporation.

Associated Press. (1999, September 23). "It's in my blood": John Daly says he feels "free."

Azrin, N.H., Sisson, R.W., Meyers, R., & Godley. M. (1982). Alcoholism treatment by disulfiram and community reinforcement approach. *Journal of Behaviour Therapy and Experimental Psychiatry, 13,* 105–112.

Bartlett, E. (1997, September–October). Brainwashing 101, or how I survived 12-step rehab. *Journal of Rational Recovery, 10,* 4–6.

Booth, P.G., Dalbe, B., & Ansari, J. (1984). Problem drinkers' goal choice and treatment outcome: A preliminary study. *Addictive Behaviors, 9,* 357–364.

Booth, P.G., Dalbe, B., Slade, P.D., & Dewey, M. (1992). A follow-up study of problem drinkers offered a goal choice option. *Journal of Studies on Alcohol, 53,* 594–600.

Bower, B. (1997, January 25). Alcoholics synonymous: Heavy drinkers of all stripes may get comparable help from a variety of therapies. *Science News, 151,* 62–63.

Brandsma, J.M., Maultsby, M.C., & Welsh, R.J.. (1980). *Outpatient treatment of alcoholism: A review and comparative study.* Baltimore: University Park Press.

Brodsky, A., & Peele, S. AA abuse. (1991, November). *Reason,* pp. 34–39. Also [On-line]. Available: http://www.peele.net/lib/aaabuse.html

Bufe, C. (1998). *Alcoholics Anonymous: Cult or cure?* (2nd Ed.). Tucson, AZ: See Sharp Press.

Bursztajn, H.J., & Brodsky, A. (1994). Authenticity and autonomy in the managed-care era: Forensic psychiatric perspectives. *Journal of Clinical Ethics, 5,* 237–242.

Bursztajn, H.J., Gutheil, T.G., & Cummins, B. (1991). Legal issues in inpatient psychiatry. In L.I. Sederer (Ed.), *Inpatient psychiatry: Diagnosis and treatment* (3rd Ed., pp. 379–406). Baltimore: Williams & Wilkins.

Bursztajn, H.J., Saunders, L.S., & Brodsky, A. (1997). Medical negligence and informed consent in the managed-care era. *Health Lawyer, 9*(5), 14–17.

Cahalan, D. (1970). *Problem drinkers.* San Francisco: Jossey-Bass.

Canterbury v. Spence. (1972). 464 F2d 772 (D.C. Cir.), cert. den., 409 U.S. 1064.

Collins, G.B. (1993). Contemporary issues in the treatment of alcohol dependence. *Psychiatric Clinics of North America, 16,* 33–48.

Connors, G.J. (1998, Spring). Overview of Project MATCH. *The Addictions Newsletter* (Division 50 of American Psychological Association), pp. 4–5.

Daley, D.C. (1987, March-April). Relapse prevention with substance abusers: Clinical issues and myths. *Social Work*, pp. 138–142.

Davidson, J. (1990, May–July). Drunk until proven sober. *Special Report on Health. Texas Monthly.*

Davies, D.L. (1962). Normal drinking in recovered alcohol addicts. *Quarterly Journal of Studies on Alcohol, 23,* 94–104.

Dawson, D. A. (1996). Correlates of past-year status among treated and untreated persons with former alcohol dependence: United States, 1992. *Alcoholism: Clinical and Experimental Research, 20,* 771–779.

Deaton, R.J.S., Colenda, C.C., & Bursztajn, H.J. (1993). Medical-legal issues. In A. Stoudemire & B.S. Fogel (Eds.), *Psychiatric care of the medical patient* (pp. 929–938). New York: Oxford University Press.

Delbanco A., & Delbanco, T. (1995, March 20). A.A. at the crossroads. *The New Yorker*, pp. 50–63.

Dick B. (1992). *Design for living: The Oxford Group's contribution to early A.A.* Kihei, HI: Paradise Research Publications.

Dick B. (1997). *The Good Book and the Big Book* (2nd ed). Kihei, HI: Paradise Research Publications.

Dimeff, L.A., Baer, J.S., Kivlahan, D.R., & Marlatt, G.A. (1998). *Brief alcohol screening and intervention for college students (BASICS): A harm reduction approach.* New York: Guilford Press.

Ditman, K.S., Crawford, G.C., Forgy, E.W., Moskowitz, H., & MacAndrew, C. (1967). A controlled experiment on the use of court probation for drunk arrests. *American Journal of Psychiatry, 124*(2), 64–67.

Drew, R.H. (1968). Alcoholism as a self-limiting disease. *Quarterly Journal of Studies on Alcohol, 29,* 956–967.

Durcanin, C. (1987, December 18). The suicides at Ridgeview Institute: Staff members didn't believe Michigan doctor was suicidal. *Atlanta Journal and Constitution*, p. A8.

Durcanin, C., & King, M. (1987, December 18). The suicides at Ridgeview Institute: Suicides mar success at Ridgeview with troubled professionals. *Atlanta Journal and Constitution*, p. A13.

Edwards, G., Orford, J., Egbert, S., Guthrie, A.H., Hensman, C., Mitcheson, M., Oppenheimer, E., & Taylor, C. (1977). Alcoholism: A controlled trial of "treatment" and "advice." *Journal of Studies on Alcohol, 38,* 1004–1031.

Eisenberg, M. (1999). *Three year recidivism tracking of offenders participating in substance abuse treatment programs.* Austin, TX: Criminal Justice Policy Committee.

Elal-Lawrence, G., Slade, P.D., & Dewey, M.E. (1986). Predictors of outcome type in treated problem drinkers. *Journal of Studies on Alcohol, 47,* 41–47.

Evans v. Tennessee Board of Paroles. (1997). 956 S.W.2d 478 (TN).

Fillmore, K.M. (1974). Drinking and problem drinking in early adulthood and middle age: An exploratory 20-year follow-up study. *Quarterly Journal of Studies on Alcohol, 35,* 819–840.

Fillmore, K.M. (1975). Relationships between specific drinking problems in early adulthood and middle age: An exploratory 20-year follow-up study. *Journal of Studies on Alcohol, 36,* 882–907.

Fingarette, H. (1988). *Heavy drinking: The myth of alcoholism as a disease.* Berkeley: University of California Press.

Finney, J.W., & Monahan, S.C. (1996). The cost-effectiveness of treatment for alcoholism: A second approximation. *Journal of Studies on Alcohol, 57,* 229–242.

Finney, J.W., & Moos, R.H. (1991). The long-term course of treated alcoholism: I. Mortality, relapse and remission rates and comparisons with community controls. *Journal of Studies on Alcohol, 52,* 44–54.

Fox, V. (1993). *Addiction, change & choice: The new view of alcoholism.* Tucson, AZ: See Sharp Press.

Gerstel, D. (1982). *Paradise incorporated: Synanon.* Novato, CA: Presidio Press.

Gordis, E. (1997, September 29). Letter to editor. *U.S. News and World Report.*

Graber, R.A., & Miller, W.R. (1988). Abstinence or controlled drinking goals for problem drinkers: A randomized clinical trial. *Psychology of Addictive Behaviors, 2,* 20–33.

Graham, A.W., & Schultz, T.K. (Eds.). (1998). *Principles of addiction medicine* (2nd ed.). Chevy Chase, MD: American Society of Addiction Medicine.

Grant, B.F. (1996). Toward an alcohol treatment model: A comparison of treated and untreated respondents with DSM-IV alcohol use disorders in the general population. *Alcoholism: Clinical and Experimental Research, 20,* 372–378.

Griffin v. Coughlin. (1996). 88 N.Y.2d 674, 673 N.E.2d 98, 649 N.Y.S.2d 903; *certiorari denied,* 117 S.Ct. 681 (1997).

Grisso, T., & Appelbaum, P.S. (1995). A comparison of standards for assessing patients' capacities to make treatment decisions. *American Journal of Psychiatry, 152,* 1033–1037.

Gutheil, T.G., Bursztajn, H.J., & Brodsky, A. (1984). Malpractice prevention through the sharing of uncertainty: Informed consent and the therapeutic alliance. *New England Journal of Medicine, 311,* 49–51.

Hagen, R.E. (1980). *Suspension and revocation effects on the DUI offender.* Sacramento, CA: Department of Motor Vehicles. Special report No. 75.

Heather, N., Rollnick, S., & Winton, M. (1983). A comparison of objective and subjective measures of alcohol dependence as predictors of relapse following treatment. *British Journal of Clinical Psychology, 22*, 11–17.

Heather, N., Winton, M., & Rollnick, S. (1982). An empirical test of "a cultural delusion of alcoholics." *Psychological Reports, 50*, 379-382.

Helling v. Carey. (1974). 83 Wash. 2d 514, 519 P. 2d 981.

Hester, R.K., & Miller, W.R. (Eds.) (1995). *Handbook of alcoholism treatment approaches: Effective alternatives* (2nd Ed.). Boston: Allyn and Bacon.

Higgins, S.T., Delaney, D.D., Budney, A.J., Bickel, W.K., Hughes, J.R., Foerg, F., & Badger, G. (1993). Achieving cocaine abstinence with a behavioral approach. *American Journal of Psychiatry, 150*, 763–769.

Higgins, S.T., Delaney, D.D., Budney, A.J., Bickel, W.K., Hughes, J.R., Foerg, F., & Fenwick, J.W. (1991). A behavioral approach to achieving initial cocaine abstinence. *American Journal of Psychiatry, 148*, 1218–1224.

Hodgins, D.C., Leigh, G., Milne, R., & Gerrish, R. (1997). Drinking goal selection in behavioral self-management treatment of chronic alcoholics. *Addictive Behaviors, 22*, 247–255.

Holder, H.D., & Blose, J.O. (1991). Typical patterns and cost of alcoholism treatment across a variety of populations and providers. *Alcoholism: Clinical and Experimental Research, 15*, 190–195.

Holder, H.D., Longabaugh, H.R., Miller, W.R., & Rubonis, A.V. (1991). The cost effectiveness of treatment for alcoholism: A first approximation. *Journal of Studies on Alcohol, 52*, 517–540.

Horvath, A.T. (1999, June). Awareness of non-12-step recovery resources in San Diego. *San Diego Psychologist, 8*(6), 1–3.

Huber, J.H., Pope, G.C., & Dayhoff, D.A.. (1994). National and state spending on specialty alcoholism treatment 1979 and 1989. *American Journal of Public Health, 84*, 1662–1665.

Hunt, G.M., & Azrin, N.H. (1973). A community-reinforcement approach to alcoholism. *Behaviour Research & Therapy, 11*, 91–104.

Hunter, T.W. (n.d., but mid to late 1990s). *It started right there: AA & MRA: Behind the 12 steps and the self-help movement*. Salem, OR: Grosvenor Books.

Husak, D., & Peele, S. (1998). "One of the major problems of our society": Symbolism and evidence of drug harms in U.S. Supreme Court decisions. *Contemporary Drug Problems, 25*, 191-233.

Institute of Medicine. (1990). *Broadening the base of treatment for alcohol problems*. Washington, DC: National Academy Press.

Jellinek, E.M. (1946). Phases in the drinking history of alcoholics. *Quarterly Journal of Studies on Alcohol, 7,* 1–88.

Jellinek, E.M. (1952). The phases of alcohol addiction. *Quarterly Journal of Studies on Alcohol, 13,* 673–84.

Jellinek, E.M. (1960). *The disease concept of alcoholism.* New Haven, CT: Hillhouse Press.

Johnson, V. E. (1980). *I'll quit tomorrow* (Rev. ed.). San Francisco: Harper & Row.

Kaimowitz v. Michigan Department of Mental Health. (1973). Div. No. 73-19434 AW, Circuit Court of Wayne City, Mich., 13 Criminal L Rep 2452.

Kerr v. Farrey. (1996). 95 F.3d 472 (7th Cir.).

King, M., & Durcanin, C. (1987a, December 18). The suicides at Ridgeview Institute: Doctor's treatment program may be too tough, some say. *Atlanta Journal and Constitution,* p. A12.

King, M., & Durcanin, C. (1987b, December 18). The suicides at Ridgeview Institute: Many drug-using doctors driven to Ridgeview by fear of losing licenses. *Atlanta Journal and Constitution,* p. A1.

Knupfer, G. (1972). Ex-problem drinkers. In M. Roff, L.N. Robins, & M. Pollak (Eds.). *Life history research in psychopathology* (Vol. 2, pp. 256–280). Minneapolis: University of Minnesota Press.

Lifton, R.J. (1969). *Thought control and the psychology of totalism.* New York: W.W. Norton.

Mäkelä, K., Arminen, I., Bloomfield, K., Eisenbach-Stangl, I., Bergmark, K.L., Kurube, N., Mariolini, N., Olafsdottir, H., Peterson, J.H., Phillips, M., Rehm, J., Room, R., Rosenqvist, P., Rosovsky, H., Stenius, K., Swiatkiewicz, G., Woronowicz, B., & Zielinski, A. (1996). *Alcoholics Anonymous as a mutual-help movement: A study in eight societies.* Madison, WI: University of Wisconsin Press.

Mann, M. (1981). *Marty Mann answers your questions about drinking and alcoholism* (Rev. Ed.). New York: Holt, Rinehart and Winston.

Marlatt, G.A., Baer, J.S., Kivlahan, D.R., Dimeff, L.A., Larimer, M.E., Quigley, L.A., Somers, J.M., & Williams, E. (1998). Screening and brief intervention for high-risk college student drinkers: Results from a 2-year follow-up assessment. *Journal of Consulting and Clinical Psychology, 66,* 604–615.

Marlatt, G.A., Demming, B., & Reid, J.B. (1973). Loss of control drinking in alcoholics: An experimental analog. *Journal of Abnormal Psychology, 84,* 652–659.

Masters v. Talbott. (1994, December 21). DeKalb County, Superior Court, Case No. 94-14004-3.

Mattson, M.E. (1997, March). Treatment can even work without triage: Initial results from Project MATCH. *EPIKRISIS, 8*(3), 2–3.

McCabe, J.R. (1986). Alcohol-dependent individuals sixteen years on. *Alcohol & Alcoholism, 21,* 85–91.

McIntosh, S. (1989, October 25). Doctor claims in suit that hospital colleagues tried to ruin his practice. *Atlanta Journal and Constitution,* p. B3.

Meredith, R. (1999, May 30). Michigan encountering opposition to plan to test welfare applicants for drugs. *New York Times.*

Miller, W.R. (1991). Warm turkey: Other routes to abstinence. *Journal of Substance Abuse Treatment, 8,* 227–232.

Miller, W.R., Brown, J.M., Simpson, T.L., Handmaker, N.S., Bien, T.H., Luckie, L.F., Montgomery, H.A., Hester, R.K., & Tonigan, J.S. (1995). What works?: A methodological analysis of the alcohol treatment outcome literature. In R.K. Hester and W.R. Miller (Eds.), *Handbook of alcoholism treatment approaches* (2nd Ed., pp. 12–44). Boston: Allyn and Bacon.

Miller, W.R., & Hester, R.K. (1986). Inpatient alcoholism treatment: Who benefits? *American Psychologist, 41,* 794–805.

Miller, W.R., & Rollnick, S. (1991). *Motivational interviewing: Preparing people to change addictive behavior.* New York: Guilford.

Morrow, D.J. (1998, July 31). Curbing the urge to drink: Drug to treat alcoholism sets off controversy in U.S. *New York Times,* pp. D1, D4.

Murray, F.J. (1996, November 4). Courts hit sentencing DWIs to AA, fault religious basis. *Washington Times,* p. A10.

Nace, E.P. (1993). Inpatient treatment. In M. Galanter (Ed.), *Recent developments in alcoholism, Volume 11: Ten years of progress* (pp. 429–451). New York: Plenum Press.

Narcotics Anonymous. (1982). *Narcotics Anonymous.* Van Nuys, CA: World Service Office, Inc.

Narcotics Anonymous. (1998). *Narcotics Anonymous: A commitment to community partnerships* [On-line]. Available: http://www.wsoinc.com/sandiego.htm

Natanson v. Kline. (1960). 186 Kan 393, 350 P2d 1093.

National Highway Transportation Safety Administration.(1996). *A guide to sentencing DUI offenders.* Report No. DOT HS 808 365.

National Institute on Alcohol Abuse and Alcoholism. (1999a). [On-line] Available: http://www.niaaa.nih.gov

National Institute on Alcohol Abuse and Alcoholism. (1999b). [On-line] Available: http://silk.nih.gov/silk/niaaa1/database/abdep1.txt

Nichols, J.L. (1990). Treatment versus deterrence. *Alcohol Health and Research World, 14,* 44–51.

O'Connor, A., & Daly, J. (1985). Alcoholics: A twenty-year follow-up study. *British Journal of Psychiatry, 146,* 645–647.

Öjesjö, L. (1981). Long-term outcome in alcohol abuse and alcoholism among males in the Lundby general population, Sweden. *British Journal of Addiction, 76,* 391–400.

Orford, J., & Keddie, A. (1986). Abstinence or controlled drinking in clinical practice: A test of the dependence and persuasion hypotheses. *British Journal of Addiction, 81,* 495–504.

Ouimette, P.C., Finney, J.W., & Moos, R.H. (1997). Twelve-step and cognitive-behavioral treatment for substance abuse: A comparison of treatment effectiveness. *Journal of Consulting and Clinical Psychology, 65,* 230–240.

Pattison, E.M., Sobell, M.B., & Sobell, L.C. (1977). *Emerging concepts of alcohol dependence.* New York: Springer.

Peele, S. (1986). Denial—of reality and freedom—in addiction research and treatment. *Bulletin of the Society of Psychologists in Addictive Behaviors, 5,* 149–166.

Peele, S. (1989). *Diseasing of America.* Lexington, MA: Lexington Books.

Peele, S. (1992). Alcoholism, politics and bureaucracy: The consensus against controlled-drinking therapy in America. *Addictive Behaviors, 17,* 49–62.

Peele, S. (1998, Spring). Ten radical things NIAAA research shows about alcoholism. *The Addictions Newsletter* (The American Psychological Association, Division 50), *5*(2), 6, 17–19.

Peele, S., & Brodsky, A. (1991, February). What's up to doc? *Reason,* pp. 34–36.

Peele, S., Brodsky, A., & Arnold, M. (1991). *The truth about addiction and recovery: The life process program for outgrowing destructive habits.* New York: Simon & Schuster.

Peele, S., & Sas, A. (1999). The Stanton Peele addiction web site [On-line]. Available: http://www.peele.net

Peet, J. (1986, September 28). Victim of the system: Jersey bureaucrats baffle, hound woman in DWI case. *Star Ledger,* pp. 1, 14.

Perrine, M.W., & Sadler, D.D. (1987). Alcohol treatment program versus license suspension for drunken drivers: The four-year traffic safety impact. In P.C. Noordzij & R. Roszbach (Eds.), *Alcohol, drugs, and traffic safety* (pp. 555–559). New York: Elsevier.

Pines, D. (1999, April 20). Atheist's rights violated by A.A. imposed by state. *New York Law Journal,* pp. 1, 11.

Pittman, B. (1988). *A.A. The Way It Began.* Seattle: Glen Abbey Books.

Polich, J.M., Armor, D.J., & Braiker, H.B. (1981). *The course of alcoholism: Four years after treatment.* New York: John Wiley & Sons.

Pomerleau, O., Pertschuk, M., Adkins, D., & d'Aquili, E. (1978). Treatment for middle income problem drinkers. In P.E. Nathan & G.A. Marlatt (Eds.), *Alcoholism: New directions in behavioral research and treatment*. New York: Plenum.

President's Commission for the Study of Ethical Problems in Medicine and Biomedical and Behavioral Research. (1982). *Making health care decisions: The ethical and legal implications of informed consent in the patient-practitioner relationship* (Vol. 1: *Report*). Washington, DC: U.S. Government Printing Office.

Project MATCH Research Group. (1997). Matching alcoholism treatments to client heterogeneity: Project MATCH posttreatment drinking outcomes. *Journal of Studies on Alcohol, 58,* 7–29.

Prugh, T. (1986). Recovery without treatment. *Alcohol Health and Research World, 10*(3), 24, 71–72.

Ragge, K. (1998). *The real AA: Behind the myth of 12-step recovery*. Tucson, AZ: See Sharp Press.

Restatement [Second] of Torts. (1965). §299A.

Ricks, W.S. (1987, October 11). Ridgeview Institute loses $1.3 million in suit over suicide. *Atlanta Journal and Constitution*, p. A1.

Rinard, A. (1996, August 30). Inmates can't be forced to attend drug abuse program, court rules. *Milwaukee Journal Sentinel*, p. A1.

Robbins v. Footer. (1977). F. 2d 123 (D.C. Cir.).

Rogers v. Commissioner of the Department of Mental Health. (1983). 390 Mass. 489, 458 NE2d 308.

Roman, P.M., & Blum, T.C. (1997). *National treatment center study summary report*. Athens, GA: University of Georgia.

Rosenberg, H., & Davis, L.A. (1994). Acceptance of moderate drinking by alcohol treatment services in the United States. *Journal of Studies on Alcohol, 55,* 167–172.

Ross, H.L. (1992). *Confronting drunk driving: Social policy for saving lives*. New Haven, CT: Yale University Press.

Rudy, D. (1986). *Becoming alcoholic: Alcoholics Anonymous and the reality of alcoholism*. Carbondale, IL: Southern Illinois University Press.

Rychtarik, R.G., Foy, D.W., Scott, T., Lokey, L., & Prue, D.M. (1987). Five-six-year-follow-up of broad-spectrum behavioral treatment for alcoholism: Effects of training controlled drinking skills. *Journal of Consulting and Clinical Psychology, 55,* 106–108.

Rydell, C.P., Caulkins, J.P., & Everingham, S.M.S. (1997). *Enforcement or treatment? Modeling the relative efficacy of alternatives for controlling cocaine*. Santa Monica, CA: Rand Corporation.

Salamone, G. (1997). *Religious and spiritual origins of the twelve-step recovery movement.* Lotus, CA: Lotus Press.

Salzberg, P., & Klingberg, C. (1983). The effectiveness of deferred prosecution for driving while intoxicated. *Journal of Studies on Alcohol, 44,* 303–304.

Sanchez-Craig, M., Annis, H., Bornet, A.R., & MacDonald, K.R. (1984). Random assignment to abstinence and controlled drinking: Evaluation of a cognitive-behavioral program for problem drinkers. *Journal of Consulting and Clinical Psychology, 52,* 390–403.

Sanchez-Craig, M., & Lei, H. (1986). Disadvantages to imposing the goal of abstinence on problem drinkers: An empirical study. *British Journal of Addiction, 81,* 505–512.

Saunders, W.M., Phil, M., & Kershaw, P.W. (1979). Spontaneous remission from alcoholism—a community study. *British Journal of Addiction, 74,* 251–265.

Scaria v. St. Paul Fire and Marine Insurance Co. (1975). 227 NW 2d 647 (Wisc.).

Schmidt, L., & Weisner, C. (1993). Developments in alcoholism treatment. In M. Galanter (Ed.), *Recent developments in alcoholism, Volume 11: Ten years of progress* (pp. 369–396). New York: Plenum.

Schwartz, H.I. (1994). Informed consent and competency. In R. Rosner (Ed.), *Principles and practice of forensic psychiatry* (pp. 103–110). New York: Chapman & Hall.

Sharkey, J. (1994). *Bedlam: Greed, profiteering, and fraud in a mental health system gone crazy.* New York: St. Martin's Press.

Shute, N. (1997, September 8). The drinking dilemma. *U.S. News and World Report,* pp. 54–65.

Sibley, C. (1999, May 6). Hospital sued by man treated against his will. *Atlanta Journal and Constitution,* p. J3.

Skinner v. Railway Labor Executives. (1989). 489 U.S. 602.

Smart, R.G. (1975/76). Spontaneous recovery in alcoholics: A review and analysis of the available research. *Drug and Alcohol Dependence, 1,* 277–285.

SMART Recovery. (1996). *SMART Recovery coordinator's manual.* Beachwood, OH: SMART Recovery.

Sobell, L.C., Cunningham, J.A., & Sobell, M.B. (1996). Recovery from alcohol problems with and without treatment: Prevalence in two population surveys. *American Journal of Public Health, 86,* 966–972.

Sobell, M.B., Sobell, L.C., Bogardis, J., Leo, G., & Skinner, W. (1992). Problem drinkers' perceptions of whether treatment goals should be self-selected or therapist-selected. *Behavior Therapy, 23,* 43–52.

Stewart, C. (1986). *A reference guide to the Big Book of Alcoholics Anonymous*. Seattle: Recovery Press.

Stinson, F.S., Yi, H., Grant, B.F., Chou, P., Dawson, D.A., & Pickering, R. (1998). *Drinking in the United States: Main findings from the 1992 National Longitudinal Alcohol Epidemiologic Survey (NLAES)*. Bethesda, MD: National Institute on Alcohol Abuse and Alcoholism.

Strasburger, L.H., Gutheil, T.G., & Brodsky, A. (1997). On wearing two hats: Role conflict in serving as both psychotherapist and expert witness. *American Journal of Psychiatry, 154,* 448–456.

Substance Abuse and Mental Health Services Administration. (1997a). *National admissions to substance abuse treatment services: The treatment episode data set (TEDS) 1992–1995*. Rockville, MD: SAMHSA.

Substance Abuse and Mental Health Services Administration. (1997b). *Uniform facility data set (UFDS): Data for 1995 and 1980–1995*. Rockville, MD: SAMHSA.

Substance Abuse and Mental Health Services Administration. (1997c). *The national treatment improvement evaluation study, highlights*. DHHS No. (SMA) 97-3154.

Substance Abuse and Mental Health Services Administration. (1999). *The treatment episode data set (TEDS): 1992–1997 national admissions to substance abuse treatment services*. Rockville, MD: SAMHSA.

Talbott, G.D. (1997, September 29). Letter to editor. *U.S. News and World Report.*

Thomsen, R. (1975). *Bill W.* New York: Harper & Row.

Tuchfeld, B.S. (1981). Spontaneous remission in alcoholics: Empirical observations and theoretical implications. *Journal of Studies on Alcohol, 42,* 626–641.

Tucker, J.A., & Gladsjo, J.A. (1993). Help-seeking and recovery by problem drinkers: Characteristics of drinkers who attended Alcoholics Anonymous or formal treatment or who recovered without assistance. *Addictive Behaviors, 18,* 529–542.

United States Department of Health and Human Services. (1990). *Seventh special report to the U.S. Congress on alcohol and health*. Rockville, MD: USDHHS.

United States Department of Health and Human Services. (1994). *Intensive outpatient treatment for alcohol and other drug abuse*. Rockville, MD: USDHHS, DHHS No. (SMA) 94-2077.

United States Department of Health and Human Services. (1995). *Effectiveness of substance abuse treatment*. DHHS No. (SMA) 95-3067.

United States Department of Health and Human Services. (1997). *Ninth special report to the U.S. congress on alcohol and health*. National Institute of Health No. 97-4107.

Ursery, S. (1999a, April 27). I was wrongly held in alcohol center, doctor charges. *Fulton County Daily Report.*

Ursery, S. (1999b, May 12). $1.3M verdict coaxes a deal for doctor's coerced rehab. *Fulton County Daily Report.*

Vaillant, G.E. (1995). *The natural history of alcoholism revisited.* Cambridge, MA: Harvard University Press.

Vingilis, E. (1983). Drinking drivers and alcoholics: Are they from the same population? In R. Smart (Ed.), *Research advances in alcohol and drug problems* (Vol. 7, pp. 299–342). New York: Plenum.

Walsh, D.C., Hingson, R.W., Merrigan, D.M., Levenson, S.M., Cupples, L.A., Heeren, T., Coffman, G.A., Becker, C.A., Barker, T.A., Hamilton, S.K., McGuire, T.G., & Kelly, C.A. (1991). A randomized trial of treatment options for alcohol-abusing workers. *New England Journal of Medicine, 325,* 775–781.

Walter, H.A. (1932). *Soul Surgery.* Oxford, UK: Oxford University Press.

Warner, M.L., & Mooney, A.J. (1993). The hospital treatment of alcoholism and drug addiction. *Primary Care, 20,* 95–105.

Warner v. Orange County Department of Probation. (1999). 870 F.Supp. 69 (S.D. NY 1994), *affirmed at first then remanded,* 115 F.3d 1068 (2nd Cir. 1996), *reviewed,* 968 F.Supp. 917 (S.D. NY 1997), *affirmed,* 173 F.3d 120 (2nd Cir. 1999), *certiorari denied* (99-24).

Washington Revised Code. (Supp. 1975). Section 4.24.290.

Washington v. Harper. (1990). 110 S.Ct. 1028.

Weisner, C.M. (1990). Coercion in alcohol treatment. In Institute of Medicine, Division of Mental Health and Behavioral Medicine. *Broadening the base of treatment for alcohol problems* (pp. 579–609). Washington, DC: National Academy Press.

Wells, E.A., Peterson, P.L., Gainey, R.R., Hawkins, J.D., & Catalano, R.F. (1994). Outpatient treatment for cocaine abuse: A controlled comparison of relapse prevention and twelve-step approaches. *American Journal of Drug and Alcohol Abuse, 20,* 1–17.

Wholey, D. (1984). *The courage to change.* Boston: Houghton Mifflin.

Wilson, L. (1979). *Lois remembers.* Al-Anon Family Group Headquarters.

Wilson, W. (1939, 1976). *Alcoholics Anonymous.* New York: Alcoholics Anonymous World Services.

Wilson, W. (1953). *Twelve steps and twelve traditions.* New York: Alcoholics Anonymous World Services.

Wilson, W. (1957). *Alcoholics Anonymous comes of age.* New York: Alcoholics Anonymous World Services.

Wilson, W. (1963, April 23). Letter to Sam Shoemaker. Quoted in Dick B. (1992). *Design for Living: The Oxford Group's contribution to early A.A.* (p. 10). Kihei, HI: Paradise Research Publications..

Wilson, W. (1967). *As Bill sees it: The A.A. way of life (selected writings of A.A.'s co-founder)*. New York: Alcoholics Anonymous World Services.

Wilson, W. (1988). *The language of the heart: Bill W.'s Grapevine writings.* New York: AA Grapevine, Inc.

Wren, C.S. (1999, June 29). White House drug official fights mandatory sentences. *New York Times.*

Zeleznik v. Jewish Chronic Disease Hospital. (1975). 366 NYS 2d 163.

Index